HUNGER AND WORK
IN A SAVAGE TRIBE

HUNGER AND WORK
IN A
SAVAGE TRIBE

A FUNCTIONAL STUDY OF NUTRITION
AMONG THE SOUTHERN BANTU

By

AUDREY I. RICHARDS

M.A. (CANTAB.), PH.D. (LONDON)
LECTURER IN SOCIAL ANTHROPOLOGY AT THE LONDON
SCHOOL OF ECONOMICS

WITH A PREFACE BY

PROFESSOR B. MALINOWSKI

AUTHOR OF " THE SEXUAL LIFE OF SAVAGES "

THE FREE PRESS
GLENCOE, ILLINOIS

First American Edition, 1948

Printed in U.S.A.

TABLE OF CONTENTS

FOREWORD

In its original form this book was presented as a thesis for the Ph.D. degree of the London University. It was completed only a few weeks before I left for Africa to do my first field-work among the Babemba of North-Eastern Rhodesia. Much of the material was redrafted during intervals of my work there, and thus, while living amongst one of the matrilineal, agricultural, peoples of Central Africa, I was able to check and compare many of the theoretical conclusions I had reached through a study of the patrilineal, cattle-loving Bantu further south. Some of these observations I have added here and there in the text, when they seemed specially relevant, although I am keeping the major part of my material for publication after a second expedition to the field during the coming year.

The completion of the present book leaves me in debt to many of my friends. Professor C. G. Seligman, under whom I have worked at the London School of Economics, has always given me generously his advice and criticism. Professor Graham Wallas was the first to encourage me to take up research on a biological line, and has also helped me since. Professor Gilbert Murray, an anthropologist himself, though of a very different era of human culture, very kindly read and criticized my thesis. Mr. Edwin Smith annotated the text very carefully and freed it from a number of inaccuracies, while Dr. I. Schapera gave me useful advice from his specialized knowledge of South African cultures. The late Mr. Emil Torday lent me the proofs of his then unpublished *Descriptive Sociology of Africa*. Miss Edith

Clarke, Miss Camilla Wedgwood, and Mr. T. R. Yates have also helped me.

Finally, by writing a preface to this volume, Professor Malinowski has added to a debt which was already large. I owe to him my theoretical knowledge of anthropology, as well as my field technique, and he has given me help at many stages of the present work. A good teacher is one who stimulates ideas in others, while in the act of imparting his own, and a fruitful scientific approach is one which so changes the pupil's outlook that it seems to have been always his. For this reason I feel I owe to Professor Malinowski more than I can acknowledge by reference to his published works.

AUDREY I. RICHARDS.

PREFACE

BY PROFESSOR B. MALINOWSKI

ANTHROPOLOGY is a young science. This inflicts upon its followers a great many disabilities. It gives them also one or two advantages. In the new Science of Man it is still possible to find and work out problems entirely untouched ; to become an explorer of untrodden fields ; and thus to reap the reward of discovery—the reward of discovery, but not the unearned increment of first claim.

In scientific pioneering the first-comer, far from enjoying any privileges of idle occupation, has always a specially difficult task and plenty of hard work to do. This is true of anthropology as of any other branch of learning. In the breaking of a new field there is no relying upon the well-known compendia, no looking up of the evidence in Tylor, Westermarck and Frazer. The student has to go to the sources, scour the articles in special journals, and look through innumerable records of field-work. And since the subject is new, he will find but scanty notices and scattered bits of information. Nor can he take over from scientific tradition well-established methods, patterns of research, ready-made concepts, classifications and terminologies. He has to work out all these for himself.

In this volume Dr. Richards has undertaken just such a difficult task and has carried it out successfully. She has set out upon an entirely new subject : the social and cultural functions of nutritive processes. To my knowledge there is no book upon this problem published by an anthropologist, or for the matter of that by any student of an allied discipline. The author presents us with the first collection of facts on the cultural aspects of food and eating ; she demonstrates conclusively that this universally neglected subject can and indeed must be treated in the science of human civilization ; she lays the foundations for a sociological theory of nutrition upon which others will have to continue building.

In having written the first scientific memoir on the subject of the sociology and psychology of nutrition, she reaps the reward of pioneering achievement. No serious anthropologist can afford to neglect the present study, which opens new prospects and dictates new questions in field-work. No student of human society can overlook an analysis which considerably enlarges and deepens our conception of early human organization, especially in its economic aspect. Above all, no psychologist should ignore this careful examination of one of the most fundamental drives of all human beings. For modern psychology has been too much dominated by an exclusive, one-sided and unsound interest in sex.

" Nutrition as a biological process is more fundamental than sex." With this opening sentence of Dr. Richards' book, those of us who have a first-hand acquaintance with primitive cultures—and also of highly developed ones —will whole-heartedly agree. It is extraordinary what an uneven treatment has been meted out in all studies of mankind to the twin impulses of sex and hunger respectively ; to the physiology of reproduction on the one hand and to that of nutrition on the other. We are enjoying now a surfeit of sex—I alone have to plead guilty to four books on the subject, two of which have the word *sex* on the title-page. Sex has been emphasized for many reasons, some very good, others rather extraneous. The recent breakdown of most reticences and many restraints ; the brutal curiosity of our machine-driven age ; the anti-moral and anti-religious bias of the progressive intelligentsia of to-day—all this has given undue currency to the innumerable scientific, pseudo-scientific, and non-scientific theories and mythologies of sex, with which we are now flooded. After the flood has subsided, it will no doubt leave a wide expanse of rich alluvial soil for future research.

For the present, the extraordinary over-emphasis of sex and the correlated neglect of other appetites, drives, and interests of man, has obscured the issue. Are we to believe that " *libido* ", a vaguely sexual or may be exclusively sexual force, is the only reserve of human energies and interests ? Are all the other impulses, above all that of nutrition, only " substitutes ", " surrogates ", or " sublimations " of *libido* ? Is all social cohesion, all solidarity, perhaps even all morality and altruism, merely a somewhat differentiated form of sexual interest ?

It is high time to put some order into these and similar problems—into the chaos raised by the rapid succession of modern pan-sexual theories. One of the best ways to check up the results of these speculations is the study of other drives. Common sense tells us that nutrition is an independent impulse, more important, if anything, than sex. And yet what do we know of nutrition as a creative force in human societies and cultures ?

In comparative works an accidental, scrappy and unsatisfactory account is given of it ; while in the records of field-work we mostly look in vain even for a mention of the manner in which people eat their food, and its influence on social life, or the gradual emergence of economic values out of nutritive appetites, co-operative effort, and the early needs of exchange.

Speaking as a field-worker who has himself only too grievously neglected all these subjects, I am in a position to affirm that the facts are there, ready to be garnered. What has not existed up till now, is the field-worker's interest in them and the field-worker's capacity to deal with them. For it can never be too often repeated that in anthropology as elsewhere there can be no empirical observations without the lead of theory. And it is only now, after I have become thoroughly acquainted with Dr. Richards' essay, that I see how much I missed in my own observations among the Melanesians. Were the present book only to force the field-worker to keep his eyes and his mind open to the immense rôle which food plays in primitive societies, it would become a landmark in the history of anthropology. But the book does much more : it equips the student with new methods and with a conceptual apparatus ; it provides us with a new outlook on the nature of nutritive processes which I am confident will bring forth rich results in future observations of native life.

It is perhaps not the least merit of her book that after her theoretical introduction Dr. Richards leaves the realm of abstract theory and speculation and comes down to the bedrock of concrete and detailed facts. She proceeds, immediately after she has defined her problem, to a detailed analysis of the nutritive institutions, customs, and ideas in one ethnographic area, the Bantu tribes studied by such excellent observers as Smith and Dale, Junod, and Dudley Kidd. No theories presented in this memoir but are fully documented by concrete evidence ; no conclusions reached but those which were painfully arrived at through a complete survey of the evidence ; no assumptions made but those dictated by facts.

But though it strictly avoids generalities, the book is full of general ideas, implied rather in the treatment of facts than explicitly developed. To me its greatest value is that it opens a number of philosophic perspectives and gives rise to fundamental reflections. After reading it, my conviction deepened that society is not animated by one obsessive force, that of sex. The drives of hunger and appetite ; the co-operative economic interest and the bonds of commensualism are independent of any sexual motives in the sense that they are not by-products of erotic pursuits, but determined by an entirely autonomous physiological process and anatomical apparatus.

From the psychological point of view the book will be of great interest as a contribution to the vexed subject of instinct. Here again the author refrains from taking up any dogmatic position or indulging in too general speculations. But as we pursue the facts presented in this volume, we become more and more convinced that no raw and unmoulded " instincts " appear as direct driving forces in human society. In following up the gradual development of appetites, of co-operative interests, their shaping into socially effective motives and the manner in which they integrate into the concerted activities of a group, Dr. Richards supplies the psychologist, above all, the psychologist of the behaviouristic school, with a rich store of facts from which to choose illustrations of the processes of " conditioning ", as they actually occur in primitive human groups. On the other hand, Dr. Richards pays no mere lip-service to psycho-analysis in tracing her study of nutritive interests back to earliest childhood, in finding in the influences of parental care, above all, of the child-mother relationship, some of the sources of later attitudes towards food. Thus steering a wise course between the Scylla of mechanistic behaviourism and the Charybdis of nebulous psychoanalysis, the author yet does full justice to all that is fertile and sound in both positions.

But however great might be the psychologist's interest in the nutritive sentiments, nutrition itself is a subject which above all falls into the province of the economist. The production, preparation and the uses of food constitute the first and foremost economic processes of mankind, both as regards their genetic sequence and their importance. No one can study the history of the formation of human values, the development of co-operation and labour, the early forms of capitalism and exchange, without coming up against the theory of nutrition. This book, which is the first to study it from the anthropological point of view, will therefore be of great value to the historical economist.

It would be tempting to point out all the fruitful new arguments developed in this volume. I shall choose only one or two which appear to me specially important. The principle which underlies a great deal of what is said in this book is that only a synthesis of facts concerning nutrition can give a correct idea of the economic organization of a people, of their domestic life, of their religious ideas and ethical values. Dr. Richards shows that food and eating must be studied in their institutional setting and through their manifestations in other aspects of culture. Appetite and hunger, commensualism and table

manners, gluttony and asceticism, combined with the
beliefs and rites concerning food, are one and all parts of
the food-providing process among the Southern Bantu.
This again is a phase, though an all-important phase, of
their economic and legal organization, that is of ownership, of inheritance, and of their system of values. Dr.
Richards in this book traces to their physiological basis
all the details which hinge on the human interest in food.
And again she shows how the physiological facts are
transformed in human societies and refashioned into a
body of traditional rules which are impressed upon
each member of the community by the lengthy and
important process of education, in the widest sense of
the word.

" Nutrition in a primitive tribe must be envisaged as
a single process starting from the period of suckling and
family life and continuing till full economic status is
reached by the adult." These words—and the important
theoretical argument from which I have detached them
—were written by Dr. Richards before she had ever seen
a live Bantu. After she had lived for over a year in
Africa, studying the Bamba tribe in intensive field-work,
that is, through the medium of their own language with
a thorough personal knowledge of her informants, she
found she could fully endorse them. Personal contact
with the Bantu allowed her to control and revise most of
her theories as well as to prove a great many conclusions
at which she had arrived from theoretical studies, though
for reasons which she states in her preface, she includes
only little of her own material. But the book is pervaded
with the live touch which only personal acquaintance with
an area can give to the treatment of a theoretical problem
in anthropology.

Speaking from my experience of an entirely different
part of the world, Melanesia, I could repeat word for
word Dr. Richards' statement concerning the unity of
nutritive processes, the need of genetic treatment and the
capital influence of food and eating on primitive organization. Among the Melanesians whom I studied, the

most important motive in the life of the community and in the interests of the individual is food, not sex. Accumulated food is for the Trobriander the symbol of stability and happiness. The word *malia*, which I think is a variant of the Polynesian term *mana*, and which means to the Trobriander not so much " magical force " as " plenty and prosperity ", is associated in his mind with accumulated food. The emotional life of a Trobriander is dominated by his nutritive desires, anxieties and satisfactions. The most important interests of the Trobrianders are concerned with the ownership and distribution of supplies of yams, and the relations between the members of the community are very largely determined by alimentary needs and by the food-providing activities of the natives.

Another very important *Leit-motif* in Dr. Richards' book is her thesis that the traditional tribal or cultural attitudes towards food are among the most important cohesive forces in the community, which unite its members to each other and differentiate them from the surrounding tribes. The attitude to food, table manners, customs of common eating—the morals of food, as we might call it, the things permitted, forbidden, and enjoined—all form a complex and developed ideology of food.

To the savage and to the civilized man alike there is nothing more important perhaps than what he eats and how he eats. I could draw parallels to this from Europe and my personal knowledge, as well as from Melanesia ; not so easily from other parts of the world, because here again we are up against the deficiency in Ethnographic literature : the fact that nutritive ideas and motives have not been sufficiently studied by field-workers. The natives of the Trobriand Islands, whom I studied in my Melanesian field-work, do not eat man and shudder at the idea of eating dog or snake. They abhor their neighbours as cannibals and dog-eaters or snake-eaters. These neighbours in turn despise the Trobrianders for their lack of culinary discrimination in neglecting such excellent viands as man, snake and dog. The natives of the

British Isles whom I studied in another bout of field-work, look down on their neighbours, inhabitants of France, calling them " snail-eaters " and " frog-eaters ". What the French think about British plum-pudding and white sauce and the " cut from the joint ", I dare not repeat here. Any decent member of the Mediterranean *Kultur-kreis* looks with contempt on those who drink water ; a member of the Blue Ribbon League despises those who drink anything but water. It was Voltaire, I think, who expressed his scorn of the nation " who had a hundred religions but only one sauce ".

It is easy to be facetious about national prejudices in food, but it is not so easy to study this subject scientific-ally, and it is high time to do it. The analysis of the production and consumption of food within the family in relation to the formation of kinship ties ; the examina-tion of incentives to work in food production ; the study of economic organization in a pastoral community ; above all, perhaps the inquiry into the symbolism of food, are one and all new and important contributions to social anthropology.

The value of the book is not less because on many points it does not aim at a dogmatic or conclusive settle-ment of the problems. It stimulates—at times even to contradiction—more often than it didactically lays down the law. But after all, as I have already insisted, it is a pioneering piece of research, and as such it should lead and inspire rather than fetter and dictate, or aim at a premature dogmatism. It is only to be hoped that the present volume will start a new line of anthropological and sociological research, and that it will provoke dis-cussion of the many points of view which it advances, and development of the many new ideas which it suggests.

B. MALINOWSKI.

DEPARTMENT OF ANTHROPOLOGY,
　UNIVERSITY OF LONDON ;
　LONDON SCHOOL OF ECONOMICS.
　April 1932.

HUNGER AND WORK IN A SAVAGE TRIBE

A FUNCTIONAL STUDY OF NUTRITION AMONG THE SOUTHERN BANTU

CHAPTER I

HISTORY OF THE PROBLEM

1. NUTRITION AS A BIOLOGICAL PROCESS

NUTRITION as a biological process is more fundamental than sex. In the life of the individual organism it is the more primary and recurrent physical want, while in the wider sphere of human society it determines, more largely than any other physiological function, the nature of social groupings, and the form their activities take.

Yet in current sociological theory man's nutritive needs play a very insignificant rôle. While discussions on sex are thrust constantly before us, both by the scientist and the man of practical affairs, the proportion of serious attention devoted to nutrition is almost fantastically small. Paradoxically enough, it is, I believe, the basic character of the nutritive impulse that has led to this neglect. The alimentary process has been taken, so to speak, for granted by the students of human behaviour. The impulse to seek food is, after all, a desire that cannot be inhibited or repressed, at any rate beyond certain limits. Unlike the drive of sex, it is a periodic urge, recurring regularly every few hours. It cannot be denied fulfilment, as can the sex impulse, throughout the course of the individual's life. We therefore do not associate with nutrition those violent emotional disturbances to which the whole reproductive system appears to give rise. Hunger leads first, it is true, to the concentration of the whole energy of the body on the problem of getting food. Every thought and emotion of the starving man is fixed on this one primary need. But if he fails to obtain it, there are no complex psychoses for observation, but merely the gradual lowering of the whole vitality of the body, and the lethargy which leads to death.[1] The individual man can exist without sexual gratification, but he must inevitably die without food. Therefore, while the inhibited sex instinct finds expression in every variety of neurosis, psychic disturbance, and romantic sublimation, the nutritive impulse seems to provide little material for the mental pathologist.

Further, while sex is necessarily a disruptive force in any human society,[2] and one which must be checked and regulated to some extent if the community is to survive, man's food-seeking activities not only necessitate co-operation, but definitely foster it. Society may condemn a too exclusive interest in the sexual impulses, but it is at its peril that it does not seek rather to encourage a greater concentration of human energies on securing food. Dewey maintains that, " If a society existed in which the existence of impulse towards food were socially disavowed until it was compelled to live an illicit, covert life, alienists would have plenty of cases of mental and moral disturbance to relate in connection with hunger." [3] In fact, however, such a community cannot be conceived. In our own society, in which a sufficiency of food is more

---

[1] Phenomena of mental dissociation are of course observed during prolonged fasting. Cf. Chap. V of this work.

[2] The animal herd appears also to be subject to grave disruption during the breeding season. Cf. A. Espinas, *Des Sociétés Animales*, 1877, Chap. 6 ; F. Alverdes, *Social Life in the Animal World*, 1927.

[3] J. Dewey, *Human Nature and Conduct*, 1922, p. 165.

or less assured, in spite of faulty distribution, psychoses arising from the thwarting of the nutritive impulse are exceedingly rare.   They usually occur only in abnormal conditions, due to the breakdown of our social machinery, such as occurred in some European countries following the late war.   The whole process of nutrition has therefore never focussed the attention of psychologists to the same extent as that of sex.   It lacks the emotional colouring with which the latter problems are always invested.   It is as absent from the sphere of scientific speculation as it is from popular controversy.[1]

Nor is it only a question of the focus of interest ; the whole problem of nutrition in human society has not only been neglected but also, I think, definitely misunderstood. We are still too apt to describe man's chief biological functions in terms derived from the earlier studies of animal psychology.   The attempt for instance to account for man's food-getting activities as the product of an inherited " nutritive instinct " has led to a dangerous over-simplification of the whole problem.

The recent work of Pavlov and of the American Behaviourist psychologists has shown the extent to which habit conditions the instinctive reflexes in the case of the food-getting behaviour of higher animals.   Of all the biological impulses nutrition is that which is most dependent for its fulfilment on the formation of a habit complex in the individual's lifetime.   It requires at one and the same time an adaptation of the individual to the physical environment which must provide its diet, and also relationships with other individuals of the species on whom it must rely in immaturity for its subsistence, or with whom it must co-operate in later life in procuring

---

[1] A numerical analysis of the number of references to different biological instincts in various scientific and popular works was made recently by L. L. Bernard, *Instinct*, 1925, Chap. IX.   It shows the figure 853 for references to sex impulses and 228 for those connected with food-getting activities, such figures being of course an index of the popular interest in these problems rather than a comparison of their actual importance.

food supplies.[1]   But if this is true of the higher animal, the situation is even more complex in the case of man. Our first attempt to define the term " nutritive instinct " in terms of human conduct leads us at once to an untenable position.

To begin with, to the majority of writers of the so-called Instinctivist school, it is the motor aspect of instinctive behaviour which is characteristic—the identical and inherited response of the individual to a given stimulus, in this case food, under certain internal conditions of the organism.[2]

Now as a pattern of activity it is obvious that food-getting is a complex process in man. Besides the *direct* actions of putting food into the mouth, chewing and swallowing it, man also carries out *preparatory* activities. He makes a fire and cooks the food. Further to this, he must procure the articles of his diet by a complicated system of *productory* activities, or economic tasks. Lastly he must undertake a whole series of *accessory* activities, in order to make the tools which he requires in order to exploit the environment, and the vessels in which he cooks his daily meals. The most primitive hunter cannot satisfy his hunger without a chain of muscular actions of the most complex type. He may have to forge the iron for his spear or arrow, set a snare, dig a game-pit, or stalk and kill his prey, before he can even begin to skin and roast the meat. To assume an inherited neuro-muscular disposition to carry out such multitudinous activities would be obviously absurd.[3] The great majority of such actions belong to the definitely *learned* type, and learned, moreover, through cultural institutions

---

[1] The functions of sex and reproduction involve relations with other individuals, but do not depend directly on the absorption of elements of the physical environment : respiration and circulation fulfil the latter conditions but not the former.

[2] Cf. the definitions of W. James, C. J. Herrick, J. Drever, E. L. Thorndike, W. Pillsbury, G. F. Stout, etc.

[3] Cf. L. Bernard's analysis of the number of different motor activities by which man can satisfy the so-called " criminal " instinct, *op. cit.*, Chap. XIII.

of an educational order rather than through a trial and error process as in the animal world.

If we attempt, therefore, to account for man's food-getting behaviour as the product of an inherited neuro-muscular mechanism, we are reduced to an impossible position at once. We must either limit the term instinct to the only reflex which appears to be innate—the sucking reflex present in the human infant at birth—or we must extend it to include all forms of activity which actually end in putting food into the mouth.

Some psychologists, faced with this difficulty, have simply omitted nutrition from the list of fundamental biological impulses. MacDougall's standard work on social psychology does not even include nutrition among the *primary* instincts, although dealing at great length with such far less elemental tendencies as self-assertion or self-abasement.[1] W. James gives no definite food-getting instinct, but mentions *sucking* and *hunting* as though they were comparable food-getting activities, although the one is a reflex present at birth, and the other demands the formation of a series of bodily habits according to the cultural traditions of each particular human society. Ordway Tead does not discuss the nutritive instinct in his account of the drives behind industrial work, where surely, if ever, it should find a place. Dickinson similarly, in his analysis of economic motives, will only allow that man has certain infantile food-getting reflexes such as sucking or " a slight instinctive bent at later ages towards hunting wild game, or towards other fairly definite food-seeking behaviour ". S. S. Colvin puts hunger in the seventeenth place in his list of primary impulses, instead of first : while the writers of the psycho-analytical school equate the nutritive instinct with the self-preservation tendency in general, and dismiss its

---

[1] W. MacDougall, *Introduction to Social Psychology*, 21st ed., Chap. III ; W. James, *Principles of Psychology*, 1890, Part II, pp. 404, 411 ; Ordway Tead, *Instincts in Industry*, 1919 ; Z. C. Dickinson, *Economic Motives*, 1922, p. 114.

importance after the earliest years of the infant's life.[1]

Other writers have tried to solve the problem by sup-
posing the existence of a number of separate biological
drives behind the most universal food-getting activities in
human society. Because man hunts, he must have a
hunting instinct they maintain : because he co-operates
with his fellows in economic activities, he must be said
to have inherited a *gregarious* instinct : because he stores
his grain when he has reaped it, he has an innate disposition to *hoard*.[2] Because therefore man's food-getting
activities ultimately fulfil a biological function, because
many are found universally throughout human society,
and are often associated with a strong emotional tone
and carried out in an apparently impulsive way, we
are asked to conceive behind some of his most complex
economic institutions an innate biological drive of the
type that determines the simple food quest in the animal
scale. Now no psychologist would attempt to limit the
sexual impulse merely to the copulating reflex ; but
neither, conversely, would he postulate a separate
biological instinct to account for each form of love-
making or marriage institution he found.   Yet in the
case of nutrition both these psychological errors have been
committed, as we have shown.   In an age when discussions
on the nature of human instincts have been so prolonged
and heated, the nutritive impulse, the most basic of all
biological functions, has either been dismissed in a
paragraph on infant psychology, or else split into a number
of separate inherited " urges " expressed in human institutions of the most varied and complex type.[3]   Neither

---

[1] S. S. Colvin, *The Learning Process*, 1922, p. 35, quoted L. Bernard ;
S. Freud, *The Ego and the Id*, trans. Joan Rivière, 1927, p. 55.

[2] Hunting instincts have been postulated by Vierkandt, "Nahrung v.
Wirtschaft ", *Festschrift Eduard Hahn zum LX Geburtstag*, 1917, p. 59 ;
Thorndike, *Original Nature of Man*, 1913, pp. 50–53 ; J. Drever, *Instincts
in Man*, 1921, p. 169 ; W. Pillsbury, *The Fundamentals of Psychology*,
1923, p. 229, and others.   Acquisitive, hoarding and gregarious instincts
by Ordway Tead, J. Drever, W. Pillsbury, R. Woodworth and others.

[3] Cf. J. Dewey, *Human Nature and Conduct*, 1922, Chap. VI, for an
interesting protest against the infinite multiplication of human
" instincts " in recent psychological literature.

of these solutions is satisfactory, and neither enables us to analyse the part played by nutrition in the structure of human society.

But if we turn from the *motor* aspect of instinctive activity, can we show that the *affective* or interest side of man's alimentary process is of an inherited biological type ?   MacDougall defines instinct as " an inherited or innate psycho-physical disposition which determines its possessor to perceive, and to pay attention to, objects of a certain class, to experience an emotional excitement of a particular quality upon perceiving such an object, and to act in regard to it in a particular manner, or, at least, to experience an impulse to such action ".[1] We can classify instinctive activity, therefore, according to the definition of another school of psychology, not only by its characteristic action patterns, but according to the type of stimulus which calls forth this behaviour, or the affects and emotions associated with its performance. What does this mean, in our particular case ?   Can we prove that man selects food according to an inherited neural disposition ?   Is hunger and its associated affects the drive behind his food-getting activities ?

Now it is obvious that for man, as well as the animals, there are a number of unconditioned food-signs—to use Pavlov's terminology. Physiological structure is the limiting factor in diet selection in both cases.   There are certain substances the mammalian organism cannot metabolize : others, such as a certain minimum balance of proteins, carbohydrates, and salts, which it needs. But whereas the animal, except in the case of some of the higher apes, is adapted to the digestion of only one main type of food—vegetable or animal—man is distinguished anatomically by the extremely wide range of foodstuffs he is able to utilize.   He has the incisors of a rodent, the molars of a plant-eater, and the canines of a carnivore, as Armitage points out.[2]   He has an added

[1] W. MacDougall, *op cit.*, p. 25.
[2] F. P. Armitage, *Diet and Race*, 1922, p. 9.

length of gut for the digestion of green food, gastric juice for the conversion of starch to sugar, pepsin for the metabolism of proteids, and a pancreatic fluid for the emulsification of fats. No animal has such a power of adapting itself to different environmental conditions, nor such a bewildering number of appetites or tastes.

But in spite of the wide choice of foodstuffs open to him, man's diet is limited in actual fact : and limited not by environmental or biological factors, but by the traditional regulations of the society into which he is born. Culture imposes restrictions where nature would have left him free. We find, for instance, that primitive peoples may refuse food of excellent dietetic value because of a belief that it is magically dangerous, either to the whole community, or to the members of a special social group, such as a totemic clan.[1] Conversely, other foods, less nourishing in character, may be prescribed by cultural rule because of certain magic properties which the eater is supposed thus to acquire. While to go a step further, the primitive man may be compelled by the rules of his community to eat food from which most higher animals would turn in disgust. The practice of sarco-cannibalism enjoined on the members of a number of Melanesian communities is carried out rather against their biological endowment than according to it, and the use of emetics or purges in many religious rites among primitive tribes may be classed in the same category.

We see, therefore, that while physical structure must remain the ultimate limiting factor, both in the human and animal kingdom alike, man's selection of food is determined very largely by the habits and values which his " social heritage " has imposed upon him. In some cases, in fact, his appetites may have become so culturally conditioned from the earliest years of childhood that he

[1] To take a present-day instance, the Kikuyu men refuse to eat green foods in some districts because they believe such a diet prevents them from being swift of foot when defeated by the Masai. Cf. " The Physique and Health of Two African Tribes ", by J. B. Orr and J. L. Gilks, *Report of the Medical Research Council*, No. 155, 1931.

becomes unwilling or unfitted to eat certain types of food which he has been taught to despise. The writer well remembers, on an occasion in post-war Germany, the sudden and prostrating physical nausea she experienced on being told that the excellent meat stew she was eating was composed of horse-flesh rather than beef. Many similar examples are of course narrated of savage societies, where magic belief teaches the primitive child to dread very nourishing forms of food. Man's diet is therefore as limited as that of some of the higher animals, but the limitation is cultural in origin rather than biological.

Nor can we say that hunger is the spur behind most of man's food-producing activities. The animal will make strenuous efforts to feed itself when impelled by the immediate biological want. But man needs, first and foremost, besides this direct satisfaction of his hunger, the feeling of security as to his food supplies. A higher type of memory distinguishes him from other animals, even from the higher apes. He can remember past disasters, and foresee and fear the future.[1] Few tribes, however primitive, live entirely from hand to mouth, and even the Bushmen of Australia or the Kalahari desert perform magic rites to relieve their anxiety, and to reassure themselves as to the safety of their food supply.[2] The majority of even savage peoples carry out long and arduous economic operations in order to make their nutritive needs secure.

Secondly, by man's more complex type of mental association, food acquires for him a series of values other than those which hunger provides. He not only produces

[1] Kohler considers this faculty of memory the chief distinguishing feature between man and the higher apes ; cf. W. Kohler, *The Mentality of Apes*, Appendix I. Varendonck distinguishes also between the *reduplicative* memory of the higher animals subject to recollection only when the same stimulus calls it forth, and the *synthetic* memory of man who is able by a process of psychic automatism to call images to mind at will. Varendonck, *Evolution of the Conscious Faculties*, 1923.

[2] Cf. Australian *Intchiuma* ceremonies described by Spencer and Gillen, *The Arunta*, 1927, Chap. VIII. Bushmen's magic rites for rain and fertility, I. Schapera, *The Khoisan Peoples of South Africa*, 1930.

sufficient food to tide himself over the seasons of drought
or shortage, but in most communities he actually produces more than he needs.   The Melanesian grows yams
in excess of his requirements, not in order to eat, but
in order to display—to proclaim to his fellows his wealth
or social rank.   He may even store food produced with
great labour, apparently for the express purpose of letting
it rot.   Similarly the African will spend his days herding
cattle, but in many cases refuses to use them for food.
Among some of the Nilotic tribes a man may apparently
prefer starvation to the slaughter of one of his beloved
oxen.   When faced with such facts we cannot longer
maintain that man's interest in food, and the drive behind
his food-producing activities, can be explained by the
operation of an innate biological impulse alone.

The result is, in fact, the same whatever criterion of
instinctive action we take—whether we regard the similarity of the motor response to the stimulus as the
diagnostic feature, or whether we stress the nature of the
stimulus itself, or the emotions and desires so aroused.
The term " nutritive instinct " is inapplicable as a description of food-getting behaviour in man unless it is
used in an entirely different sense to that which serves to
describe the conduct of the lower animals.[1]

The fact is that nutrition in a human society cannot
even be considered apart from the cultural medium in
which it is carried on.   As long as the alimentary function
is studied as an individual physiological process largely
to be explained in terms of animal psychology, its nature
must be misunderstood.   The problem is one which the
psychologist cannot solve unaided, for its sociological
aspects are an integral part of the whole.   It is therefore

[1] Marston's recent attempt to substitute the term *hunger drive* for
nutritive instinct appears to me to be open to the same charge of over-
simplification.   This writer stresses the unit character of the response
of the human organism to internal stimuli whether of the hunger or
the erotic type, whereas in reality, as we shall see, human motives
cannot be classified into such simple biological categories (W. M.
Marston, *Integrative Psychology*, 1931).

to the treatment of nutrition in sociological literature that we now have to turn.

2. Nutrition as a Social Activity

The food quest as a form of social behaviour has, of course, figured prominently in the history of sociological theory. The psychologists, as we have seen, have attempted to explain man's food-getting activities and economic organization in terms of his biological endowment of instinctive drives. The sociologists, on the other hand, have tended towards the other extreme, isolating economic activities from all connection with man's fundamental biological needs.

It is true that political scientists, modern or ancient, base themselves on the assumption that economic effort was originally induced by the need for food. " The starting-point of all human activities ", says Professor Seligman, " is the existence of wants. To satisfy hunger and thirst, to secure shelter and to provide clothing were the chief aims of primitive man, and constitute, even to-day, the motor forces of all society." [1] So also Buecher, in his account of the evolution of industrial institutions, states : " The need for nourishment . . . is the most urgent, and originally the sole, force impelling man to activity and causing him to wander about incessantly until it is satisfied." [2] Society is organized round two principles according to Sumner and Keller—" hunger and sex-love " [3] While to go a step further back, those eighteenth-century philosophers such as Montesquieu and Rousseau, who were intent on making as complete a *tabula rasa* as possible of their primitive man, yet postulated hunger as one of the chief impelling forces which

[1] E. R. A. Seligman, *Principles of Economics*, 1929, 12th ed., Part I, p. 3.
[2] K. Buecher, *Industrial Evolution*, 1901, p. 44. It must be remembered that Buecher denied the existence of organized economic effort at this stage at all,—pp. 7, 14, 20 and 39.
[3] Sumner and Keller, *The Science of Society*, 1927, Vol. I, Part I, p. 22.

drove him over the face of the earth—" *la nourriture, une femelle, et le repos* ".[1]

Man's alimentary needs have therefore been recognized as the original driving force which set in motion the social machine. But having granted so much to the biologist, the nineteenth-century economist began his chapter anew. From thenceforth he considered economic activities as a sphere apart, divorced from the physiological needs from which they originally sprang. Industrial organization, and the laws of property, initially " summoned by hunger into being "—to use the graphic phrase of Sumner and Keller, might thereafter be considered on an entirely non-biological plane. Food-producing activities were to be reckoned on the same footing as other economic tasks, separated in an entirely artificial manner from the whole system by which food in a human society is divided, prepared, and consumed, and from the ties of human relationship which are thus formed. Biological factors were not the chief determinants of economic activities, according to these writers, but environmental limitations and the laws of evolution of human society.

It is true that writers of the Geographical School give great importance to the food quest in determining the nature of human society. For instance, Buckle, Jevons, or to a lesser extent Elsworth Huntingdon, consider environment as the chief determinant of different types of human culture—and in the environment one of the most essential elements is the food supply, and the type of work required for its production. The history of different peoples, their migrations, and their varying social structures were largely attributed to this cause.

Again, Leplay and his followers tried to correlate different types of environment with characteristic forms of economic activities, and hence of social organization as a whole—family grouping, the system of leadership,

---

[1] Rousseau, *Discours sur l'origine et les fondements de l'inégalité parmi les hommes*, 1922 ed., p. 21.

and the ownership of property. Demolins' famous study of the different types of social structure to be found among peoples living on the Steppes, Tundra, coast, forest, or plains, was designed to show the variations and adaptations of different social institutions, chiefly the family, according as the food quest, and therefore the method of living, is altered with each environment.[1]

In more directly anthropological literature, too, the same type of economic determinism is evident. Human society, according to anthropologists of the evolutionary school, passed through a series of economic stages classified under such headings as hunting and collecting, lower and higher agriculture, pastoral, industrial and so forth. These economic stages themselves largely determined the form that social institutions as a whole should take. Grosse's valuable study of family organization among primitive peoples attempted to associate such institutions as patriarchy, matriarchy, or the individual or extended family (*Grossfamilie*), with different stages of economic development. He accounted, for instance, for a patriarchal type of family organization by the exigencies of a pastoral and nomadic life.[2] His followers of the *Kulturhistorische Schule* give similar prominence to man's food-producing activities in determining the structure of human society, although, according to these writers, historical incident and culture contact are responsible for the combination of economic organization with special types of religious organization, kinship grouping, material culture, and other characteristic institutions of the society.[3]

We see therefore that neither the economist nor the

[1] E. Demolins, *Comment la route crée le type social*, 1901.
[2] E. Grosse, *Die Formen der Familie und die Formen der Wirtschaft*, 1896.
[3] Pater Koppers, *Die Anfänge des menschlichen Gemeinschaftsleben*, 1921. The correlation of different occupational stages with different forms of social grouping—hunting with totemism and patriliny for instance—forms the basis of one *Kulturkreis*, quoted by R. Firth, *Primitive Economics of the New Zealand Maori*, 1929, Chap. I, who gives an excellent historical account of economic determinism in anthropological literature.

anthropologist have underrated the importance of man's food-getting activities in determining his social institutions. But, in all such theories, economic organization is considered as evolving in human society according to its own laws, apart from the physical structure and needs of man. This obscures the main issue. In a primitive society the bulk of economic effort is directly concerned with the production of food. Now food stands in a different category from the ordinary commodities of economic exchange. It is an insistent human want, occurring regularly at short intervals, and shared by the whole community alike. Its value varies primarily therefore with directly physiological needs. Food is actually a different object to the hungry and to the full man, and, as Sorokin puts it, the greater the shortage of supplies the greater the proportion of the human budget of time spent in nutritional activities—" the greater are the obstacles to be overcome in order to obtain food, the greater are the proportion of food-producing actions in the whole ".[1] Moreover, the more nearly does a human institution fulfil man's nutritional needs, the more universal will that institution be—the family, the most fundamental unit of food consumption and distribution being a case in point.

Now it is in a primitive society that such statements find most dramatic proof. In most savage tribes starvation is a constant possibility, if not an actual menace. The food quest is the chief occupation of every active member of the community, and their most important institutions are concerned with the ownership and distribution of supplies. The emotional life of the primitive man is, therefore, chiefly dominated by his nutritive desires and anxieties. His relations with other members of his community are, in fact, determined very largely by his alimentary needs, and food itself, as the object of such a keen and varied interest, becomes the centre of complex values in his social life. For this reason we

[1] P. Sorokin, *Contemporary Sociological Theory*, 1927, p. 631.

cannot separate the study of eating proper from the series of economic activities by which it is made possible, as we can in the case of a modern society. Nutrition in a primitive tribe must be envisaged as a single process starting from the period of suckling and family life, and continuing till full economic status is reached by the adult. In fact, in a savage society the whole social organization is held together very largely by the strength of these nutritive ties, and if we divorce the economic activities of food-getting from the study of man's physiological needs and appetites, we shall fail to understand the nature of society itself.

We have, therefore, to adopt a new method of approach. We must abandon the old conception of human instincts as either inherited behaviour patterns, or as a series of biological drives of the type that determine the reactions of the lower animals. But we must not, for this reason, deny the biological basis of human character, nor eliminate from the study of society the fundamental importance of man's physiological wants. On the contrary, it is the mechanism by which food-getting habits are formed in the structure of each different culture that we have to analyse. Whereas in the case of sex there is abundant comparative material as to the variety of sexual customs in different communities, the abnormalities and aberrations of the impulse, and its contribution to the shaping of human institutions, sentiments and values, no work of this sort has been done in the case of food.

3. New Developments in Psychology

This new attack on the problem of nutrition has only recently been made possible. The latest developments of psychological theory have opened up new lines of approach to the problem of man's biological endowment. From our point of view perhaps the most important of these psychological concepts is the theory of sentiment-formation first outlined by Shand in his book on *The*

Foundations of Character, but implicit in the work of other psychologists, and in particular those of the psycho-analytic school.[1]   According to this most recent psychological doctrine man's character and conduct must be considered as the product neither of rational decision nor of the drive of inherited impulses ; but of the gradual organization of affective systems round the objects, persons and activities connected with the satisfaction of his primary needs, and the corresponding integration of the habitual actions by which in each differing environment these desires may be fulfilled.   Shand describes this process of emotional organization as beginning on the organic level, so that objects and persons connected with such primary appetites as the desire for food, warmth or safety become the centre of the first system of sentiments. Such sentiments come later to integrate the character at higher psychic levels, and determine a man's values and aspirations according to the traditions of his group—his devotion to such symbols as his flag, his totemic emblem, or the ritual of his Church.

Now it is obvious that it is some such conception that we must have in mind in our study of the formation of habits and values round the organic need of food.   But this sentiment concept, stimulating as it is, involves the development of a new method of observing sociological facts.   The mechanism of sentiment-formation round any one set of biological factors must be studied, as Malinowski has shown, through the medium of individual life histories in the setting of each particular culture.[2]   Shand described the process of organization of human emotions in abstract terms, but to be fruitful in the field of sociology his concept must be translated into concrete facts.

[1] A. Shand, *The Foundations of Character*, 1920.   The work of J. Dewey deals rather with the organization of systems of habitual activities and forms of human behaviour, than with their correlated emotional dispositions.

[2] B. Malinowski, *Sex and Repression in Savage Societies*, 1927. This work is an attempt to apply Shand's concept of the sentiment in a description of the developing sex impulses of the Trobriand child.

Such an approach is obviously particularly important in the case of those primitive societies in which formal institutions of Government, Law, or Economic organization of the type with which we are familiar in our own society do not exist. Durkheim and his followers realized many years ago the importance of studying the common emotional values binding together the members of a primitive group, and the social mechanism by which these necessary sentiments are handed on from one generation to another in a community without written records or an organized system of education. But for want of an adequate technique of observation of primitive societies, his theories were bound to remain as stimulating hypotheses rather than actual descriptions of fact. He pictures his savage as acting under the grip of some mysterious social force inherent in his group, rather than bound by a series of moral codes and emotional values implanted from the earliest days of his youth according to the traditions of his tribe. It was, in fact, impossible to analyse the sentiments underlying primitive law and order on the basis of such scanty ethnological data as Durkheim himself possessed. The same is true of the complex of human institutions and values which centre round such a primary biological need as hunger or sex. To understand the formation of typical sentiments in any particular culture we want first-hand sociological records of a much more systematic type than we have yet had. In our study of nutrition we have therefore to discuss, not only the recent developments in psychological theory, but also the newest technique of anthropological research.

4. The Functional Method in Anthropology

Ethnological data of a sort have, of course, long been available to the sociologist. Since the sixteenth century, or even earlier, explorers have recorded curious facts about the primitive peoples they visited. Many of their observations have been embodied in the current doctrines of political science of their day. This fact sometimes leads us to forget that field-work proper, in the sense of scientific expeditions by trained observers, is of very recent date. The Cambridge anthropological expedition to the Torres Straits published its material in 1904: Rivers' book on the Todas appeared in 1906, and the Seligmans' account of the Veddas, in 1911. And even then such anthropological field-work was naturally still in the pioneer stage. The scientific technique of observation remained to be further developed.

On these first ethnological expeditions the object was rather to collect and compare savage customs and beliefs than to formulate any general sociological laws. Such earlier field-work was in fact either descriptive, pure and simple, or else concerned chiefly with attempted reconstructions of hypothetical past ages of which the present savage institutions were considered to be relics, or the tracing of the migrations of different primitive races by means of the distribution of culture traits throughout the area visited. Little or no attempt was made to elucidate the general principles of organization of a primitive tribe. Indeed, it is doubtful whether sufficient material for this purpose was in existence.

But during the last decade or so, a new tendency has been visible in anthropology, first manifested in two important monographs which appeared in the same year (1922)—*Argonauts of the Western Pacific*, by B. Malinowski, and *The Andaman Islanders*, by A. Radcliffe-Brown. In both these works a new challenge was issued to the scientific observer in the field, since both authors claimed that the function of the anthropologist was to deduce and formulate the general laws governing the structure of primitive societies, rather than merely to collect and describe the peculiar antics of the savage peoples he visited.

Thus, for instance, Radcliffe-Brown prefaced his description of the customs of the Andaman Islanders by announcing certain general sociological principles. He

reformulated, in the light of recent psychological knowledge, Durkheim's conception as to the forces of cohesion
which bind together the primitive group, defining the
means by which tribal solidarity in a savage society is
maintained and preserved from generation to generation.
But unlike Durkheim, he based these general social laws
on his own personal observation in the field—a significant
new departure in sociological method.

Malinowski's book—a study of the *Kula*, or inter-
trading cycle of the Trobriand Islanders—was even more
important from the point of view of development of
anthropological method. This monograph was the result
of intensive work on one tribe over a four-year period,
involving in all three expeditions to the field. It thus
presented a marked contrast to the type of survey work
previously carried out by Rivers, Seligman, and others,
among a large number of different Melanesian Islands.
It initiated, in fact, a new technique of observation in
the field. Malinowski worked throughout in the language
of the people, instead of using an interpreter. He not
only questioned selected informants, after the manner of
Rivers, but constantly observed and participated in the
events of daily and ceremonial life. He noted the reactions
of individual members of the community to different
social events and analysed the varying motives and
values that appeared to animate their conduct, and the
obligations by which each native was bound to the other
members of his tribe. He thus presented savage society
to us as a living reality rather than as an abstract scheme
of social relationships. This was in many ways a new
approach. Some years previously Graham Wallas made
a powerful appeal for the study of the human emotions
and desires underlying the social institutions and customs
of modern society—the *Human Nature in Politics* [1] as he
termed it—but the human nature in anthropology did not
become apparent until new methods of field-work evolved.

The Functional method is the new theoretical approach

---

[1] Graham Wallas, *Human Nature in Politics*, 1st ed., 1908.

which has resulted from these recent developments in the technique of observation. It led first of all to an attack on the old purely descriptive comparative anthropology, or the historical or evolutionary schools of the end of the last century. For instance, Malinowski starts with an emphasis on the fundamental unity of the social institutions of primitive society. He shows by concrete examples from his own field material that in the setting of a living culture each social institution is intimately linked to every other institution of the society of which it forms part. It is therefore impossible even to describe a savage custom correctly unless we consider it in relation to the other organs of the functioning whole. To treat primitive law, kinship, or religion as though they developed separately in human society according to fixed evolutionary laws is to misunderstand the nature of society itself.

Similarly a comparative study of primitive customs is misleading, if by this is meant the mere collection and tabulation of isolated facts from different accounts of savage tribes without understanding the part which these customs play in each particular culture. The attempt to trace the history and affinities of different peoples by means of the institutions and artefacts found amongst them—the most important task of the *Diffusionist* writers—is equally dangerous unless we can first give an account of the working of each institution in the society in question, or the way in which the tool is used and regarded by the natives. It is the whole question of human motives and values which is important and which can only be analysed by first-hand observation in the field. Social institutions must be studied as they actually *function* in a living society, and in relation to the fundamental cultural needs they satisfy—" cultural needs " being defined as " a body of needs which must be fulfilled if the group is to survive ".[1]

[1] B. Malinowski, " Culture ", *Encyclopædia of the Social Sciences*, edited by Seligman and Johnson, IV, pp. 621–645 ; also article on

Functional anthropology is therefore not merely a reaction against the pseudo-historical approach to the problems of primitive society, but an attempt to analyse social institutions in their relation to the primary social wants—such fundamental biological needs as procreation and nutrition being naturally in the first rank. These essential human needs are the basis, not only of the integration of the individual character accorded to the traditions of each culture, but also of the formation of a system of human relationships which integrate the society as a whole. Man has to satisfy his primary needs in any particular environment by means of a body of artefacts or tools, by which he wins himself food, makes himself shelter, and secures himself against attack. These activities involve a system of human groupings to make possible co-operative effort, and institutions by which the knowledge and technical skill of each generation can be handed on to the next. Thus such primitive impulses as hunger and sex form the foci round which the most universal human institutions are grouped, as can be seen clearly in the examination of one particular case.

Malinowski has made one such analysis of primitive society in terms of the sex and procreational needs of one specified tribe—the matrilineal society of the Trobriand Islanders, and his *Sexual Life of Savages* is in effect an account of what I shall call the *reproductive system* of a savage tribe. It shows how the cruder biological impulses of the individual must be shaped and educated in relation to other fundamental needs in order that the social group

---

" Social Anthropology ", *Encyclopædia Britannica* 14th ed. The application of the method is most clearly seen in his treatment of primitive kinship, religion, economic organization and law, *vide Argonauts of the Western Pacific*, 1922 ; *Myth in Primitive Psychology*, 1926; *Crime and Custom in Savage Society*, 1927; *The Sexual Life of Savages*, 1929. Cf. also the work of Radcliffe-Brown, who makes a similar attack on imaginative historical reconstructions in anthropology (Presidential Address to the British Association, 1931), although his general theoretical approach is more definitely Durkheimian, and therefore less significant from the field-work point of view.

may survive. The sexual desires of the Trobriander are regulated from the earliest years by traditional rules prescribing his methods of courtship, and influencing his choice of mate. Human marriage has to perform a wide variety of social, legal, and economic functions besides the purely biological tie, and for this reason laws of incest and exogamy debar a man from mating with certain women in his community, while on the other hand many other marriages within his kinship group are especially approved. Moreover, his whole attitude towards the members of the opposite sex is determined by a systematized process of education from his early childhood, and profoundly influenced by the religious and magic beliefs of his tribe with regard to the nature of sex.

Further, this complex of sexual institutions is linked inevitably with those of reproduction. Marriage founds the family in order to ensure the necessary care and nurture of the child after birth, and during the long period of immaturity of the human young. Social custom and ethical codes reinforce and educate the parental impulses. Thus legal rights and obligations define the economic, financial, and even religious duties of the pair, and also their correct attitude to other members of the opposite sex. They determine, moreover, the legal status of the child, and his relationship with a certain group of ancestors in the past, and another group of descendants as yet unborn.

The fundamental need of procreation, therefore, founds the family as a system of social grouping, and the type of marriage in each community will determine the sentiments formed by the individual in early life towards his parents, siblings, and near relatives. On these his attitudes towards other members of the society, his co-workers, leaders, or subordinates, are afterwards framed— the reproductive and sexual group being the workshop for later social ties. The family is also associated with systems of housing and local grouping, the functions of education and economic co-operation, and the transfer of material objects to the next generation. With each family are linked other families, and the whole *reproductive system* can only be understood in relation to the wider kinship system of the society, which merges gradually into the clan or the tribe.

Thus readers of Malinowski's *Sexual Life of Savages* will find no bare account of the sex customs in Trobriand society, but rather a description of the whole system of human relationships between one sex and another, lasting from birth, through the process of formation of kinship patterns in youth and adult life, till the final regrouping of society at the death of one of its members. The human activities correlated with the fundamental drive of sex bind the whole society in close emotional ties, regulated by the legal conceptions of the tribe and its ethical and magical beliefs. For the instinctive bodily desires of the individual are substituted a series of " culturally shaped appetites " : and for the inherited behaviour patterns of the animal, a system of bodily habits, correlated with an outfit of material culture handed on from one generation to another.

Now the *nutritional system* of a primitive people is as complex and important as the *reproductive*, but the institutions centred round the biological need of food have never yet been described. It is this analysis that I want now to undertake. I want to examine the human relationships of a primitive society as determined by nutritional needs, showing how hunger shapes the sentiments which bind together the members of each social group. By what means is this fundamental biological want fulfilled in a given environment ; and what forms of human activities and social groupings are so derived ?

CHAPTER II

HUMAN RELATIONSHIPS AND NUTRITIVE NEEDS

1. FOOD CONSUMPTION

WE must turn first to the life of the individual in order to outline our task. Can we show, for instance, that the ties of the family, the initial social group, are in any way determined by alimentary needs? It is obvious, to begin with, that the first human relationship ever formed by the young organism is almost entirely nutritional. Food is the infant's most imperative and constant need. In the dim period preceding consciousness, hunger and the various degrees of satiation form its dominant sense-emotional states. Its whole affective life is organized round the nutritive system. The baby does not appear to react in an emotional fashion to those objects and activities which do not affect its urgent physical wants. On the other hand those external and internal stimuli which become associated with such a function as nutrition form the chief foci round which its rudimentary sentiments first form.[1]

But it is just this urgent demand for nourishment which, above all other physiological needs, the infant is powerless to satisfy unaided. It is entirely dependent on some other human being at this stage of its life. It is, therefore, round the individual who can appease its

---

[1] Cf. I. King, *The Psychology of Child Development*, 1906, pp. 53-5 ; also J. Baldwin, *Thought and Things*, Vol. I, p. 46 ; " All is neutral as long as nothing touches upon his appetites, instincts, native propensities, and organic sensibilities."

Cf. also W. Stern, *Psychology of Early Childhood*, tr. 1924, pp. 75, 126 ; W. Preyer, *The Mind of the Child*, 1893, Part I, p. 158, for accounts of these sense-emotional states preceding consciousness.

hunger that this first confused emotional system forms. The very urgency of the infant's need makes for the strength of the tie. In connection with food the child first becomes conscious of other individuals in its environment, and the mother acquires her initial meaning very largely as a satisfier of hunger. As a source, therefore, of the mingled feelings of desire, satisfaction, or disappointment that inanition and repletion bring. While the act of suckling cannot, of course, be dissociated from the other coincident pleasures the mother provides —the warmth and tenderness of her physical contact and the services she renders—yet I think I am right in maintaining that nutritive dependence is the dominant element on which the child-to-mother sentiment is built.[1]

The first emotional tie between the infant and another individual in its environment is determined, therefore, by its physiological dependence at this time. Suckling initiates what is in all probability the most far-reaching human relationship it ever makes in the course of its life. The physical link between the baby and the mother influences profoundly not only the integration of the child's character, but also the subsequent relationships it forms both within the family unit, or the larger social group.

But here the problem becomes more complex. We

[1] It is here that the psycho-analytic treatment of the subject seems to me to be definitely one-sided. Freud speaks of an " oral or cannibalistic " stage of infant history, when, in the words of one of his adherents, " the libido of the child is almost entirely occupied with the instinct of nutrition " (I. H. Coriat, *Sex and Hunger, Ps. A. Review,* VIII, 4, p. 376). But this is, according to him, merely a preliminary fixation of a libido which will afterwards be thrown into the channels of sex. The sensuous pleasure derived from the act of suckling is stated to be almost entirely erotic in type, and not a function of the equally important physiological process of obtaining food. The mouth as an organ of feeding is reckoned as of less importance than the mouth as an erogenous zone, with which it is assumed to be quickly identified ; cf. S. Freud, *Three Contributions to the Theory of Sex,* tr. 1918, pp. 44–6. Such a theory concentrates attention exclusively on one aspect of the problem. The recognition that the child derives pleasure from the act of suckling should not blind us to the fact that it continues to suck in order to get food, nor should it lead us to assume that the sensuous pleasure so derived is necessarily erotic in type ; cf. also W. Stern, *op. cit.,* Chap. VII, for a criticism of Freud's theory in this respect.

have to realize that the relationship between child and mother differs profoundly according to the methods by which it is fed in early life. Tradition and social environment will early condition the purely biological interdependence of mother and child. Experimental tests on this period of child-history are, of course, exceedingly difficult to carry out, for obvious practical reasons. Comparative data from different cultural areas must form the only type of observation open to us, or will furnish at least possible lines of research. A careful examination of even the scanty data available shows how widely the customs of suckling and infant feeding differ from race to race. The nature of the nursing relationship is everywhere determined by social tradition and rule, and until we know the limits of variation of such customs, we cannot grasp the essential elements of the problem we have to solve. Any theory as to the development of filial sentiment in a primitive society is likely to be valueless if based on observations of the care and treatment of a civilized child.[1] The sociologist can no longer afford to relegate the period of suckling to the sphere of physiology alone. I believe that when this fact has been realized, a systematic first-hand study of the question in the field must result.

In the second place, I am convinced that some of the most important aspects of the problem will be missed if we assume, as is too often the case, that the tie of nutritive dependence is severed when weaning takes place. Strangely enough, the nursing period has been considered in psychological literature as an epoch apart from the child's subsequent nutritive life. In reality the alimentary dependence of the human infant persists for a very long time, owing to its protracted physical

---

[1] We cannot even apparently assume that male and female infants are always treated in the same way. Mr. P. G. Harris (District Officer, Northern Provinces, Nigeria) tells me that among the Bareshe, a riverine tribe inhabiting the islands of the Upper Niger, the male children are weaned at 3 years, 3 months, while the female children are weaned when 4 years and 4 months old, 3 having a magic significance for the male and 4 for the female in this tribe.

immaturity, and the difficulty of the food quest in most types of society. The dependence persists, but its nature is changed—gradually or suddenly—according to the weaning customs of each race. Here again we need further observations as to how the process of weaning is actually carried out. The sensual elements in the child-to-mother relationship have to be eliminated,[1] and transformed according to the social status and function of the woman in each particular society. In most cases, however, the child continues to receive his food from his mother during his earlier years, and throughout his life the function of motherhood is associated with the provision and preparation of food.

But weaning brings yet further changes in the nutritive life of the child. His diet is no longer confined to the single element of the mother's milk which originally formed food and drink alike. The whole width of gustatory sensations is gradually opened up to him. His interest in food is more varied and complex.[2] Further, the number of human foods which can be assimilated without cooking in some form or other is very small, and in a savage society, where the household implements are very primitive, the process of preparing the daily food occupies a large part of each day. The daily meals thus involve a series of technical activities and a system of co-operation between members of the community. Now social tradition fixes, first that the child should become dependent at weaning for its subsistence on the members of his family, his kinsmen, and sometimes a number of other members of his kinship group. Secondly, in every society we know of, the family is the chief unit which serves to prepare the food for immediate consumption. Each member of the house-

---

[1] *Vide* B. Malinowski's theory as to the formation of the sentiment of incest in the human family (*Sex and Repression in Savage Society*, 1927).

[2] Dependent, of course, on the length of suckling in each particular culture. *Cf.* W. Preyer, *op. cit.*, p. 154, " The animal eagerness for food manifestly increases in the first year."

hold has usually his or her part to perform in these directly nutritive activities, either in the culinary sphere itself, or in the accessory tasks which make possible the preparation of the meal. This fact exerts a strong influence on the relationships of the different individuals in the family group. We cannot analyse the formation of kinship sentiment in a primitive society unless we realize that the common sharing and preparation of food is one of the essential ties which hold together the groups, and one of the most important legal obligations of the family system and, moreover, the dependence of the child for food upon its parents often for a period of ten to fifteen years, is intimately connected with the formation of that sentiment towards authority upon which a primitive, if not a civilized society, must be built.

Further, apart from the question of food and its preparation, the problem of its distribution must be considered here. At weaning the child becomes conscious of competition with his fellows for the satisfaction of his needs. The time of his sole possession of the mother as a source of food supply is over. He finds himself in rivalry with other members of the household group— his brothers and sisters or older relatives—in the sharing of meals. The immediate satisfaction of his appetite is constantly checked by the presence of other members of the family, and more important still from our point of view, by those codes of manners which regulate the consumption of food in any group,

Strong emotional ties are thus formed between those individuals who regularly eat together, their intensity varying, of course, according to the scarcity of food supplies, but always contributing largely to the intricate growth of family bonds. On the one hand the family meals are intimately connected with the building up of ties of affection, confidence and trust towards the parents, and the sense of security and routine of home life. On the other hand, the group itself is composed of different individuals, each with separate rights and interests,

jealously guarded in a society where food is scarce.[1]
Codes of manners are necessitated therefore by the play
of strong biological impulses, and their acquisition is an
important part in the training of the child in his social
relationships. Those customs, therefore, which govern
the manners of eating in any community, are exceedingly
important details sociologically, if we are to understand
the formation of the family group. At present too great
a number of field-workers appear to have considered
them too insignificant to record.

But the function of food distribution is not ended
with the apportionment of the family's daily meals.
In a primitive society where efficient methods of preserv-
ing food are practically non-existent, and scanty transport
facilities prevent the bringing of supplies from other areas,
the savage must guard against starvation by forming
ties of reciprocity with other members of the group.
The original functions of the family are thus extended
to provide for the exchange of food, and especially of
perishable supplies, the support of those rendered desti-
tute by a sudden shortage, and the mutual exercise of

---

[1] A similar phenomenon is, of course, to be observed in the behaviour
of animal societies when feeding. We know that herd animals will
combine together against outsiders in the protection of their food.
P. A. Kropotkin, *Mutual Aid*, 1902, p. 24, described the sparrows of the
Jardin du Luxembourg combining to fight all other birds invading their
garden, but jealously guarding their own individual rights within the
garden. E. Alverdes, *Social Life in the Animal World*, 1927, p. 111,
speaks of communities of pariah dogs who also unite to attack dogs
which have not grown up with them, while they will share food with
each other. Similar phenomena are observed among the wolves, while
Romanes and Howard give data as to the common defence of territory
by lions, monkeys and birds, and Kropotkin (*op. cit.*) states that white-
tailed eagles will summon their fellows if they have spotted a carrion
horse. (Romanes, *Mental Evolution in Animals*, 1883 ; H. E. Howard,
Territory in Bird Life, 1920.)

At the same time a regular order of feeding is observed among many
animals. Alverdes (*op. cit.*, p. 124) describes the " pecking order "
among birds. Kropotkin mentions some female gulls observed in the
North Russian marshes, who " keep a certain order in leaving their
nests in search of food ". Also P. Hachet-Souplet, *Examen Psychologique des Animaux*, 1900, p. 258, carried out tests to show that the
area of a cage occupied by each mouse confined there was directly
proportionate to its physical strength, and altered in exact proportion
when the whole area was halved or quartered.

hospitality within the group.   Such a system forms what Malinowski has called the *principle of social insurance* in a savage society.   In fact, one of his most stimulating contributions to the study of primitive kinship is this conception of the extension of the ties of the family to a more distant group of kinsmen in a " number of gradually widening circles " in order to form a scheme of mutual self-help within the tribe.[1]

The rules governing the distribution of food in the primitive family, village, or clan, is one of the most important examples of such an extension of kinship duties and privilege.

2.   Food Production

We have seen therefore that the mechanism of food distribution leads us finally beyond the limits of the family circle to the local or kinship group, and to the exchange of goods between subject and chief.   But with the organization of food production proper, yet a further series of human relationships is involved.   Nutrition in its widest sense includes the whole scheme of regulations by which man's food-getting activities are organized and controlled, and unless we can picture the whole nutritional system in functioning order, we shall have but a one-sided view of the whole.

In order to exploit the environment successfully, man must evolve complex schemes of co-operation—a division of labour, and a system of co-ordinating the activities of the group.   He must protect the resources of the environment against wanton usage, or the destruction of the potential value of land or stream.   He must also guard his supplies from other groups of human beings, and regulate their use by his fellow-men.   Finally each community must provide some means by which the laws of ownership of food resources are defined, and these

[1] B. Malinowski, " Kinship ", in the *Encyclopædia Britannica*, 14th ed.

rights transmitted from generation to generation according to rule.

Now in a primitive society the family is in most cases the central unit of economic co-operation. The beginning of economic life for each individual therefore involves the resetting of old attitudes and the formation of wider ties within the kinship group. The family is no longer solely the food-consuming and distributing group, as it appeared to the child in early life. It acquires new functions. It becomes the body of men and women united for the co-operative production of food supplies.

Further, in many primitive societies the ownership of certain economic resources, such as hunting or fishing rights, or the actual co-operation in some specific food-getting activities, reach out beyond the limits of the kinship or village group on a clan or tribal scale. Or, they may be co-ordinated by the leadership of the chief of a large area by the common performance of some religious rite connected with economic activities, or by a system of exchange or distribution of food. Authority and social status are almost universally based, whether in the family or in the tribe, upon the power of using or controlling supplies of food or the natural sources from which they are produced.

It is thus that the structure of what I have called the *Nutritional System* begins to take shape. We see that hunger, like sex, must be satisfied in a human society by a number of activities, immediate, preparatory, and productory. Food must be eaten, prepared and cooked, and won from the natural environment by a series of complicated economic tasks. With these must be correlated a number of accessory activities, such as the making of utensils for eating and cooking, the construction of household dwellings, and the implements used in tilling the soil, killing game, or otherwise producing food.

Further, each type of activity demands the creation of a series of social groups and human relationships. Definite units—the family or household group in most communities—are responsible for regulating the consumption of food, the provision for dependent members of the community, and the immediate distribution within the circle affected by customary daily meals. The wider system of production and distribution of raw materials is carried out by a regular system of economic co-operation, the recognition of some authority in control of these organized activities and usually a scheme of transport and exchange.

It is a study of this complex of nutritive activities that we have in mind, and since such a network of human institutions and values can only be successfully analysed through intensive work on one particular culture, I have selected for this purpose the South-Eastern Bantu.

3. AREA SELECTED

The South-Eastern group of Bantu, according to the classification proposed by Dr. I. Schapera, comprise roughly the Zulu-Xosa people, the so-called " Kafirs " of the Eastern province and Native territories of the Cape—AmaXosa, AmaTembu and AmaMpondo : the " Fingoes "—mostly fugitive remnants of tribes disbanded through Chaka's raids : the " Zulus ", inhabitants of Natal and Zululand, and the BaThonga, extending up the Eastern coast as far as the Sabi River on the North, and inland into Southern Rhodesia.[1]

I was influenced in my choice of this group by the following considerations. Like most Bantu peoples the South-Eastern group provides an interesting contrast between pastoral, hunting, and agricultural activities,

[1] I. Schapera, " A working classification of the Bantu peoples of Africa," *Man*, May, 1929 ; S. Molema, *The Bantu, Past and Present*, 1920, p. 25, speaks of the " East coast group " of Bantu as comprising AmaXosa, AmaMpondo, AmaTembu : the AmaZulu and Matabele : the AmaThonga : and the AmaSwazi. J. T. Brown, *Among the Bantu Nomads*, 1926, p. 18, similarly distinguishes the AmaZulu-AmaXosa group of Bantu from the Bechuana-Basuto group, and the Ovaherero-Ovambo group on the West. Cf. also J. Ayliffe and J. Whiteside, *The History of the Abambo, generally known as the Fingos*, 1911, p. 15.

all combined as part of one economic scheme. They differ thus profoundly from some of the Melanesian communities about which we have, so far, the greatest collection of material as to economic organization, the distribution, the exchange, and the display of food. For this reason they provide interesting material for a comparative study.[1]

The social organization of the Bantu is also interesting from our point of view because of its strongly marked family structure. The basic territorial unit among the South-Eastern peoples—the kraal or village—is a kinship unit, an extended family under one patriarchal head. Political organization is also of a distinctly patriarchal pattern, the headman dependent on his sub-chiefs, and the latter themselves owning the authority of the chief. Moreover, ancestor worship, the dominant cult of Bantu religion, emphasizes still further the kinship sentiment which unites together the members of the family, the clan, or the tribe. In daily life too the economic functions of the household and kinship units are clearly defined. The kraals or household are always, as Schapera points out, "the primary groups for the production and consumption of food" [2]; while the special developments of the cattle cult in South Africa and the peculiar complications of the lobola system of marriage payment, bind different families in a still closer network of economic obligations. Our thesis as to the importance of nutrition in the formation of family sentiment should therefore find its most dramatic expression in a study of the customs of these peoples.

The quantity of South African material available has

[1] The Trobriand culture described by Malinowski is almost entirely an agricultural and fishing community, while Dr. Firth's exhaustive account of the economic organization of the Maori is also concerned with a collecting and agricultural community. Cf. B. Malinowski, *Argonauts of the Western Pacific*, 1922 ; " Primitive Economics of the Trobriand Islanders," *The Economic Journal*, XXXI, March, 1921 ; R. Firth, *op. cit.*

[2] I. Schapera ; " Economic Changes in South Africa ", *Africa*, Vol. I, No. 2, 1928, p. 172.

also weighed with me in my choice. Junod's account of the Thonga provides the most full and illuminating account of primitive kinship organization and child life that we have.[1] I have also been able to draw on Dudley Kidd's accounts of Kafir childhood—chiefly among the AmaMpondo—which deal with a little-studied aspect of primitive life.[2] Where information as to the South-Eastern Bantu has been lacking, I have taken instances from other cultures, particularly from the valuable account of the Ba-Ila furnished by Smith and Dale.[3]

In studying this material I shall deal first with the formation of family sentiment—the emotional attitudes towards the parents, the siblings, and near relatives, developed through the daily usages of common life, and the functions of the household group as the unit which prepares, preserves, consumes and shares its own supply of food.

Next, I shall discuss the primary extension of these family functions to the members of the wider kinship group, with a parallel extension of similar attitudes of affection, trust, and dependence towards those kinsmen bound by such reciprocal legal obligations as the share in the family task of consuming and distributing food.

I shall then consider the economic organization proper —the rules of economic co-operation, ownership of natural resources, laws of inheritance and the legal contract of marriages as an economic partnership—all these institutions affecting profoundly the ties which bind together the members of the family, the kinship and tribal groups.

Lastly our survey must include a study of the supplementary value acquired by food as a symbol of those complex human relationships—the reproduction of the routine of cooking and eating food in primitive ritual to symbolize the life of the family and the functions of

---

[1] H. Junod, *The Life of a South African Tribe*, 2nd ed., 1927.

[2] D. Kidd, *Savage Childhood*, 1906; *Kafir Socialism*, 1908; *The Essential Kafir*, 1925.

[3] E. Smith and A. Dale, *The Ila-speaking Peoples of N. Rhodesia*, 1920.

its various members : the exchange of food as a sign of reciprocal kinship ties : and the general function of ceremonial in strengthening such bonds. All such information is necessary for a functional study of the *Nutritional System* of a savage tribe.

CHAPTER III

FOOD AND FAMILY SENTIMENT IN BANTU SOCIETY

1. METHOD OF ANALYSIS

A FUNCTIONAL study of nutrition obviously necessitates some form of genetic approach, whether in field observation, or in a theoretical *exposé* such as the present work. Since we believe that hunger in its widest sense, determines man's chief social relationships, we must study the formation of such ties and institutions in terms of the individual's alimentary needs. Now these needs obviously alter in succeeding periods of his existence. His physiological requirements differ from infancy to old age, and the customs of his society determine the way in which they must be satisfied at different epochs of his life. Thus it is not enough for us to furnish even a full description of the nutritional activities of any particular community as these are performed in mature adult life. To prove our case we must examine the growth of the human sentiments which underlie such institutions : and to do so we must turn to the life-history of the individual child.

By this I do not mean to suggest that we should simply follow a biographical arrangement of material such as is to be found in many excellent field monographs, such as, for instance, the works of Junod, Smith and Dale, and Rattray.[1] Van Gennep's stimulating conception of the *Rites de Passage* [2] in primitive religion has had a wide

---

[1] Cf. Junod and Smith and Dale, *op. cit.* ; R. S. Rattray, *Religion and Art in Ashanti*, 1927.

[2] A. Van Gennep, *Rites de Passage*, 1909.

influence on the schematic arrangement of field results; but not on the observation of this new type of fact. It is not our object merely to describe in sequence the magic or religious rites which mark the growth of the child— birth ceremonies, teeth ceremonies, initiation, marriage, and the like. Such institutions perform a definite function in the religious and legal life of the tribe, and in some cases act as educational agencies as well. But the description of these ceremonies does not give us that knowledge of the daily life and interests of the growing individual which is essential for our purpose. We want rather to study the changing biological needs of the child from birth to death, his changing relationships with other members of the community, and the changing activities demanded of him at different periods of his life.

Biographical studies of this type form the basis of most of Malinowski's work. In fact, the Functional method appears to me to go hand in hand with a definitely genetic approach. Malinowski's treatment of the problems of primitive kinship is a practical experiment in this direction. He studies the mechanism by which the family ties of childhood are gradually extended and modified as the household group becomes linked to those of the near relatives in different co-operative activities, and later, in adult life, to the families united by marriage, and the wider bodies of the clan, the age-group, or the tribe. It is the education of the child in these relationships, not by formal instruction, but by the acquisition of a series of behaviour patterns towards different members of the community, and the use of specific kinship terms for them, which maintains the tribal structure and the legal and moral system on which it rests.[1]

Somewhat the same biographical tendency is seen in the theoretical approach of Professor Radcliffe-Brown, his book on the Andaman Islanders [2] being largely devoted

[1] B. Malinowski, " Parenthood the Basis of Social Structure ", in *The New Generation*, edited by S. D. Schmalhausen and V. F. Calverton, 1930.
[2] A. R. Brown, *The Andaman Islanders*, 1922.

to the description of Andaman rites and ceremonies as they influence and educate the growing child. Margaret Mead's study of adolescence in Samoa is, on the other hand, an experiment in the application of this conception to field-technique in the case of one particular aspect of a primitive culture. I believe that the further development of such methods of observing and recording field-observations will open up wide possibilities for sociological research.[1]

It is this biographical method of study, therefore, which I propose to use in the case of the nutritive institutions of Bantu society, even though lack of material as to infant and child history will prevent me from developing it to its fullest extent. For the convenience of arrangement I have divided the youth and childhood of these peoples into a series of stages, calling them *infancy*, *early childhood*, *later childhood*, and *adolescence*. These periods are more or less arbitrarily selected but represent epochs of physical growth which are marked, according to Bantu usage, either by religious rites such as initiation, or by changes in social status or economic occupation—the beginning of the boy's pastoral activities or the girl's agricultural work. It must be realized, however, that these periods are divided merely for my own convenience in description. It is the continuity of the child's life I want to study, not the *rites de passage* which often mark dramatically the time of growth.

2. INFANCY

The first period to be dealt with is infancy proper—from birth, that is to say, to the third or fourth year. During this stage, the child's most important relationship is very largely nutritive in function. Initially the infant is, of course, entirely dependent on its mother for the

[1] Margaret Mead, *Coming of Age in Samoa*, 1929 ; cf. also articles by B. Z. Seligman (*J.R.A.I.*, Vol. LIX, 1929) and E. E. Evans-Pritchard (*Man*, Vol. XXIX, Nov. 1929) for further illustration of the biographical method as applied to primitive kinship.

satisfaction of its hunger—at this time its most urgent
physical need. She becomes, as we have seen, the object
round which its most complex sentiments first form.
But, since the nature of this nutritive relationship varies
very largely according to the customs of infant feeding
in each community, we have to study, in the case of the
primitive society which we have selected, the methods
of suckling and weaning practised, the length of the
period, and the association of the mother's nutritive
function with the other social duties she has to fulfil.

To begin with, the period of suckling is relatively
speaking long among those tribes which we are considering. It lasts till the second or third year, and covers
therefore, the greater part of that life-stage with which
we are now dealing. The savage mother generally delays
the weaning of her child until she is aware that she has
conceived again. But, according to Bantu custom, the
event is prescribed much more rigidly, since sexual intercourse between the parents is definitely tabooed during
the first two years after the birth of the child. This
taboo appears to be kept with a rather remarkable
stringency throughout the Zulu-Xosa peoples. Junod
states emphatically that among the Thonga " children
follow each other regularly at an interval of two and a
half years or three years, and seldom is the law trans-
gressed which says : a woman must nurse her child
during three ' hoes ', viz. three ploughing seasons ".[1]
Kidd adds that the Pondo women are kept " in strict
seclusion from their husbands " during the first three
years after their confinement, while the same custom is
recorded among other Xosa-Kafir peoples. The problem
has obvious practical bearings for those missionaries and
others who insist on strict monogamy among these tribes.[2]

[1] Junod, *op. cit.*, Vol. I, p. 61.
[2] D. Kidd, *The Essential Kafir*, 1925, p. 19 ; also *Savage Childhood*,
1906, p. 82 ; *Report of the Commission on Native Laws and Customs*,
1883, No. 743. Further north among the Rhodesian peoples, Smith
and Dale state that this prohibition holds until the child's teeth are
fully grown (*op. cit.*, 1920, Vol. II, p. 13). Two or three seasons
is the tabooed period which I observed myself among the Babemba.

The period of suckling is therefore considerably longer among the Bantu peoples than it is in most European societies. But this is not the only difference in the relationship between child and mother which is thus developed. The savage and the civilized infants are treated during this period according to entirely different customs.

The modern well-to-do baby in our own society is trained to a fixed routine of sleeping, waking, and periodic meals ; the meals themselves being invariably associated with a regular procession of events—the lifting of the child from the cot, sudden changes of light, the preparation of the bath, or changing of clothes. In more directly physiological terminology, the digestive reflexes of the infant become conditioned to a definite series of stimuli—visual, tactile, or auditory—and it wakes, if in health, at given time intervals. Its cry of hunger may be stilled, not only by the sight of the food itself, but by the mere sound of the lighting of the match which precedes the heating of the bottle, or any one of the whole chain of stimuli involved in the process.[1] The presence of the mother herself is only one element among such multifarious food signals. The child's physical contact with her is reduced to a minimum, practically to the period of nursing itself, and its emotional fixation on her is correspondingly decreased.

The Bantu infant is in quite a different position. It forms no such organized train of habits with regard to feeding. The mother, during the first few months of the infant's life, must be considered as almost the sum-total of the environment with which it is in contact. The two are hardly ever apart. Sleeping or waking the baby is pressed close to her body. She goes to work with it strapped to her back, or sitting astride her hip in a sling of goat or antelope skin, where it dozes as she tills the

[1] Cf. J. Baldwin, *Mental Development in the Child and the Race*, 1895, p. 122.

fields, with only a head visible above the fold of the skin.[1] Indeed, so adapted to this position does it become that, when lifted from the ground, it " stretches out its legs at right-angles with its body in order to sit on its mother's back ".[2] At night it sleeps on its mat by her side.[3]

Even when the mother's supply of milk fails, apparently a rare occurrence in primitive society, it is she who administers the substitute food to the baby as a general rule. The Kafir woman, as Dudley Kidd records, even holds the calabash of cow's milk up her breast to simulate most nearly the action of suckling. It is the mother, too, who feeds the baby with the supplementary foods which the savage infant is given from birth upwards— amasi (sour milk), and a pap of Kafir corn among the Zulu-Xosa peoples.[4]

The child is thus very intimately in contact with its mother during the first month of its life. As Mrs. Seligman suggests, comparison with the marsupial cub would really be closer than that with " the baby in our own civilization, lying separated from its mother in cot or perambulator ".[5]

The Bantu mother becomes therefore the centre of all those emotions associated with the gratification of her child's appetite, while other stimuli from the outer world attain relatively little importance in its affective life. The baby associates the reception of food with a tender bodily presence, rather than with a regular sequence of events in its more distant environment.[6]

---

[1] Smith and Dale, op. cit., Vol. II, p. 13 ; cf. also E. Casalis, The Basutos, 1861, p. 192 ; A. Kropf, Das Volk der Xosa-Kaffern, 1889, p. 122.

[2] Junod, op. cit., Vol. I, p. 47.

[3] D. Kidd, Savage Childhood, p. 49.

[4] D. Kidd, op. cit. pp. 37–38.

[5] B. Z. Seligman, " Incest and Descent ", J.R.A.I., Vol. LIX, 1929, p. 242.

[6] I have myself been surprised to see how little savage babies of a few months old appear to " notice "—in the sense of following lights or sounds as our own children do. I came to the conclusion that this was due to the fact that none of these stimuli were connected with the fulfilment of the child's needs. The black baby sleeps through all

Again, in the case of the actual feeding of the suckling, there is another important distinction to be made between the white and the black child. The civilized mother will often refuse to respond immediately to her child's desire. The whole modern theory of education demands the initiation of a definite scheme of child-training actually from the day of birth. The complex integration of character needed to adapt the individual to the conditions of present-day life probably requires such carefully organized discipline. Infant habits cannot be left to form haphazard, and it is considered imperative that the feeding of the baby should be subject to the most systematic rules.[1] The child is often left to cry unheeded for quite a considerable period if it should wake before its feeding-time. Its efforts to summon the mother are often unsuccessful, and she remains a more or less incalculable personality who cannot be controlled at will.

Bantu practice is almost diametrically opposed to such modern theories of child nurture. Among the Rhodesian peoples I have been studying I have never seen a child refused the breast, however inconvenient its demand might have been to a mother at work in the fields. To turn to the area we are considering, Junod says that the Thonga mother " would deem it a cruelty to refuse the breast to a crying child ". Smith and Dale say of the Ba-Ila baby " it drinks at all times ; whenever it cries it is put to the breast ".[2] The infant's needs are therefore satisfied constantly and without delay. The mother is a perpetually indulgent presence who can be controlled with gestures and cries.

sounds and adapts itself to all attitudes—including the violent movements of its mother in a dance. When it is hungry, it has only to whimper and the breast is put to its mouth. The other stimuli are meaningless. It wakes for no other reason at first.

[1] It must be remembered that the training of the execretory functions —so large a part of the education of the modern infant—is not attempted at this stage in savage society as a rule. " We must wait till the child can walk, for then it will have some intelligence," the Babemba mothers said to me. Cf. also D. Kidd, *Savage Childhood*, p. 84.

[2] Smith and Dale, *op. cit.*, Vol. II, p. 14. Junod, *op. cit.*, Vol. I, p. 47.

This fact must influence profoundly the child's first attitude to those about him. The earliest period of the child's consciousness is, according to Piaget, that in which " the parents, like parts of its own body, like all the objects that can be moved by the parents or by its own actions (food, toys, etc.), make up a class of things obedient to its desires ". In controlling them, as in controlling its own actions it first gains the sense of its own power—" the conduct of people towards it gradually gives the baby the habit of command ".[1]

Now in the modern nursery these early conceptions are very soon modified. The mother, or the nurse, does not always, as we have seen, satisfy automatically the child's desires. In fact, Baldwin, on the basis of observation of the civilized infant, states that the first distinction made between objects and individuals in the environment is due to this cause. Persons, he says, are distinguished by the irregularity of their behaviour. They are variable, difficult to control, yet responsible for the infant's needs. " They go off like guns on the stage of his panorama of experience ; they rise and smite him when he least expects it ; and his reactions to them are about equally divided between surprised gratifications and equally surprised disappointments." [2]

Now such a hypothesis, if applied to Bantu child development, no longer holds good. The primitive system of education provides no check to the constant efforts of the baby to gain its desires. During the first year or so of its existence the Kafir child is almost in a position of domination over the mother, its sense of power being experienced initially and chiefly through the immediate satisfaction of its demands on her for food. This feeling of secure possession is no doubt increased

---

[1] Piaget, *The Child's Conception of the World*, 1929, pp. 154 and 153 ; cf. also B. Malinowski, " The Problem of Meaning in Primitive Languages ", appendix to *The Meaning of Meaning*, C. K. Ogden and I. A. Richards, 1923, for a similar conception illustrating the origin of language.

[2] J. Baldwin, *Thought and Things*, Vol. I, p. 60.

by the fact that the Bantu baby is allowed unchallenged use of its privileges for a considerable period, since the mother is tabooed from conceiving a new child before the weaning of the last.

In later infancy the situation becomes more complex of course. The child is less dependent on its mother as it becomes able to crawl and walk, and other individuals assume importance in its environment. It finds other sources of pleasures and excitement than the satisfaction of its hunger and physical needs alone. It is passing through a period of eager experimentation of its own desires and the nature of the world about it. In any community an infant's first experience of its mother's power to satisfy its physical needs must be continuously extended in demands for further expressions of her affection and indulgence towards him. But in the case of the Bantu baby of two or three years, side by side with this deepening emotional attitude towards the mother, the original physiological relationships produced by suckling remains undisturbed. Not only is the child still in very close physical contact with his mother—sleeping on her mat at night, going to work in the fields on her back by day—but he is allowed to take the breast whenever he desires. While solid food probably supplements the baby's diet very largely during the last year or so before weaning, the psychological importance of the nursing relationship is hardly diminished thereby.

The act of suckling acquires additional and complex values each succeeding month as a sensuous pleasure and symbol of the mother's indulgent affection, and immediate response to her child's desire. I have myself observed among the Babemba that a child of two to six years, or even older, will instinctively clutch the mother's breast when frightened, cold, or in some distress. Once secure with its hands on her breast, it will gaze with a kind of roguish defiance at a hostile world. If the mother scolds it, it will put the nipple to its mouth as though challenging her to continue her unnatural conduct. I have even heard a young girl soothe a small boy she had been teasing by catching him to her unformed breasts, saying, " Never mind then. I'll suckle you,"—the action itself appearing to calm and appease the angry child. Maternal tenderness among these primitive peoples appears to be definitely associated with the mother's attributes as a conveyor of food.

Having thus discussed the first nutritional relationship on a more or less biological basis, let us see how the tie between child and mother is further emphasized in Bantu society by different family usages, or magical and religious beliefs.

To begin with, the bond between the two individuals is strengthened by the comparative isolation in which they live during these first years. In daily life the segregation of all women and children is fairly complete, especially in the case of the wives of a polygamous household each in their separate huts ringed round the kraal. No Bantu husband will eat with his wife and children, at any rate for the chief meal of the day. He takes his food, either on the men's place, in the centre of the kraal, as among the Thonga tribes, or in a separate partition of the hut according to Kafir usage. Moreover, economic activities make for a still further isolation. The mother with her small child is at work all day in the fields, while the father remains in his kraal, or supervising the herd of cattle.

But beyond this general sex differentiation, it appears that the Kafir father pays little attention to his infant children—contrary to the practice of some Oceanic societies where the male parent performs small services for his baby with as great a tenderness as the mother herself.[1] This fact may be due in part to magic beliefs. Lactation is not merely a physiological process according to most savage philosophers, but a time of special

[1] B. Malinowski, *The Sexual Life of Savages*, p. 17; R. Firth, *op. cit.*, p. 107.

danger demanding ritual precautions and taboos. For instance, among the Thonga, the father may not touch his new-born child, even after his wife has been purified from the blood of birth, until the third month, when the ceremony of the *Yandla*, or the presentation of the child to the moon, has taken place. He will not mourn for a baby which has died before the *Rite of the tying of the Cotton string* at the age when the child first crawls and is considered fit to be admitted as a member of the society.[1] Among the Basuto the mother and baby remain two months in the home of the maternal grand-mother.[2] Such an isolation of the two individuals affected by the birth is a very common practice in all primitive societies.

The privileges and obligations of the father are in fact very limited during the first three years of his child's life. He is obliged to refrain from sexual intercourse with the mother for fear of harming the child. He may have to provide special sustenance for the mother during her confinement,[3] and he is also responsible for the sacrifices made to the Ancestor Gods at the various ceremonies which mark the birth and growth of the child. But these are acts of legal emphasis of his paternity. In actual life he has little to do with the child, and in case of divorce, he cannot claim the offspring which is entirely his by right of his lobola payment (cf. Chapter IV) until the day when the child is weaned. It may be said in fact that the Bantu mother is never so completely in possession of her child as during the first three years of its life.

To sum up very briefly therefore our conclusions as to the importance of lactation in the formation of family

---

[1] Cf. Junod, *op. cit.*, Vol. I, pp. 42–57.

[2] E. Casalis, *op. cit.*, p. 192.

[3] Junod says that the husband must provide the wife with a fowl during her confinement, *op. cit.*, Vol. I, p. 42 ; cf. also C. Dundas, *Kilmanjaro and its People*, 1924, p. 200. It is considered a disgrace among these tribes if the wife is not well-fed by the father and the parents-in-laws during the first three months after the birth of her child, even if food has to be begged or borrowed for the purpose.

ties—I think it must be granted that the long period of suckling and the methods of infant-feeding practised by these particular Bantu communities influence very strongly the relationship of mother and child. The baby is more intimately tied to its parent in earliest infancy than can be the case in any modern society. Its dependence on her for food is associated, not only with close physical contact, but with sentiments of pleasure, affection, and a sense of power, and exclusive possession. The emotional bonds so developed are deepened still further by the organization of daily activities among these peoples, and the customs and beliefs regarding birth and parenthood.

Our problem now increases in complexity. We have to try to estimate the influence of this early sentiment on the subsequent relationships which the child must form within the family group. We have to consider the effect of weaning on the attitude of the child to the mother, and the shaping of the early emotional tie according to the position she now occupies in the whole nutritive scheme. With the differing traditions of each society the child may either remain dependent upon his mother for food, or else he may be taken from her care. His affectionate contact with her may deepen and develope, or it may have to change to fit the rôle she now plays in household life or village routine. The sociological attributes of maternity begin to modify the physiological tie, and it is these cultural traditions which we have now to study in the particular society which we have chosen to survey.

3. Weaning

The weaning of the civilized baby of well-to-do parents takes place usually at three to nine months of age. It is a very gradual process, and produces little change in the life of the infant, especially during the earlier months. The tie of suckling is not the only element in the relationship between mother and child. The savage infant, on the contrary, is not weaned until it has developed emotionally a much more complex attitude towards the mother, and until it has reached physiologically a more or less independent stage. Professor Malinowski suggests, indeed, that it takes place " at a moment when the child neither wants nor needs the mother's breast any more, so that the first wrench is eliminated ".[1]

Now this is the point that we have first to consider, with the aid of such little material as is available on the subject. Does weaning in a savage society produce a deep emotional trauma in the child's life ?

We know that Karl Abraham has claimed, on the basis of a study of individual psychoses, that severe neuropathic conditions may be caused in this way. He attempts also to correlate temperamental differences in after life with the varying degrees of satisfaction or disappointment which the infant has experienced during suckling and weaning.[2] Such conclusions may, or may not, be confirmed by the study of infant psychology among primitive tribes. But we are concerned here, not so much with individual pathological conditions, as with the sociological setting in which weaning is accomplished, the change in family relationships so involved, and the native beliefs as to the magic or legal importance of the act. This is the contribution which the anthropologist, as distinct from the psychologist, should be able to provide.

Unfortunately, it is just on this point that our material is disappointingly inadequate. The process of weaning is portrayed in most field accounts as a single event—a religious rite, rather than a stage in life history. The ritual and magic acts often performed on this occasion are usually recorded in detail as typical *rites de passage* in the child's ceremonial life. But changes in its actual

[1] B. Malinowski, *Sex and Repression in Savage Societies*, p. 26.
[2] Karl Abraham, *Selected Papers*, tr. 1927, Chap. XXIV ; cf. also p. 126.

way of living at this crisis of its existence are often impossible to picture from the information given.[1]

We know, however, the following facts, which would seem to show that whereas in our own society the emotional wrench—if wrench it be—affects the baby subconsciously, in a primitive tribe weaning takes place at a time when the child is old enough to understand the meaning of punishment or rebuke.[2] Disciplinary measures are evidently taken to prevent the baby from sucking the breast. The mother, who has been up to now, supremely indulgent, must begin to refuse the child's desires. The Babemba women say that they squeeze the juice of the mulombwa tree on their breasts at weaning. This is a red juice. They say that it frightens the child, because it looks like blood. I have not seen this done, but I have noticed mothers slapping their children for coming back to the breast when they should have been weaned at two or three years old. They call them " Papu " in varying tones of annoyance or resignation—which term seems merely to mean a " greedy sucker at the breast ". Junod says that among the Thonga the women cover their breasts with pepper when weaning a child : while the Ba-Ila women paint the nipples with nicotine.[3] The Thonga rite of weaning also includes, besides the hondlola or sacrifice to the family ancestors on behalf of the child, the administration of a medicine to make him " forget his mother ".

There is this much evidence, therefore, to show that weaning has actually to be enforced in a primitive society. It does not seem to take place gradually and without

[1] The revised edition of Notes and Queries on Anthropology, 1929, for instance, contains no reference to the importance of this event in the child's life.

[2] Accounts of the resentment and grief expressed by the modern baby at weaning seem to me to confuse the distress of the child when put on to a food that probably doesn't suit it, with the emotional trauma of separation from the mother. Most civilized babies are cuddled just as much before as after weaning, and can suck their thumbs or any other substitute just as much too. The break seems to me to differ essentially from that which takes place in savage society.

[3] Junod, op. cit., Vol. I, p. 60 ; Smith and Dale, op. cit., Vol. II, p. 12.

effort, although we should need a good deal more first-hand evidence before we could announce this fact categorically. But in any case weaning probably acts as the first barrier placed between the child and its mother ; and the prohibition must be enforced at an age when the child more or less consciously associates the act with sensual pleasure, and not in early infancy as in our own society. This statement I think holds true whether we accept the psycho-analytical doctrine that such pleasure is entirely sexual in nature, or whether we adopt a narrower, and to my mind, more scientific use of the term " sex ".[1] We have given instances to show that the savage child continues to demand the breast after it has already begun to eat other foods, and that it seems to experience pleasure and comfort in the act. Moreover, it must be remembered that this expectation of pleasure is all centred round the mother's breast itself. The savage child does not require any substitutes, since it is able to suckle whenever it pleases. If it wakes, while being carried on the mother's back, it will cry, and the nipple will be put into its hands. The mother very rarely attempts to distract its attention by a toy or a game of any sort, and I do not remember having seen a native baby sucking its thumb as a substitute for the breasts.[2] The savage mother does not often play with her baby or caress it as a white mother does, although she is quite as devoted, tender, and proud. It is her breast that provides, not only sensual pleasure, but the

---

[1] I think I have noticed that small boys are more insistent in their demands upon their mothers in this respect than little girls, but I have not yet collected sufficient evidence to state this as a fact.

[2] It would be interesting to know whether thumb-sucking in children or the various adult forms of neurotic hunger, or food phantasies attributed by Abraham to prolonged suckling or fixation at the oral stage of development, are commonly found in savage society. D. Kidd mentions that Kafir children are fond of sucking their thumbs or index fingers, or biting their nails (*Savage Childhood*, p. 52), but, as I state above, I did not notice this myself, and since writing this I find that Margaret Mead makes the same comment. (*Handbook of Child Psychology*, edited by Charles Murcheson, 1931, p. 676.) Mrs. Edwin Smith, who lived among the Ba-Ila women and children for many years, confirmed my observation in a personal communication.

feeling of comfort and dependence, and the confidence that there is a superor being always ready to answer demands.

Now the results of this very close relationship between child and mother I cannot define. I can merely pose the problems here, in order to stimulate further research in the field. But it can at any rate be said definitely that weaning in a primitive society cuts across a very complex emotional situation. Whether we consider the infantile pleasure in suckling as being sensual or definitely sexual, weaning is the first prohibition laid on this indulgence. It is the child's first experience of the whole phenomenon of *taboo*. Moreover, in these communities where weaning is long delayed, we find very universally taboos, and magic beliefs connected with a woman's breasts and her milk. In a tribe where the babies are nursed in public without the slightest embarrassment, and where women are usually naked from the waist up, I have yet noticed an extraordinary interest in breasts as such, even among quite young children. A woman's breasts would always be commented upon first in any picture I showed them. There were indecent jokes on the subject, and a sort of half obscene banter about suckling between men and women occupying different tabooed positions in the kinship group. Junod says that the word *lumaka*, i.e. the state of mother and child when weaning is taking place, " is pronounced with a curious smile, because the act of weaning is in direct relation to the sexual life "—being the time when cohabitation between the father and mother is resumed.[1]

But from the more directly sociological point of view there is another aspect of weaning that is important.

[1] Junod, *op. cit.*, Vol. I, p. 60. It must be remembered that where mother-in-law avoidances are strong, a man is stated to have a particular horror of seeing the breasts of the woman who has suckled his wife— cf. Junod, *op. cit.*, Vol. I, p. 240 ; D. Leslie, *Among the Zulus and Amatongas*, 1875, p. 172 ; D. Kidd, *The Essential Kafir*, p. 241. Among the Akamba the one curse without palliative is to draw milk from a wife's breast and lick it on the hand. After this no cohabitation is possible (C. W. Hobley, *The Ethnology of the Akamba*, 1910, p. 105).

In a primitive society the time may coincide with actual separation of the mother and child. Temporary adoption at weaning is by no means an uncommon occurrence. The Thonga baby is taken, immediately after the rite has been performed, to the house of its grandparents—maternal or paternal, alternately with each child of the family—and Junod records that the parents visit the village next day to watch their child in secret to see if he is weeping in his new home. " It is a sad day for them as well as for the child . . . he must not see his mother, otherwise he would cry." [1] It is difficult to know how complete the separation from the mother really is in these cases. Among the Babemba, where the same custom holds, marriage is matrilocal, so that the child who goes to sleep in the hut of its maternal grandmother after weaning, remains yet in the same village, and sees its mother by day. But among the Southern Bantu, marriage is patrilocal, and while the kraal of the paternal grandparent is probably near that of the father, the maternal grandmother's kraal is very likely some distance away. The attitude of the mother, both to the child, and to the female relatives who act as her substitutes during these years, would be an interesting field of observation, especially in view of the rather strained relations which often exist between the groups united in marriage (cf. Chapter IV).

We see thus that the tradition of any particular culture may insist on an actual change in the life of the child at weaning, as well as setting a taboo on the act of suckling itself. Observations on this aspect of the problem are urgently needed if we are to understand anything of the nature of the sentiment formed between mother and child in a primitive community.

Moreover, we have to consider in this connection, the effect of weaning on the relation of the child to its father, and to other members of the family group.   In a primitive

---

[1] Junod, *op. cit.*, Vol. I, p. 60 ; cf. also Smith and Dale, *op. cit.*, Vol. I, p. 391 ; A. T. Bryant, *Zulu-English Dictionary*, 1905, p. 36.

community the separation of the child from its mother may be associated with powerful causes of jealousy in household life. In some cases, as we have seen, the child is removed for a period to live in another kraal; but in others it remains in the paternal hut. At weaning the father resumes his sexual rights over the mother, and in a community where sex relations are discussed and observed by children of all ages, such a fact must influence powerfully the attitude of the child towards its father. The small boy is separated from his mother, and prevented from satisfying his sensual pleasure in suckling, while at the same time he sees his father begin to possess his mother sexually for the first time.

Further causes of jealousy are involved in the subsequent arrival of a new suckling to disturb the exclusive possession of the mother by the older child. Kidd records that among the Kafir, where the custom of temporary adoption at weaning seems less common, the natives themselves recognize such an emotional disturbance as an expected incident in family life. When the new baby is born, he says, the older girl is brought in by her grandmother to see it. It is placed in her arms, and if she shows any jealousy she is taken out of the hut for another three days. She is then brought back again, and if she again shows jealousy, the mother must take her in her arms, fondle both children together, and suckle the baby. Otherwise his informant added, "the milk would have made the baby ill". This is an interesting aspect of family psychology, but one on which we cannot attempt to dogmatize without further investigation in the field. Suffice it to say that the process of weaning in a community where the nursing period is prolonged, affects not only the attitude of the child to its mother, but also its relations to other members of the family group.

We must remember also that the nutritive and reproductive functions of maternity are definitely linked in primitive legal code. Suckling is part of the obligations

of the married woman—one which may have to be paid
for if performed by any other woman except the mother,
and which, in some tribes, is tabooed except in the case
of the woman's own child.[1]　In some cases also nursing,
is considered as a service on the part of the wife which
entitles her family to certain privileges in kinship transactions.　J. T. Brown says that among the Bechuana
natives the *malume*, or maternal uncle, derives his rights
over his nephews and nieces from the fact that they
have derived their nourishment from his sister's breasts.[2]

Thus on the one hand, the break in the child to mother
relationship at weaning initiates that separation of the
child from the mother which later becomes the incest
sentiment within the family group.　The act of suckling
is surrounded with magic observances and restrictions,
and weaning is itself considered to have some connection
with the sexual life.　On the other hand, suckling is
definitely a social service : a physiological process
regulated by tribal custom, an essential part of the
marriage contract, and symbolic of the functions of
maternity in native eyes.　It is for this reason that a
comparative study of weaning customs is important.
The severing of the tie of suckling has results as important
sociologically as its formation at time of the birth of
the child.

4. Early Childhood

The baby must now be considered to have reached the
next recognizable stage of its life—the period from three
years till about seven or eight, when the first economic
tasks are begun, and when the daily life and occupations
of the boy become sharply differentiated from those of
the girl.　Early and later childhood are separated, that

---

[1] Junod records the case of a child being suckled by the co-wife of
its dead mother, the foster-mother receiving payment from the dead
woman's family on this account, (Junod, *op. cit.*, Vol. I, p. 49).　Among
the Ba-Ila it is taboo to suckle the child of any other family but one's
own (Smith and Dale, *op. cit.*, Vol. I, p. 374).

[2] J. T. Brown, *op. cit.*, p. 53.

is to say, by an alteration in social status and routine, rather than by a definite physiological change.

During this stage of childhood we have two problems to examine. First, as we have noted, it is in the post-weaning period, when the mother's supply of milk is no longer available, that the savage child first becomes aware of insecurity or competition in obtaining his food supply. We must therefore study as fully as possible the actual methods of child-feeding during these early years. Shortage or plenty will determine his pre-occupation in satisfying his hunger, and will shape very largely his attitude towards those individuals in the group upon whom he relies to provide his food.

Second, it is at this period that the child's feelings towards his mother as the food-purveyor must be changed. In some communities she will cease to provide him with food at all; while in other cases her function is un-altered, but she fulfils it by a series of complicated social activities in the preparation and production of food-stuffs, and associates with it a number of other functions. These combine to stamp the orthodox picture of matern-ity on the mind of the growing child. So also the baby's attitude towards the other members of its household group undergoes during this period a profound modifica-tion. The part they have to play in the daily routine of eating and food-preparation determines very largely the pattern of his sentiment towards them in each particular tribe. The arrangement of family meals and food dis-tribution is therefore exceedingly important in the period of childhood we have under survey.

(a) The Sociological Functions of Maternity

Whilst observations on this aspect of child life are still very meagre, it seems clear that the small boy or girl in a Bantu society feels little anxiety as to his food supply during these early years, or responsibility as to its production. The little children are still largely dependent on their mothers or upon the woman who is looking after them. They feed with her, and not with the separate groups of boys, girls, or men, into which the community divides at meals. They are thus under her special protection, and since the Bantu women, in general, have a great deal of power over the distribution of vegetable produce and milk, she is likely to see that they do not go short. They seem indeed to occupy a rather privileged position, protected at mealtimes from the competition of the groups of older boys and girls, and occupying a strategic post at their mother's fireplace. Here they are allowed to hang round their elders at mealtimes begging for choice bits, behaviour which would be discouraged, or even expressly forbidden, in the case of older children in the presence of grown-ups.

So much can be said as to the child's security as to his food supply during these early years.

To turn now to our second problem—the changes which take place in the infant's dependence on his mother for food. In primitive societies, where the family acts as the sole food-consuming unit, there is a continuous association of the functions of motherhood with the preparation, production, and control of food.

Each Bantu woman presides over her own fireplace, even in the case of a polygamous household. The provision of cooked food for the husband is her essential matrimonial duty, as well as a cherished privilege and a source of power.[1] Neglect to provide the husband with

[1] This is not by any means an invariable custom in primitive society. Whereas women cook separately for each family among most of the South, East and Central Bantu, among the Ovambo the men, on the contrary are reported to act as cooks, while amongst the Bushmen both sexes cook separately for themselves (G. Stowe, *The Native Races of South Africa*, 1905, p. 45).

Leaving Africa we find that in Polynesia generally the cooking is done by men, and communal sheds for cooking are commonly found. Men and women share the cooking for the large Samoan household, says Miss Mead, " but the bulk of the work falls on the boys and young men " (*Coming of Age in Samoa*, p. 48) ; cf. also G. Turner, *Samoa a Hundred Years Ago*, 1884, p. 112. In the Tonga Islands cooking is done by the lowest rank of men, and the term " cook " is an opprobrious one (W. Mariner, *The Natives of the Tonga Islands*, 1818, Vol. II, p. 89). In the Trobriands men cooked on ceremonial occasions (B. Malinowski, *Argonauts of the Western Pacific*, p. 170), while in *The*

cooked food may be a cause for divorce among many of these peoples, and conversely, a husband who has left his wife in anger, may often be forced to return and sue for mercy, if he can get no one else to cook his food. Smith and Dale describe the wives of a chief vying with each other to produce tasty dishes to be carried to him when he sits at court. So essential is the part of cook in the married woman's status, that a husband's neglect to taste a dish prepared by a wife is as potent a cause of jealousy between the women of a polygamous household as omitting to sleep with her.[1] The Kafir husband can reduce his wife to shame by shouting aloud her inadequacies as a cook from the door of his hut.[2] The great wife of a Zulu chief may be degraded in rank, according to Jenkinson, if she cannot serve strangers and visitors with suitable and sufficient food.[3]

It must be remembered, too, that over a wide area of South and East Africa the women are definitely responsible for the supply of all vegetable produce. The rôle of cook is invariably associated with that of tiller of the soil. In fact, it might seem as though the one task gave the right to the performance of the other, since we read that the bride is not allowed to cook at her own fireplace for a year after marriage since she will not have sown and reaped her fields till then.[4] J. T. Brown says of the Bechuana that " all the work of providing vegetable food, from the sowing of the grain to the reaping of the crop, the threshing of the maize and Kaffir-corn, the husking of it in a wooded mortar called a *kika*, with a wooden pestle, the grinding of the husked grain . . . the cooking of the porridge and the brewing of beer, are

Island of Stone Money, W. H. Furness records that men and women have separate fires and may not eat food cooked in the same vessels (p. 120). In the Loyalty Islands, only the unmarried of both sexes may cook (S. H. Ray, " The People and Language of Lifu, Loyalty Islands ", *J.R.A.I.*, Vol. XLVII, 1917, p. 260).

[1] Smith and Dale, *op. cit.*, Vol. II, p. 51 ; G. Lindblom, *The Akamba*, 1920, p. 82.
[2] D. Kidd, *The Essential Kafir*, p. 330.
[3] T. B. Jenkinson, *The Amazulu*, 1882, p. 49.
[4] Junod, *op. cit.*, Vol. I, pp. 125, 126, 185.

all in their hands ". The same may be said of most other South African tribes such as the Zulu, AmaXosa, Thonga, Basuto, etc., except where the introduction of the plough has led to joint work by men and women in the fields.[1] As soon as she is strong enough, the little girl begins to help her mother in agricultural work : when she is married the task is definitely part of her marriage undertaking and privileges : and in old age she continues the work to which her life has been given. " During all her lifetime she has contracted such an intimate union with Mother Earth that she cannot conceive existence away from her gardens, and she crawls to them with her hoe, by a kind of instinct, till she dies." [2]

It thus happens that the small children see their mother constantly at work in the preparation of food— either hoeing her field, pounding her grain, or cooking the one or two daily meals. The little girl, besides these associations, begins at an early age to share in her mother's tasks and responsibilities herself. She amuses herself by cooking little dishes of her own, and when playing at married life with some small boy, she must always cook him a meal. At her initiation ceremony she is exhorted, " You are to provide food. Oh, woman, cook well, and do not spoil the food : you are to be perfect in cooking." [3] She knows that her *lobola* price may depend on her skill in this respect, and in some languages such as Thonga, there is a special word which describes the girl who is a good cook—*Awa hisa*, i.e. " she burns ".[4]

[1] J. T. Brown, *op. cit.*, pp. 49, 50 ; also J. Y. Gibson, *Story of the Zulus*, 1911, p. 2 ; J. Barrow, *Travels into the Interior of South Africa*, 1800, Vol. I, p. 204 ; Fritsch, *Die Eingeborenen Südafrikas*, 1872, p. 79 ; also the comprehensive study of H. Baumann, " Division of Work according to Sex in African Hoe Culture ", *Africa*, 1928, Vol. I, No. 3, p. 289.

The only exception to this rule appear to be the Mashona, the AmaMpondo, and those natives of the Matabele, Bapedi, and the Basuto who inhabit Natal. Casalis mentions that both sexes work with equal ardour in the fields among these peoples (*op. cit.*, p. 159).

[2] Junod, *op. cit.*, Vol. I, p. 214.
[3] Smith and Dale, *op. cit.*, Vol. II, p. 25.
[4] Junod, *op. cit.*, Vol. II, p. 36.

A composite picture of the functions of maternity is therefore gradually evolved in the child's mind. The mother prepares and grows the food, and she is also clearly the person who can distribute and divide it. The woman's power of owning and sharing out food differs of course from tribe to tribe, especially where the products of the herd are concerned. But as a general rule she has considerable power over the vegetable food, and may help herself from the store-houses she has filled for her husband, and in some cases, actually own food in her own right.[1] To her children she is clearly the centre of the household, and the controller of the family supplies. The bonds which united the child to the suckling mother are deepened and extended as she assumes in his eyes the sociological functions of maternity in the nutritive scheme of his tribe.

(b) Family Ties and the Household Meal

We must turn now to study the child's daily routine in the household group, and hence to discover the further series of nutritive relationships which he forms at this epoch of his life. After weaning, the child is subject, like his brothers and sisters, to the ordered sequence of family meals: and it is difficult perhaps to realize the full

[1] It is the custom of the Basuto and Zulu-Xosa peoples to allot a cow or cows to each wife for the use of herself and the babies. She may not sell these, but " she uses the milk for the support of her family and after the birth of her first son they are called his cattle ". (J. Shooter, *The Kafirs of Natal and the Zulu Country*, 1857, p. 84 ; I. Schapera, " Economic Changes in South African Native Life ", *Africa*, Vol. I, No. 2, 1928, pp. 173-4 ; E. Casalis, *op. cit.*, p. 143.) Among the Hottentots the position is carried to the other extreme, since a husband may not help himself to the milk sack without his wife's permission (S. S. Dornan, *Pygmies and Bushmen of the Kalahari*, 1925, p. 212).

With regard to the vegetable produce, Lichtenstein says of the Xosa women that they had the principal direction of all household affairs and common property (*Travels in South Africa*, Vol. I, p. 265), E. Casalis of the Basuto that all provisions of vegetables and dairy belonged to the women. The husband could not dispose of them without her permission (*op. cit.*, p. 143), whilst among the Barotse the women actually own a part of the crops (Holub, *Seven Years in South Africa*, 1881, Vol. II, p. 303). Among the Venda, a tribe bordering on the Thonga, a wife may even kill and eat goats without her husband's permission (Junod, *op. cit.*, Vol. I, p. 305).

significance of this fact.   We have got to remember that food simply cannot be obtained in a primitive society except through the full functioning of the family as the unit for its supply.   The components of the daily diet cannot be bought over a shop counter ready made.   It is thus that the child's first consciousness of family grouping and social distinctions is built up gradually through the customs which regulate the use and ownership of food and the taking of meals in the household group.   His mother, his father, and the members of his own and the contiguous households, all play their parts in this nutritive organization at different succeeding periods of his life.   Primitive ritual shows clearly the extent to which the common meal becomes symbolic of the ties of union between two members of a group, and it is in the circle of the family household that these sentiments first begin to find shape.

The father has as yet assumed little importance on the child's horizon, and little can be said about the nutritive aspect of the child-to-father tie.   Among the Thonga, we are told, that the father " does not bother much with these little boys and they enjoy an immense amount of liberty ".[1]   The father lives in his own hut in the centre of the kraäl circle, and as he eats almost entirely on the *Bandla* or men's place, he does not appear in the family circle at mealtimes.[2]   He is merely responsible for the provision of special treats for the little children, and not for the regular distribution of their food.   He is described as dividing up small shreds of meat from the ancestral offering to the small boys and girls, whereas it is the mother who deals out the porridge, the staple food.[3]   The child's tie to the father is not a nutritive one at this stage.   He does not act as the chief provider of food, nor does he demand the help of his

---

[1] Junod, *op. cit.*, Vol. I, p. 61.

[2] Among the Pondo and Fingoes described by Kidd, the men of the tribe eat with the women, but separated from them on the other side of the hut and receiving their food first.

[3] Kidd, *Savage Childhood*, p. 96.

small son in the food-producing activities in which he is engaged. It is among the groups of women and children that these first few years of the child's life are passed, and the segregation of the different families at mealtimes is the child's first education in his relationships to the different women in the kraal.

It is at mealtimes that the small children playing about together in the open life of the kraal come together to their respective mothers' huts. The typical arrangement of the kraal dwellings among the Southern Bantu gives particular emphasis to the family pattern. The huts are arranged in a circle enclosed by a thick-set hedge which gives protection from enemies or beasts. Within this ring the houses are arranged in a definite sequence, the patriarch's hut in the middle, his chief wife next to him, and the lesser wives in order of precedence. While in cases where the married brothers and sons remain in the old man's kraal, their huts will be built on the outskirts of the group. Bryant describes the Zulu village of former days as " a many-roomed house, inhabited by a single family ",[1] the headman, his wives and children, and his married sons. In the larger units to be found in the Thonga country, or the bigger AmaXosa settlements, the same form of family grouping is manifest in the arrangement of the huts. While even in the Bechuana towns separate clusters of houses belonging to the family are marked off geographically from the rest.[2]

Now the members of each household are self-contained units as regards the preparation and consumption of food. Each man keeps his own store-house, and each hut has its own milk sack and churn.[3] At mealtimes each different household is clearly distinguished, although the men and women usually eat apart. The members of a

[1] A. T. Bryant, " The Zulu Family and State Organization ", *Bantu Studies*, 1923, Vol. II, No. 1, p. 47; J. Shooter, *op. cit.* p. 10.
[2] J. T. Brown, *op. cit.*, p. 47. W. J. Burchell, *Travels into the Interior of South Africa*, 1822, Vol. II, p. 513.
[3] Junod, *op. cit.*, Vol. II, pp. 25-7; Smith and Dale, *op. cit.*, Vol. I, p. 130. A joint sharing of the milk supply seems to have been practised in the Zulu kraals in earlier days.

family are those who receive their food from one woman, and who prepare it and eat it together according to the various rules of precedence which are observed in each particular tribe. Mr. Bryant tells me that he has often heard Zulu mothers rebuke their children for straying into other huts at mealtimes, although by the laws of hospitality they would be bound to be offered food. The child has to learn through the carrying out of the daily routine of mealtimes the structure and unity of the family group, and its relationship to the other households contiguous in the kraal.

These households include first of all those of the co-wives of the child's mother—whose huts stand in a circle with her own. The children of these huts are brought up together, and share in the common life of the kraal. But at mealtimes, as we have seen, the separation of each wife's family is fairly complete. A Zulu woman would protest if the child of one of her co-wives appeared continually in her hut when food was being prepared.

Again, this segregation of the different households is sometimes accompanied by feelings of real hostility, overt or suppressed. Jealousy between the co-wives of a polygamous household is a commonplace of primitive life. The Thonga language contains a special word *Bukwele* which is applied to this particular form of rancour, and also serves to indicate the small courtyard where the wives assemble to shout insults and abuse at each other.[1] This is a hostility which the children are not likely to ignore. Kidd speaks of the hatred between the children of rival wives, the sons being potentially competitors for the privileged positions in the kraal, and in the case of chief's sons, rival claimants for the throne.[2]

Moreover, the situation is complicated by the fact that the status of each wife is not by any means equal. Torday points out that the superior social and legal standing

---

[1] Junod, *op. cit.*, Vol. I, pp. 215–17 ; J. Shooter, *op. cit.*, p. 78.
[2] D. Kidd, *Savage Childhood*, p. 17.

of the " chief wife " is a common feature of all Bantu societies.[1] The chief's wife's household is, in general, more richly supplied with food than the others.[2] Among the Zulu-Xosa groups this privilege is extended to those of the " right-hand " and " left-hand " wives,—substitute " chief wives " whose sons will inherit in default of an heir produced by the first. Each of these households possesses its own cattle, allotted to the woman on her marriage, and passing, on the death of the father, to her oldest son. If the husband takes new wives with the cattle from either of these three herds, such women must become attached to the household to which the cattle belongs, and subservient to the wife who owns the herd. Thus a series of lesser households become dependent on the greater for milk and food.[3] All the huts grouped round any particular household can eat meat slain by a member of the group. The Zulu child therefore finds himself in the centre of a series of small units, each of which owns separately their food supply, produces, prepares and eats it apart. He plays together with the children of all these households, and makes expeditions with them into the veldt. But at mealtimes the segregation is apparent, and the natural undercurrent of envy and hostility between them centres in the position of each family with regard to the possession and distribution of food.

Neither must we forget the other household groups in close contact with the child's own, and perhaps even contiguous with his in the circle of the kraal. These are the huts of his father's brothers—the elder who occupies a position of authority—usually designated by

---

[1] E. Torday, " Principles of Bantu Marriage ", *Africa*, 1929, Vol. II, No. 3. He cites the Zulu, Bathonga, Basuto, Matabele, Wachagga, Akamba, Akikuyu, Barotse and others.

[2] Smith and Dale give the proportion of cows allotted to the chief wife as 30, while the second wife would have 15, and the third 10, etc. (*op. cit.*, Vol. II, p. 67).

[3] *C.N.L.C.*, Appendix B, p. 19 ; A. Kropf, *op. cit.*, p. 161 ; T. B. Jenkinson, *op. cit.*, p. 34 ; H. Callaway, *The Religious System of the Amazulu*, 1887, p. 180 ; J. Shooter, *op. cit.*, pp. 84, 105-7.

a special term in most Bantu languages—and the younger, whose status is similarly defined, linguistically and otherwise. There will also be the households of the paternal grandparent, probably an important personage and a polygamist—and if the child comes at the tail end of the family, his own elder brothers may be married and have households of their own.

Thus the women with whom the child will come most in contact will be the paternal grandmother, the father's brothers' wives, and the mother's co-wives. If he has been sent to his maternal relatives to be adopted during these early years, the position of course will be altered. He will find himself dependent on the maternal grandmother, the mother's brothers' wives, and the wives of her nephews if they are already married. And here the difficulty of our problem is apparent. It is almost impossible to decide from the material available to what extent the child is dependent on either of these households for food. The field-observer on his first arrival in a village will notice that the small children apparently take food at random from any hut they fancy. They will wander about munching some raw fruit or vegetable, or pick up a potato or a corn cob from a field. Further investigation, however, will show him that the child can always tell him from whom he took the food. He will say from " my mother "—using the term in its extended sense—and pointing out the actual person referred to, even though he is too young to be able to explain her exact relationship to him. An older child will formulate some general rule about the different members of his kinship group. He will tell you those from whom he may take food without asking ; those who will give it to him if he just asks ; those who will surrender if he worries, or those who might give him some special treat just because they were kind ! He will sometimes even explain to you why such and such a household is bound to provide him with food.

Now information of this kind seems to be non-existent

with regard to these particular tribes of the Southern
Bantu. Junod tells us that the father's brothers—the
Tatana lwe 'nkulu, or " Great Father ", the elder brother,
and the *Tatana lwe Vntjonga*, or " Little Father ", the
younger brother, must be treated with respect and reverence like the father himself, and will take the latter's
place should he die. It is probable that these relatives
are bound to provide the child with food if he is short.
But it is the mother's relatives, he says—her father or
her brothers—who treat him with the most indulgent
affection, and with whom he feels most at ease. They
may give the child treats on a visit, although they are
not under legal obligation to provide for him with food.
Later also, he will learn, that he enjoys a kind of ritual
licence with his maternal uncles' property and can command his wives to cook him food when he pleases.

The mother's sisters are the real *mamana* or substitute mothers, and will bring up the child should his
mother die. They are treated with a tenderness and
affection quite different from the attitude towards the
other *mamana*—the wives of the father's brothers, or the
mother's co-wives.[1]

Now in a matrilineal tribe such as the Babemba, a
child will tell you that he may run into his maternal
aunts' huts and take food without permission, but that
in the house of his paternal uncle he will have to ask
politely. The wife of his uncle will have to give him
food, because she is afraid of her husband, but she does
not like doing it because " I don't belong to her clan.
She would rather give food to her own children." Kinship distinctions of this sort must hold just the same in
the very different type of patrilineal society which we
find among the Southern Bantu. I should surmise that
the tenderness and indulgence of the mother's family as
compared with the more severe treatment of the father's
relatives—the legal guardians of the child—is expressed
in a very similar way with regard to the provision of

[1] Junod, *op. cit.*, Vol. I, p. 229 ; cf. also Chapter III of this work.

food. I am at any rate certain that there is a wide range of *nuances* in the way food is shared or given in a primitive society, varying from the strict fulfilment of a legal obligation, to the indulgence of natural affection, or the gift made as a sign of respect.[1] I am also sure that these kinship usages are well appreciated even by a child of six or seven years. He becomes early acquainted with the grouping of the family at mealtimes, and the rules governing the ownership and distribution of cooked food. It is by lessons such as these that the whole kinship structure is felt rather than explained. Family sentiment is imprinted by a series of daily habits rather than taught by any definite lesson or rule.

Another important problem during this period of childhood is the question of the actual rules by which food is consumed. Primitive, as well as civilized communities, have a more or less complicated eating etiquette. Few field-workers seem yet to have realized the importance of observing the working of such codes. All those innumerable details that go to make the whole habit of eating in any particular culture—its table manners, so to speak—are difficult to describe even in a community in which one has lived for many years. They reflect so entirely the whole system of values which food has acquired in that society, either through scarcity, abundance, or a special association between the possession of food and social prestige. Moreover, in a primitive com-

---

[1] It is interesting to note that these kinship obligations are expressed in some societies in the form of definite rules. Malinowski describing the *Veveni* or customary exchange of food at the daily meal of the Mailu natives (off the New Guinea coast) states that when food is short a man need only supply his brothers and sisters ; when it is fairly adequate he extends the obligation to half-brothers and sisters ; and when it is abundant he must give to paternal and maternal cousins and uncles ("The Natives of Mailu", *Transactions of the Royal Society of South Australia*, Vol. XXXIX, 1915, p. 546).

In the large family groups of Samoa, Margaret Mead describes the children wandering about among their kinsmen according as the latter are noted for "fewest babies, best food", etc. "From a relative one may demand food, clothing, shelter or assistance in a feud. Refusal of such a demand brands one as stingy and lacking in human kindness" (*op. cit.*, pp. 42–5).

munity, eating manners represent, in miniature, the rules of food distribution among the members of the group. The pattern of behaviour between different individuals at mealtimes—man and woman, child and parent, chief and commoner, or citizen and stranger—is an expression of their respective social attributes as well as the general attitude of the community towards food itself. The acquisition of these codes of manners in early childhood teaches the baby his position in the family household, and the different distinctions in status of those about him.

Turning, therefore, to our own particular society, we find that greed is rebuked in children, according to Kidd, and usually treated with practical jokes and laughter. Avidity exhibited in the kraal of a stranger is specially reprehensible, and the children who go out to visit their friends in another village are specifically cautioned against eating the crumbs off the floor ! An appearance of hunger might reflect on the prosperity of their own family ! [1]

Further, the duty of sharing food with other members of the family is early impressed on the child. Kafir babies are taught that it is the basest deed conceivable not to divide a tempting morsel with everyone present. Junod states that Thonga children seem to him to be superior to their European contemporaries in this respect, even from an early age. [2] Small boys and girls in a civilized community are taught laboriously to share their toys and pleasures with their fellows : but in Bantu society this form of training is centred round the offering and sharing of food. The definite rules of hospitality, which later form part of the whole system of clan obligation, are built up in early childhood on the basis of such lessons.

[1] D. Kidd, *Savage Childhood*, pp. 111–12. This psychology is of course common in our own community, but naturally assumes greater proportions in a society in which the possession of food is the chief or only form of measuring wealth.
[2] Junod, *op. cit.*, Vol. I, p. 318.

From early years, too, the children have to observe certain rules of precedence in eating which betoken the status of the men and women members of the family. The typical Bantu society is rigidly divided, not only according to sex, but also to age. These divisions are invariably emphasized at the time of the daily meal. The Kafir child may not take food from the pot in the presence of his elders, and he must receive food in both hands to show his sense of the giver's munificence. One hand would not be sufficient to hold the gift ![1] The girl has to learn to offer food to the boy, although *he* may devour any dainty without handing her a share.

But these are only scattered observations on what, in my own experience, is a rich field of research. I believe that in a primitive community every shade of distinction in status can be expressed by variations in eating etiquette. Few observers have recorded fully such details as characteristic attitudes when eating, conversation suitable at meals, ways of asking and refusing food, or expressing satisfaction with what one is given, and the methods of apportioning special highly valued delicacies such as meat. In fact, such observations are exceedingly difficult to make, as meals do not take place in the open gaze of the public in most communities, but in the intimacy of the domestic hearth. But I believe, none the less, that such information is very important, and that it is largely by training in the manners of the table that the savage child gets his sense of the status and functions of his different kinsmen. A Mubemba boy in answer to my question as to who were his " fathers ", replied, " The men whom I kneel to when I bring them water to drink ". In just such a concrete fashion, the segregation of different groups at mealtimes makes him aware of the interrelation of the various households comprising his village or clan.

[1] A very widespread custom among African peoples. Professor Seligman tells me the Chinese do the same.

5. Later Childhood

We are ready now to turn to the next period of the child's life. By the term " later childhood " I mean the epoch between the child's eighth or tenth year and his attainment of puberty—years which are characterized sociologically by marked changes in his way of life. Broadly speaking, these are three in number : the division of the children according to sex, involving altered occupations ; the clear demarcation of those age distinctions which are such an important feature of the organization of all Bantu societies ; and, perhaps most important of all, the beginning of economic activities proper. In all these changes, the child's nutritional needs and habits are important, if not dominant factors in the development of kinship sentiment and relationships between the members of the village and clan.

(a) Grouping according to Sex and Age

We have seen that the sharing of meals in the mother's hut is the small child's first initiation into family life proper, and the essence of his daily routine. It is thus that he first becomes conscious of the differences in status and importance of the members of his family group. So now, as distinctions of age and sex cut across the household unit, the child begins to join other groups of his fellows and to form a new routine in his daily meals. Moreover, he becomes aware of the general sense of insecurity with which the savage man of necessity regards his food supply. The importance of rules of food ownership and distribution becomes a reality to him, as he begins to take an active part in the economic life of the village. His attitude towards his different relatives is very largely modified thereby. The break in his way of living is more or less sharp, but the change in his kinship sentiment is obviously gradual, lasting through the whole period of his youth and early manhood.

At seven or eight, then, the little boy is forbidden to eat any longer with his mother and sisters round the

household hearth.   His status is changed ; he has begun
to outgrow the play of the smaller children, and the
presence of the little girls, encumbered as they are by
the care of the babies, is a hindrance to the more adven-
turous expeditions which he now wants to join.   Also
the boys' economic tasks begin, and for the next few
years he will have to herd the goats on the hill-side,
coming gradually more and more under the authority
first of his older brothers, and next of his father and
paternal uncles.

The first step in this separation of the boy from his
mother is the prohibition laid on their eating together,
and it is interesting to note that, in Kafir society at any
rate, the boy is forbidden to eat with the women for
some years before he ceases to sleep in the women's part
of the hut.[1]   Current public opinion considers it deroga-
tory for the young boy to eat with the women and babies,
and the father will rebuke him for slinking back to the
fireside where there is more security though less prestige.
In a different type of society, Dr. Evans-Pritchard tells
me that he has often noticed Azande boys creep back to
their mother's hearth under cover of night to be fed by
her in stealth.

From henceforth, therefore, the way of the boys and
the girls divides, and even when the children combine at
harvest-time to scare the birds off the crops, the sex
division is most rigorously observed in the preparation
of the meals to be eaten in the fields.[2]

Age distinctions are similarly marked.   The group of
boys is sub-divided into two major divisions : the youths,
who are already promoted to the care of the cattle, and
are in some cases already living in the unmarried men's
kraal ;[3] and the smaller boys, who act during this time

---

[1] D. Kidd, *Savage Childhood*, p. 95.

[2] Cf. D. Kidd, *Savage Childhood*, p. 187.   There seems to be no question
of the existence of a definite taboo prohibiting the brother and sister
from eating together as is characteristic of Melanesian and Polynesian
society.   Nor is the eating together of boy and girl a significant matrimonial rite as in parts of New Guinea.

[3] J. T. Brown, *op. cit.*, p. 49.

as goat-herds to the village. The older and younger girls can be similarly distinguished, but their separation into age groups is not complete. There is no definite change in economic activities to divide the elder girls from the younger. The differentiation takes place when the adolescent girl begins to sleep in the unmarried women's hut in the kraal, or when, as among the Bechuana natives, the girls are sent to sleep in a separate quarter at the back of their mother's hut.

All these groups eat separately in the village, although deriving their food, as we have seen, from the family household. The mother will cook their food and send it by some little child either to the men's place, or to the band of young boys. Her children remain still dependent upon her, although new ties of loyalty are beginning to be formed.

This division of the community into separate groups at mealtimes is a very significant fact, but one which has almost consistently been ignored. Travellers in Africa have commented upon the communistic nature of Bantu custom, and the generous sharing of food and other commodities between neighbours in a village. Kidd, in fact, commits himself to the definite statement, " Finally, we must say that all such things as food, beer, private earnings, blacksmithing, matrimony, &c., are more or less tribalized ".[1] Junod also describes the meal in a Thonga kraal as the highest expression of " communism ", and it will be remembered that Professor Radcliffe-Brown's interesting conception of the " social value " of food depends on the assumption that the eating of food in a primitive tribe is " a kind of communion of the society "—an occasion when the group is particularly conscious of social cohesion and the uplifting force which the sense of union brings.[2]

But such statements seem to me to require a good deal of modification in the light of the facts I have given

[1] D. Kidd, *Kafir Socialism*, p. 30.
[2] A. R. Brown, *The Andaman Islanders*, p. 288.

below. In a culture as primitive as that of the Andaman Islanders it is possible that the whole local group does assemble together at mealtimes. But in the more complex organization of Bantu society, it has been seen that the community is divided into well-marked units, the men on the central place in the kraal, the women and babies by the fireside, the small boys, the big boys, and the girls.[1] Food must be shared according to Bantu etiquette it is true, but it must be divided only within the group, and according to strict rules of precedence. The pattern of the sentiment formed in the family circle is extended to other small compact groups of the community. There is nothing like a general communism in food to be observed. Social differentiation is more closely marked by the eating customs of these people, than is the union of the members of the society as a whole. The food routine teaches the child his place in a complicated social structure, and the ties that bound him to his household group are reflected and modified in the new relationships he now has to form.

(b) Food Shortage and Kinship Ties

At this period, too, the child becomes conscious, not only of new groupings in his society, but of effective competition in tightening his supply. His privileged position at the mother's hearth has now gone, and as the youngest member of the boys' group, he has to be satisfied with the food his seniors leave him, the bits the older men will throw him from their plates, or what he can fend for himself. For, while small boys of all races and cultures appear to be always hungry, the little Bantu boy, at the stage we are considering, seems to be definitely short of food. This is specially true of the boys in charge

---

[1] Cf. Junod, *op. cit.*, Vol. I, p. 337 ; A. T. Bryant, *Olden Times in Zululand and Natal*, 1929, p. 75 ; A. Kropf, *op. cit.*, p. 102.

B. Malinowski records that among the Trobriand Islanders separate groups of kinsmen divide off from the company gathered at a feast and eat with their backs to the rest (*The Sexual Life of Savages*, p. 295). I have not been able to find an account of the grouping observed at a Kafir feast.

of the herds of goats belonging to the kraal. It seems to be a special characteristic of this type of Bantu society that the small boys should pass through a period of lawless independence on the mountain-side, watching the goats, or scaring the birds off the crops, and indulging in fights or joint hunts with the goat-herds of other kraals.[1] Junod states, that during this time " hunger is the constant companion of these boys who do not get enough to eat at home " ; while Kropf speaks of the Xosa children who have no definite portion of food allotted to them, but may suck the cows dry after they have been milked. Kidd was informed that the boys were purposefully kept short of food in this way in order to make them resourceful, somewhat after the manner of Spartan boys. Smith and Dale tell us that in former days the goat-herds had only curds and whey from the milk, never getting porridge unless they stole it from their mother's kraal,[2] the girls meantime followed their

[1] J. Y. Gibson, *Story of the Zulus*, p. 10.

[2] Junod, *op. cit.*, Vol. I, p. 64 ; A. Kropf, *op. cit.*, p. 102 ; Smith and Dale, *op. cit.*, Vol. I, p. 144.

It is difficult to decide how far this period of food shortage is specially characteristic of Bantu society and due to the exigencies of pastoral life, and how far the scarcity is really intentional, and corresponds to the restrictions placed on the diet of growing children in widely different cultures.

Besides those taboos frequently kept in a primitive society in order to give magic protection to the undeveloped sex organs (cf. Smith and Dale, *op. cit.*, Vol. II, p. 17 ; also Fraser, *Totemism and Exogamy*, Vol. I, pp. 40–4 and p. 484), many cultures forbid the consumption of certain articles of diet during different stages of the child's youth. A. R. Brown accounts for the successive taboos placed on pork, honey, turtle, etc., among the Andaman Islanders as a means of educating the growing youth of the community in the value and importance of certain staple articles of diet. W. E. Roth interprets the series of taboos kept by unitiated youths among the North-Western Australians as a method of food distribution which preserves the better food for the older men (W. E. Roth, *North Queensland Ethnography*, 1903 ; Spencer and Gillen, *Native Tribes of Central Australia*, p. 471). Cf. also the taboos which last throughout the childhood of the Solomon Islanders, withdrawn gradually as puberty is reached (C. E. Fox, *The Threshold of the Pacific*, 1924, p.179), and similar taboos in New Guinea in the Waga-Waga area (C. G. Seligman, *Melanesians of British New Guinea*, 1910, p. 451).

In the Gilbert Islands, on the contrary, actual shortage of food was definitely prescribed for growing children. Grimble states that from his fifth to his eighth year the child eats as much as he likes, and " to carry a well-rounded stomach " is generally approved of. " But at

mother to work, eating with her, or picking up gleanings in the fields.

To satisfy their hunger the children console themselves by snatching food wherever they can, trapping birds, stealing potatoes or sugar-cane, pursued by the reprimands and chastisements of their elders. Even the plate of food sent to an infirm old grandparent is not safe from their clutches.[1] The boys also try to supplement their diet by scraps left over by their elders. " They scramble for what they get to eat," says Leslie of the Zulu children,[2] while accounts of the meals of chiefs, headmen, or important personages of the tribe, mention always the crowd of boys waiting on the outskirts for the remains. Smith and Dale describe the Ba-Ila chief breakfasting in the cow-shed of the kraal with the little boys and girls looking on. J. Tyler refers similarly to the Zulu headman : " He eats alone, giving what is left to the hungry children, or more hungry dogs." [3] At feast-times there appears to have been a similar crowd of children and hangers-on waiting to suck the bones of the meat or other titbits, and defending the portions of the viscera they secured from the attacks of hungry dogs.

In this period of the boy's life, therefore, he experiences for the first time a definite shortage and insecurity as to his food supply. It is a time of independence from, and even war on the rest of, the community.

6. Adolescence

The older boys, of course, are in a rather different position. It is difficult to gather at what age they begin

about eight his diet begins to be strictly regulated, though not so much in kind as in quantity ", and again later in life, a fat suitor would have no chance of success and would be much despised (A. Grimble, " From Birth to Death in the Gilbert Islands ", *J.R.A.I.*, 1921, Vol. LI, p. 37).

It is difficult to get enough comparative material to come to a definite conclusion on this point.

[1] Junod, *op. cit.*, Vol. I, p. 172.
[2] D. Leslie, *op. cit.*, p. 198.
[3] J. Tyler, *Forty Years among the Zulu*, 1891, p. 120 ; Smith and Dale, *op. cit.*, Vol. I, p. 124.

to separate themselves off from the company of their juniors and assume the coveted rôle of cattle-keeper. But the superiority of the cattle-herd as compared to goat-herd is undoubted. Status depends to a large extent on age in most primitive communities, but perhaps nowhere do the years count for so much as in the typical African society. The older boys are the most interfering, if not the most powerful tyrants with whom the small child has to deal. Among the Thonga they must be saluted, not as *Tatana*, or " father ", but as *Hosi*, or " chief ", and they have almost complete licence to bully and order about their juniors. The elders send the small boys about their tasks, command them to sneak provisions from somewhere or other, and then devour themselves the food that has been brought back. In the evening, when they return to the kraal, it is the seniors' right to help themselves first from the dish the mother sends.[1]

Initiation rites take place at some time during this period at more or less irregular intervals, when sufficient boys have been collected together to form an initiation school, or, according to Bechuana usage, when the chief's own son is old enough to undergo the rite.[2] The ceremonies performed among most of the Southern tribes show the strong influence of the Zulu system, the rites in this case being subservient to a military organization of the Zulu type, and destined to provide a series of warrior bands for the service of the chief. Junod records that hunting lore is taught the Thonga boys at the initiation school, but it does not seem that in general the circumcision rites coincided with any definite change in economic life.

After initiation, in the old days, the young men appear

---

[1] Dr. Evans-Pritchard tells me that he has witnessed scenes of such commotion between the Azande boys at the distribution of the evening meal, that the father has been called from his hut to divide out the food into separate dishes.

[2] A. Kropf, *op. cit.*, pp. 126–8 ; J. T. Brown, *op. cit.*, p. 79. There were apparently no initiation rites among the Pondo.

to have led an easy life. Some Zulu groups spent two to three years tending the King's cattle before being formed into a military regiment. During this time they lived at his expense, and must drink milk direct from his cows to strengthen them (*Kleza*—to drink milk from the udder direct into the mouth).[1] In other cases the adolescent boys seemed to have no more definite duties than bringing the cows to the kraal to be milked, and lounging about in idleness, begging for cattle for their *lobola* from the members of their kinship group.[2]

To conclude, therefore, later childhood is a time, not only of sex and age division, but of changing and more urgent nutritional needs. In such an existence as this, the boy's kinship ties acquire new meaning. No longer confined to the narrow life of the household and women's circle, he becomes aware of the wide net of kinship rights and obligations which bind him to other huts and families beside his own. He is conscious of the importance of the laws of property and food ownership; he realizes that social status is measured to a large extent by the right to eat or distribute food. Let us therefore examine in further detail his near relationships from this point of view.

7. Paternal Authority and Possession of Food

It is at this period that the father begins to loom very largely on the child's horizon in a typically patrilineal society such as the one which we are considering. It is he who enforces the separation of the boy from his mother at this time, and who begins to correct his manners. He is also in charge of the economic activities of the small boys, and sends them out to herd the goats, bearing the brunt of any damage the child may do in his forays in the neighbouring fields. " The father is treated with

[1] A. T. Bryant, *Olden Times in Zululand and Natal*, p. 78.
[2] A. Kropf, *op. cit.*, p. 130; Holub, *op. cit.*, Vol. I, p. 400; W. Shaw, *The Story of my Mission in South East Africa*, 1860, p. 459.

respect, fear, obedience. Though he does not take much trouble with his children, he is, nevertheless, their instructor, the one who scolds and punishes. Absolute obedience is due to him on the part of his sons and daughters." [1]

With this authority is invariably associated the father's possession and control over the food supply—the cattle-herd and their produce, and in general, the grain supply too. The head of the family is, of course, bound to support his sons, not only in childhood, but until the age of marriage and even after. The receipt of food marks the dependence of the child on the father, and right up to adolescence the youth receives food from his hut. The daily portion, cooked by the mother, is sent to him in the unmarried men's kraal, or to the Initiation School in the case of the boys passing through the circumcision rite. It is difficult in fact to imagine the extent to which the young boy or man is bound to rely on his father, or the family group, for support. Unless he can earn money in white employment, or living temporarily under European conditions, he simply cannot acquire food except from his parents' hands. [2] It does not exist as a commodity to be bought or sold, but as an article which the members of his family are bound to produce and supply him with, and which one woman alone—his mother, or her substitute—must cook. His dependence is thus displayed concretely by the receipt of actual food, and not, as in our own community, by an allowance of money to be spent as the young man chooses on his maintenance. In fact, until the youth has a wife of his own, legally bound to provide him with

[1] Junod, *op. cit.*, Vol. I, p. 226 ; also p. 63. The *patria potestas* varies of course throughout the South and South-Eastern groups of Bantu according to the patrilineal or matrilineal emphasis of the society. Among the Zulu-Xosa groups the power of the father is supreme : among the tribes of Northern Rhodesia, where the child belongs to his mother's clan, the father rules, but his power is conditioned by that of the maternal uncle (Smith and Dale, *op. cit.*, Vol. I, p. 284).

[2] It is interesting to remember that wages in most European concerns in South Africa are still given in the form of a food ration as well as money payments besides.

cooked food, he is not absolutely in control of his daily supply, and in former days, before the *lobola* payment could be earned in wages, marriage was sometimes postponed till the twenty-fifth or thirtieth year.[1]

Besides this, the father is the sole possessor of the cattle, and to build up a herd of his own the son would have to wait many years. To find his *lobola* he is thus dependent on his relatives, and to carry out the many legal transactions involving the exchange of cattle or food.

The child-to-father sentiment is, therefore, inextricably connected in Bantu society with the picture of the father as the possessor, giver, and controller of food. With these attributes his authority is invariably associated, and it is this status which it is the ambition of each son to attain—the source of his mingled envy, fear and pride. The importance of this sentiment cannot be exaggerated if we want to understand the nature of the social organization of these tribes. It is on the pattern of this filial attitude that the whole structure of government in these tribes is built. The admired and respected head of a family is the man who is never in want, and is able to distribute food freely from the pots provided by his wives. " The greatness of an African is before all else a matter of pots." His ambition is to be able to eat himself full to repletion every day—*shura* or full till the sternum bulges forward. This is the privilege of the wealthy only, and consequently fat is always a sign of social status. The headman " will become large and stout, and shining, which in South African is a sure sign of wealth and nobility. The stouter he gets the more will he be respected ". A well-respected man was described to Junod in the following terms : " He is not killed by famine ! ! He has beer to drink every day ! He can give food to poor people. Even then some of it remains on the plates and is eaten by little boys and dogs in the

---

[1] A. Kropf, *op. cit.*, p. 131 ; J. Colenso, *Ten Weeks in Natal*, 1855, p. 108. Marriage among the youths in a Zulu regiment depended on the permission of the King, and was sometimes postponed till twenty-five to thirty.

square. There is always abundance there." [1] Greatness is largely conceived, as we see, in nutritional terms.

The ideal of a wealthy head of a family is the same, to a more limited degree, as that of the sub-chief or chief. The obvious enjoyment of plenty of food and its generous distribution to friends and dependents is the recognized attribute of authority, whether of the father, or the chief. The filial attitude is extended from one to the other, and the new pattern formed on the basis of the old.

8. DISTRIBUTION OF FOOD IN THE KINSHIP GROUP

Another important element in the nutritional situation is the distribution of food in the kinship group. While vegetable produce is individually owned among these people, and each hut is self-supporting in this respect, meat food is divided among a wider circle, according to strict rules of the kinship usage. The greater scarcity of the meat, and its perishable quality, makes such an arrangement common among primitive hunting or pastoral peoples. [2] The system of distribution extends beyond the family limits to the members of both families united by marriage, and even, as we shall see later, to the headman or chief. The division of an ox upon the central place of the village, or of the quarry slain in the hunt, must give the young children a dramatic demonstration of the functions of kinship, and of the series of reciprocal obligations so entailed.

[1] Junod, *op. cit.*, Vol. I, pp. 128–9; also D. Leslie, *op. cit.*, p. 170; J. Shooter, *op. cit.*, pp. 4, 5, 7.

[2] It seems clear that in former times when the shortage of all classes of food-stuffs was greater, vegetable produce as well as meat was so divided. Kropf states that it was the custom of the Kafir headman to divide the grain brought by the women into three heaps, for the men, the women, and the boys, while the women had to deal out milk to the babies from a special cow (*op. cit.*, p. 102). Shaw and Fleming also speak of the " master of the milk sack ", whose job was to divide out the milk (W. Shaw, *op. cit.*, p. 416; F. Fleming, *Southern Africa*, 1856, p. 218; J. McClean, *Compendium of Kaffir Laws and Customs*, 1858, p. 155), but in the case of the small kraal of earlier days, the father and the headman were probably one and the same.

In our particular society the distribution of the carcass is made either by the owner of the beast—in the case of a slain oxen—or by the patriarchal head of the family, or the village headman. In general, in the small kraals of the Southern Bantu, these functions would be combined in one individual, and the whole distribution would be on a village scale. Among the Thonga the headman, or *numzane*, must divide the slain beast so that the elder brother gets a hind-leg, the younger a fore-leg, while the other two limbs belong to the eldest two sons. The heart and the kidneys are the wives' portions, while the relatives-in-law will receive the tail and rump, and maternal uncle a special bit of the loins.[1] Casalis describes a similar division of a beast by a son among the Mochuana Kafir, the father in this case having the right to the head and breast, while the older and younger brothers and sisters have also their allotted portions.[2]

Hunting quarry must also be divided according to rule, although in this case the lines of division do not follow kinship structure so strictly. The chief has his portion of the animal in most of these tribes, in virtue of his titular ownership of the soil, and those who have helped to bring down the quarry have also their rights to levy. But the division in this case is by no means so public as that of the ox in the centre of the kraal, where the object is, as Callaway says, "that those who are eating, and those who are not, may be seen".[3] For such a public distribution of the food supply acts as a sanction for the fulfilment of kinship obligation as well as educating the child in the kinship sense. Kidd mentions that where children have been denied their portion by the older members of the group, they will

---

[1] Junod, *op. cit.*, Vol. I, p. 329. In parts of East Africa the distribution appears to be much more complex since sheep, goat, and oxen respectively have to be divided among the kinsmen according to separate sets of rules (C. Dundas, *Kilimanjaro and Its People*, 1924, p. 134 ; Merker, *Die Masai*, 1904, p. 169).

[2] Casalis, *op. cit.*, p. 207.

[3] Callaway, *op. cit.*, p. 181 ; J. Colenso, *op. cit.*, p. 112.

at any rate be smeared with blood to look as though they had had their share ! [1]

The whole configuration of the community during the division of an animal carcass shows clearly how the family functions as a food-consuming unit. The larger kinship group assembles to get its share of the rarer and more perishable meat food ; but each share so divided must be re-allotted within each household according to the rules of precedence of sex and age within that smaller group. The family is the centre of a wider scheme of food distribution, and authority within the family itself depends, as we have seen, on the possession and control of food.

9. HOSPITALITY AMONG KINSMEN

We come now to consider the question of the rules of hospitality within the kinship group. Is the family function of food-provision extended indiscriminately among all strangers passing through the village, or is the exercise of hospitality limited rigidly to members of the family, or clan ? Observers record that the traveller in South Africa is immediately offered food on reaching a kraal. They seem to have been so impressed by the difference between African and European custom in this respect, that they have made little accurate investigation into the subject. It is impossible to decide, among these Bantu tribes, whether hospitality is one of the legal obligations of kinship, or whether it is practised indiscriminately to all. I am inclined to think, from the little evidence available, that the provision of food for strangers is strictly regulated according to kinship rules.

To begin with, the duty of hospitality does not seem to be invariably carried out. As in the case of all such irksome codes of behaviour, evasion seems to be carried to a fine art ! Food may be cooked and eaten hastily

[1] D. Kidd, *The Essential Kafir*, pp. 44-5.

when guests are believed to be imminent, and the Kafir traveller has regularly to guard against this calamity by throwing a pebble on a special heap of stones—*izivivani*—placed on the roadside for the purpose. Such an act " ensures your getting food at the kraal to which you are going or it prevents the food being cooked and eaten before you arrive ".[1] Leslie records the taking of omens on the roadside to set such doubts at rest, while Shooter mentions a magic rite of even greater efficacy since it guarantees arrival at the kraal at the moment when the pot is on the boil ! [2]

The man's food must be carried to the men's place and there divided among all those present, but it is not necessary, evidently, to distribute the whole supply. The good Ba-Ila wife is adjured at marriage to hide food for her husband, expressly so that he should not have to divide it out. " When he has done eating with many people and you enter the house, give the food-put-by (*mafubikila*), which you have hidden, whether it be beer or bread, give it to him and he will eat." [3]

Hospitality is therefore a duty which is avoided if it is found to be irksome. But there is also evidence of definite rules which make it unnecessary in certain circumstances. Shooter states that it was the Zulu custom formerly to deny hospitality to any but members of one's own tribe, giving lodging only to others : " if he go beyond it and seek the hospitality of strangers, he will hardly succeed, unless his chief be known to them and enjoy a good reputation ".[4] It is not quite clear from this account, though, what is actually meant by the " tribe ". Shooter adds further that he has known a father beat his son for giving food to two young men who were unrelated to him—looking as though the rights

[1] D. Kidd, *The Essential Kafir*, p. 264 ; *Kafir Socialism*, p. 30. This rite is only performed in your own country, not in a strange land.
[2] D. Leslie, *op. cit.*, pp. 168, 146 ; T. B. Jenkinson, *op. cit.*, p. 33 ; E. Casalis, *op. cit.*, p. 272 ; F. Fleming, *Kaffraria*, 1853, p. 113 ; J. Shooter, *op. cit.*, p. 217.
[3] Smith and Dale, *op. cit.*, Vol. II, p. 57.
[4] J. Shooter, *op. cit.*, p. 228.

of hospitality were only exercised among kinsmen.   Fleming says " the laws of hospitality are very strict and any
breach of them is summarily punished ", but he does not
describe what these laws are.   Junod states that the
Thonga " can be very hard on people who do not belong
to their special clan ", adding on the other hand that a
village which had refused hospitality which was legally due
from it, was liable to be punished by the chief.[1]

I think therefore that there is evidence that hospitality
was not practised indiscriminately among the Zulu-Xosa
peoples although a white traveller might have gathered
this impression when going from kraal to kraal.   I can
state definitely that among the Babemba, food will never
be asked by a stranger unless he is of superior rank, or
his relationship to the host can be quite clearly traced.
Further careful investigation is needed, but I believe it
will be found that the giving of food to different relatives
—whether of the kinship group or clan—is one of the most
important extensions of the primary functions of the
household to meet the needs of travellers going from
place to place.

10.   CONCLUSION

We have now reached the final stage of the savage
child's youth.   We have traced from his earliest infancy
the development of his nutritive ties.   We saw that the
first human relationship—that of child to mother—must
be determined very largely by the suckling's dependence
for food.   This tie, under conditions of human society,
is modified from earliest days by the social usages of the
group, and later becomes associated with all the varying

---

[1] Junod, *op. cit.*, Vol. I, p. 355.   Junod usually refers to a territorial
grouping of clan members or a sub-tribe when he uses the term " clan ".
A similar state of affairs appears to exist among the Akikuyu, where it
is said that " the virtue of Hospitality is practised as a duty, or by
force of custom in the case of immediate relatives and clansmen ;
anything beyond this is a matter of expediency only ".   (W. S. and K.
Routledge, *With a Prehistoric People, the Akikuyu of British East
Africa*, 1910, p. 246.)

duties which social motherhood involves. The mother acquires her position in a savage society by virtue of her production and preparation of food, and the family meal becomes symbolic of the household life. Later, as the boy outgrows the family circle, the differentiation of society into separate groups by age and occupation, is invariably associated with a clear segregation at the time of meals. The sense of insecurity as to food, felt for the first time in later childhood among these peoples, begins to give a new value to relationships with those who provide supplies. Paternal authority becomes correlated with possession and control over food, and the child's attitude to his other kinsmen is determined very largely by their treatment of him in this respect, or their potential obligations to him in time of need. Lastly, the functions of the family as a food-distributing unit are extended to the wider kinship group in the case of the division of meat food, and the boy receives a graphic illustration of his position in the circle of kinship ties. During the last few years of this period, co-operation in economic activities concentrates his loyalties and ambitions on food production.

This brings us therefore to the second part of our problem—the relation of nutrition to the economic activities of the tribe. During manhood the interests of the individual are not concentrated so directly on food itself, but on the complicated forms of labour which its production entails. Under the conditions of primitive society success in the food quest is directly correlated with social status and fame. Hence our study of human relationships necessitates a knowledge of the nature of food-producing activities in the societies we are now considering—their difficulty or danger and the emotions so aroused. So only shall we be able to examine the shaping of kinship sentiment in manhood according to the individual's more complex nutritional needs.

CHAPTER IV

FOOD PRODUCTION AND INCENTIVES TO WORK

1. ECONOMIC ORGANIZATION AND SOCIAL STATUS

FOOD production in even the most primitive type of society demands organized co-operation. Among the simplest hunting and collecting peoples still in existence —the natives of the Andaman Islands, the Kalahari desert, Central Australia, or parts of Ceylon—we find not only a clear division of labour between men and women, the family thus acting as an economic unit, but also co-operative undertakings extending beyond the family scale, and uniting the members of wider territorial units or even tribes. In the more highly developed primitive societies, as we know, the economic organization is even more complex.[1]

Organized co-operation in the food quest is necessary, in the first place, in order to carry out the more complex economic activities. Even such relatively simple forms of hunting as the setting of snares and game-pits are rarely carried out individually, while the agricultural and pastoral life demand co-operation on a wider scale still.

Secondly, a further system of human relationships

[1] A. R. Brown, *The Andaman Islanders*, 1922 ; C. G. and B. Z. Seligman, *The Veddas*, 1906 ; I. Schapera, *The Khoisan Peoples of South Africa*, 1930 ; S. Dornan, *Pygmies and Bushmen of the Kalahari*, 1925 ; Spencer and Gillen, *The Native Tribes of Central Australia*, 1899. It will be remembered that Carveth Read traces the development of the characteristic features of human society to the institution of organized co-operation when the pre-human ancestor left the trees and took to a hunting life (*The Origin of Man*, 1925). A. Kolnai takes a somewhat similar view (*Psycho-analysis and Sociology*, tr. 1921, p. 34).

depends on the necessity for safeguarding the sources of food supply. Where there is a shortage of any particular type of food, or of water, the ownership of the chief resources of the environment must be regulated by legal rules. These in themselves create a series of social ties uniting the members of the family, kinship group or clan. Among the most primitive tribes we find well-defined hunting and fishing rights, while in desert country the common ownership of water-pools may be the chief tie binding together the members of the territorial group.

Lastly, in order to master his environment successfully, the primitive man requires institutions which shall hand on his knowledge of the technical activities required for food production, and his special experience and skill. The training of the youth of the community in these economic operations—whether by some special series of ceremonies such as initiation rites, or by more informal educative mechanisms such as example and precept— necessitates further sociological grouping. It binds the boy to those of his elders from whom he has to learn, whether these be members of his own household, or specialists from another group.

Thus the adolescent in a primitive community becomes a member of a series of new groups as he reaches the food-producing stage of his life. We have described the formation of kinship sentiment in early childhood, when the family functions as the unit for the distribution, preparation, and consumption of food. We have shown also how such ties are extended later to a wider group of kinsmen according as these functions necessitate co-operation on a larger scale. But food production proper demands the formation of new bonds of relationships, and alters the nature of the old. The young man who becomes himself a food-producer finds himself bound by new obligations to his fellows, sharing wider ambitions, and privileged to a higher extent. Hence we must include in our study of nutritional relationships those directly arising out of economic organization of the Southern Bantu.

But the different economic activities carried out in human society are themselves the centre of complex sentiments. The primitive man lives, after all, very near the starvation level, either continually, or at certain seasons of the year. Thus the constituents of his daily diet, and his rules and habits of eating, are all linked in one emotional system with the institutions and activities by which food is procured. The bulk of his energies and imaginative effort is centred on the problem of making his supplies secure. It follows from this heightened interest, that success in the food quest determines almost universally social prestige in a savage society. Any means, real or illusory, by which the primitive man gains power over the natural resources of the environment, are bound to give him power and authority in the group. Such success may depend either on individual qualities—endurance, daring, and patient concentration—or the attainment of special skill and facility. It may equally well result from inherited rights to the use of certain food sources, or the possession of stored supplies, or herds of domestic animals. Moreover, since the savage believes that he cannot succeed in his food-getting activities without the help of supernatural forces, magic power must be reckoned, like any definitely material asset, as a means of gaining security as to the food supply. Like other forms of economic control, it becomes associated with special social prestige in the group. Pre-eminence in any one or more of these many attributes may either satisfy man's individual ambitions, or else form the basis of social differentiation, or an institutionalized form of leadership in the society. It will depend on the type of food-producing activity of each particular culture and the traditional rules of the tribe.

Thus to take only a few examples, we find that among the Crow Indians, society was largely organized by the giving of political power and authority to those who had proved their reputation for individual bravery or hardi-hood in the hunt.   Again, Firth states that the attributes of a Maori chief included always a reputation for economic skill in some form or other.   He was expected to be industrious in collecting food, and hospitable in dis-tributing it.[1]

The correlation between political authority and indi-vidual prowess in economic pursuits is, of course, found most frequently among hunting and collecting peoples. The association of chieftainship with wealth and the possession of large stores of food supplies is a much more universal phenomenon.   Among many Oceanic com-munities the authority of the chief finds its chief sanction, in fact, in the open display of yams and other root crops in store-houses, the distribution of cooked food at feasts, and the giving and receiving of presents of the same kind.[2]   In pastoral societies, such as those we are now considering, the possession of large herds of cattle repre-sents wealth, rank and leadership.   In yet other com-munities such as those of the North-West Coast of America, the actual destruction of food, as well as of other forms of wealth, indicates power and a high social status in the society.

In most primitive communities, too, the magician, whether of rain, sun, or general fertility, occupies a special position of authority in the tribe.   In others he is a servant of the chief, acting under his orders, while in yet other instances this magic power is owned by the chief or king himself.   In the case of tribes where ancestor-worship is the most developed form of cult, as among most Bantu peoples, it is the head of the family,

---

[1] R. Firth, *op. cit.*, p. 164. " Though skill in all the industrial arts was the object of praise, diligence and expertness in the winning of food did most perhaps to secure the ascendance of a chief—probably because the fruits of his labours were more accessible to the people."

[2] Malinowski has made an illuminating analysis of the economic power of the chief in the Trobriand Islands and his hypothesis has been worked out in greater detail in Firth's study of Maori organization. It is a similar type of study that I shall make later in the case of the Bantu chief. (Cf. B. Malinowski, " Primitive Economics of the Trobriand Islanders ", *Economic Journal*, Vol. XXXI, March 1921.)

the village headman, or the chief himself who has the right of access to the ancestral spirits who can alone procure their blessings on economic tasks. Knowledge of the magic rites of food production, or the power to direct the forces of nature, or the spirits which govern them, are correlated in a variety of ways in different primitive communities with leadership, authority, or rank.[1]

It must be remembered too in analysing these *secondary* values centred round food production, that in the absence of other valuables, possession or control of food may be the only possible means of differentiating one member of the primitive community from another. The distribution of food may be one of the few ways in which the savage man can display his power,[2] just as the handing on of economic rights to land or stream may be the only thing which he can pass on to his heirs. Food is, in fact, in most primitive communities, the only form of capital man has. It is for this reason, I believe, that eatables are so often produced in savage societies in excess of actual needs.

Moreover, there is special virtue to the savage in the mere accumulation of food. The obtaining of food is the chief social activity, " and is the chief source of those variations or oscillations between conditions of euphoria and dysphoria that constitute the emotional life of the society ", says Radcliffe-Brown, in his brilliant description of the association in the mind of the Andaman Islander between the abundance of food, and his feelings of well-being and his confidence in the strength of the social group of which he is a member.[3]   In more complex

---

[1] Cf. R. Firth's account of the function of Tapu in maintaining the authority of the Maori chief (*op. cit.*, p. 188) and E. Evans-Pritchard, " The Morphology and Function of Magic ", *The American Anthropologist*, 1929, Vol. XXXI, No. 4, p. 619, for a comparative study of the function of Trobriand and Azande magic in this respect.

[2] In the Northern Rhodesian copper mines, where the workers receive a daily ration far superior to their village diet, they yet complained to me of having too little food. " We can see only a little food at a time," they said, " and never enough to call all our friends to a feast." Hunger was satisfied, but not social ambition.

[3] A. R. Brown, *The Andaman Islanders*, p. 270.

societies also, where food is produced by a long series of agricultural tasks, harvest is a time of rejoicing, as well as a time of plenty. After the long period of lowered activity, social life begins again. Food makes possible feasting, drinking, dancing, and general feelings of good-will. It is the sight of abundance after the strain of anxiety and penury which gives the native such a keen delight. This pleasure in the sheer accumulation of supplies finds its most dramatic expression in Melanesian cultures, and Malinowski has given us vivid descriptions of the joy of the Trobriand Islanders in piling up food, handling it, displaying it, exchanging it, and almost reverencing it at the time of the annual feasts. The value attached to abundance in any community is natur-ally determined by the traditions of that particular tribe. In general the attitude of the society towards any special type of food is expressed and emphasized by religious ceremonial centring round different events in the agri-cultural year. In " harvest festivals, totemic gatherings, first-fruit offerings and ceremonial display of food, we find religion sacralizing abundance and security and establishing the attitude of reverence towards the bene-ficent forces without ".[1] But even apart from the question of ritual emphasis, there is a special value attributed to the idea of plenty in a primitive tribe. In a community where starvation is always a possibility, there is no ideal of enjoyment possible, which does not include an excess of eatables.

We see therefore that food production in a primitive community becomes the centre of a wide circle of secon-dary values, themselves dependent on its original function of satisfying a fundamental biological want. We cannot therefore study the nutritive relationships of the adoles-cent or adult member of the tribe without a knowledge of the interest in different food-getting activities which culture decrees. It is therefore our object in the succeed-ing pages to get a thorough grasp of the nature of

[1] B. Malinowski, *Magic, Science, and Religion*, 1926, p. 90.

economic activities among the Southern Bantu. We shall study each particular pursuit in detail, attempting to show first of all the actual value of the activity as a form of food production ; the nature of the operation, the difficulties, dangers and pleasures involved, and hence the multiplicity of human hopes, desires, and ambitions centred in the work. This will pave the way for an examination of the scheme of human groupings by which the different economic activities are carried out, and the ties so formed between different members of the family and kinship group. It is only through such a knowledge of the social values acquired by each type of food production in these societies that we shall be able to complete the study of nutritive relationships begun in the first part of this work.

2. PASTORAL ACTIVITIES

Pastoral activities are perhaps the most important economic pursuit of the Southern Bantu. The Zulu-Xosa group forms part of the whole complex of cattle-raising peoples which stretches from the Nilotic region in the North (including such tribes as the Shilluk, Nuer, and Dinka) almost up to the coast on the East (Nandi, Masai, Ba-giriama) : and the chain of great lakes on the West (Baganda, Banyoro, Banyamwesi, etc.) ; and so through Rhodesia as far as the Cape. Herskovits' comprehensive study of the cattle cult over this wide area, classifies as the Southern group of the complex such tribes as the Ba-Ila, Mashona, Vandau, Thonga, Swazi, Sudo-Pedi, Bechuana, Basuto, Zulu, AmaXosa and AmaMpondo.[1] And while it is clear that cattle vary tremendously in distribution throughout this tract, the nature of the pastoral cult has certain common characteristics, which can readily be distinguished from the customs

[1] M. J. Herskovits, " The Cattle Complex in East Africa ", *American Anthropologist*, Vol. XXVIII, 1926, p. 254.

of the Eastern group—the Masai or Nandi for instance, or the Lacustrian natives of the Uganda region.

Pastoral activities under the white man's rule are not very arduous. Cattle were formerly the chief object of wars and inter-tribal raids, and the young men of the tribe were organized for their defence. Under present conditions such a means of acquiring stock is of course prohibited, and the herds have only to be protected from the depredations of wild animals. Smith and Dale reckon that in Northern Rhodesia a big herd may lose annually as many as one hundred head from the attacks of lions.[1] Shooter also speaks of platforms made by the Zulu to guard the cattle from attacks during the night. But beyond the work of watching, the bulk of the labour seems to have been done by the boys and youths of the tribe—the milking of the cows, the leading of the cattle from pasture to pasture, and the burning down of the grass to supply fresh green.[2] Pastoral activities do not require the long arduous endeavours or routine work involved in agricultural pursuits.

As to the methods of co-operation involved in cattle-raising, it is very difficult to get an accurate idea. Owner-ship of the herds is individual—subject to certain rights of the chief—and the young man's first endeavour after raising his lobola cattle is to collect stock of his own. But the herds of each village apparently grazed together, the grazing-grounds being allotted by the chief in some cases. Travellers in South Africa have frequently com-mented with amazement on the precision with which a man can recognize his own and his neighbour's beasts in a herd. The cattle of a headman, those of his sons, and his younger brothers might feed together, and be stalled together in the kraal at night. Moreover, accord-ing to the old Zulu usage, the herd of a polygamist was very distinctly divided. There was the hereditary

[1] Smith and Dale, *op. cit.*, Vol. I, p. 129 ; also J. Shooter, *op. cit.*, pp. 35–40.

[2] J. Shooter, *op. cit.*, p. 32 ; L. Grout, *Zululand*, 1864, pp. 99–111 ; J. T. Brown, *op. cit.*, p. 50.

estate, so to speak, handed down from the father; the herd of the Great Wife,[1] cattle acquired by purchase or some such means; the herds of the Right- and Left-hand wives; and some special stock which was regarded as personal property of the husband, inherited by his eldest son. The actual co-operation between the sons of the different households must have therefore been exceedingly complex in actuality, but it is difficult to know upon whom the leadership in these activities devolved.

Turning then from the question of economic organization, let us consider the attitude of the native towards his cattle in daily life. Now the *primary* value of pastoral activities among the Lacustrian or Kenya natives is certainly food, since meat and milk form the staple diet of these people, and the use of vegetable food is subject to many taboos. But among the Southern tribes it is not so easy to state definitely that this is the case. Some writers opine that oxen are never killed for food, but only as sacrifices to the ancestral spirits;[2] others say that a rich man might kill an animal occasionally for food alone, or that stock may be slaughtered in winter when the hair is not long enough to make good karosses.[3] But of course the meat of the sacrificed animal is always eaten by the family present, and meat food is highly valued: while among the Zulu groups, the *amasi* or curded milk forms the chief article of diet.[4] The skins of the animals also provide leather for clothing, while the cow-dung forms the cement plastered over the floors and walls of the huts.

But the *secondary* values acquired by this form of food-producing activity brings us at once to familiar

[1] If a wife was taken with the cattle from this private herd she founded a second great house, and her son the *iponsakabusa* was called the " child of his father's cattle " and performed special functions in the kraal (T. B. Jenkinson, *op. cit.*, pp. 34–9).

[2] J. Barrow, *op. cit.*, Vol. I, p. 155.

[3] J. Shooter, *op. cit.*, p. 28; W. Shaw, *op. cit.*, pp. 413, 414.

[4] Where the herds have been diminished by pest, as among the Thonga, milk is not such a regular feature of daily diet.

ground. Nothing has so struck the white traveller in South Africa as the fondness of the native for his cattle and the part they play in his whole legal and religious life. We have, therefore, a great variety of material to draw on, from the accounts of the earliest missionaries in the field to the more trained observers of the present day. The so-called cult of cattle in Africa varies, of course, from an intense affection and interest in the animals, to a ritual veneration and almost worship of the herd. To account for this phenomenon we must look first at the nature of cattle as a form of economic resource.

To begin with, domestic animals provide a storable form of wealth, and one, moreover, that increases with the years—which cannot, of course, be said of any other form of food supply at a low level of culture. The possession of cattle is therefore a method of investing capital. The object of cattle-rearing, says Junod, is "not milk, but the acquisition of wealth".[1] Casalis, describing the larger towns of the Basuto, notes with some acumen that the patriarch " is obliged to reckon less and less upon his flocks and herds for food. The cattle cease to be tame game and become *capital and interest* which must only be touched sparingly ".[2] It follows from this that the ownership of stock is the chief means of reckoning status in these tribes. Social ambition among most Bantu peoples is largely centred in the acquisition of cattle, and since they are essential, or at any rate usual, for the payment of the marriage *lobola*, no man can reach adult status without the possession of a certain number of beasts.

Moreover, cattle are not only used as a form of capital but as a means of exchange—not as currency in the ordinary sense of the word, for cattle are rarely bought and sold—but in order to contract or express social relationships. No such transaction takes place among

---

[1] Junod, *op. cit.*, Vol. II, p. 48.
[2] E. Casalis, *op. cit.*, p. 158.

these people without the gift, counter-gift, or slaughter of cattle, whether this be on the occasion of birth, marriage, death, or in the relationship of subject to chief.

Besides this, the cattle kraal forms the centre of the village among most South African tribes. Here the men gather round the fire of cow-dung in the evening ; here they make their sacrifices, hold feasts, and, in some cases, give judgment, or dance. The regular coming and going and the milking of the cattle forms the routine of the day, just as the succession of agricultural activities makes the routine of the year.[1]

Further, unlike any other form of food-supply in this area, cattle become the objects of warm personal affection. Evans-Pritchard tells me that among some of the Nilotic tribes, such as the Nuer, cattle are treated exactly as we would treat a favourite dog or cat, and the same could probably be said of the Southern Bantu. A favourite ox may be named after a friend or a lover, as a compliment. It is ornamented, and never parted with.[2] In the kraal the fortunes or misfortunes of the herd form the chief topic of conversation—" Ihre Phantasie sich Tag und Nacht damit beschäftigt,"[3] says Kropf, of the Kafirs, and this feeling for cattle was common throughout the Bantu peoples. The Batlapin hated losing stock to the Bushmen in the course of a raid, because the latter killed the beasts, whereas natives of Bechuana, or Basutos, or Kafirs spared the cattle they took by fight.[4] Many of the Zulu people use cattle as a form of sport, racing with beasts specially trained as steeds. A chief might send racing oxen to honour the marriage of a fellow-chief if he were not able to attend

---

[1] T. B. Jenkinson, op. cit., p. 52, and J. Shooter, op. cit., p. 15.

[2] Smith and Dale, op. cit., Vol. I, p. 128 ; J. T. Brown, op. cit., p. 92 ; C. Barter, Alone among the Zulus, 1879, p. 39. A form of personification of animals is found among hunting peoples, especially those dependent upon one type of animal for support. But the various forms of totemistic worship so developed are different from the affectionate, almost familial feeling of the Bantu for his cattle.

[3] A. Kropf, op. cit., p. 108.

[4] G. Stow, op. cit., p. 457 ; R. Moffat, Missionary Labours, 1842, p. 55.

personally.[1]   The children begin early, as we have seen, to tend the cattle, and even their games consist in trafficking with miniature oxen of clay.[2]   Throughout life the herd is the chief object of interest, and at death among some of these tribes a man may be wrapped in the skin of an ox.[3]

Lastly, in some mysterious sense, the cattle are members of the social organization of their human owners, and akin to them in a particular way.   Mrs. Hoernle in an interesting article on the South-Eastern Bantu, says, " there is a most intimate bond between a group and the cattle that it owns, and, further, that cattle are the most important medium for all ritual relations between human groups ". [4]   The exchange of cattle at marriage forms a living bond between the two families.   A somewhat similar tie may be contracted by the drinking of milk. Briefly stated, milk taboos prohibit a man from drinking milk in any household but his own, or that of the paternal or maternal relatives.   A wife may not drink in any kraal except her husband's, and then only after the first year of married life.[5]   " For a man to eat *amasi* at a neighbour's kraal or among strangers," says Grout, " would be a most indecent thing." [6]   Mrs. Hoernle says, in stronger terms still, that among the Zulu and Pondo the drinking of milk with a member of another clan is tantamount to pledging blood-brotherhood with him, and prevents marriage in that clan.

[1] Lichtenstein, *Travels in South Africa in the Years* 1803, 1804, 1805, 1806, Vol. I, p. 268 ; W. Shaw, *The Story of My Mission in S.E. Africa*, 1860, p. 418 ; A. Kropf, *op. cit.*, pp. 109, 111.
[2] A Kropf, *op. cit.*, p. 108 ; J. Shooter, *op. cit.*, p. 30.
[3] Smith and Dale, *op. cit.*, Vol. I, p. 130 ; E. Casalis, *op. cit.*, p. 250 ; E. Brauer, *Züge aus der Religion der Herero*, 1925, Karte 2.
[4] Mrs. Hoernle, " The Importance of the Sib in the Marriage Ceremonies of the South-Eastern Bantu ", *S.A.J.S.*, Vol. XXII, November 1925, p. 481.
[5] Father F. Mayr, " Zulu Kafirs of Natal ", *Anthropos*, 1906, p. 467.
[6] L. Grout, *op. cit.*, p. 135 ; also D. Leslie, *op. cit.*, p. 175 ; D. Kidd, *Savage Childhood*, p. 39 ; A. T. Bryant, *Zulu-English Dictionary*, p. 336 ; also J. Maclean, *op. cit.*, p. 93 ; and a reference to a similar custom among the Herero, F. Galton, *Narrative of an Explorer in Tropical S. Africa*, 1889, p. 84.

It is not surprising, therefore, that cattle, as the objects of such complex sentiments, are everywhere handled and protected with ritual observances. In most cases, as we have seen, they may not be slaughtered except as a sacrifice to the Gods. All pastoral activities are surrounded by special taboos preventing, in particular, the contact of women with the herd. Milking and dairy work is done by men among the Zulu-Kafir peoples, and women are prohibited from entering the kraal in all circumstances which would render them magically dangerous to the cattle. Since the prosperity of the whole tribe is bound up with the fortunes of the herd, all the resources of religion and magic must be invoked for its protection.

We have to realize, in fact, that the *secondary* values centred round cattle among the South-Eastern Bantu come to predominate over the *primary*. The herd is less important as a source of meat, milk, and leather, than as the object of social ambitions, rivalries and emotions. Cattle become an attribute of leadership, a means of expressing ties of relationship, and a centre of religious life. At birth a man becomes a member of a group which is intimately associated with the herd of beasts which it owns ; throughout life his obligations to his fellow-tribesmen are largely carried out by the exchange of heads of stock : at death this is the chief form of inheritance he leaves. The people are therefore more passionately attached to cattle, than to any other possession, even though they are more dependent on their fields for support.

3. AGRICULTURAL ACTIVITIES

The Southern Bantu are not described as typical agriculturalists, yet in fact vegetable produce provides the bulk of their diet. Meat is a rare luxury, and the daily food consists almost entirely of cereal foods and vegetables. A porridge of some kind is made by stirring the ground flour of one of the different cereal crops with boiling water, and this is eaten with a relish of vegetables —monkey-nuts, beans, peas, etc. Among the Zulu-Xosa peoples, curdled milk forms an addition to the diet.

The chief crops grown among these peoples—Kafir corn, Kafir pea, sorghum, maize, ground-nut, manioc, sugar-cane, and different types of pumpkin—provide a rich variety of menu. In fact, the diversity of plants cultivated among the Southern Bantu is a characteristic feature of their agriculture.

As an economic activity, agricultural work is more continuous and exacting than any other type of food production in these tribes. There is no season of the year in which there is not something to be done in the fields or gardens. Little is known of an accurate system of crop rotation, but the work proceeds by clearing strips of the virgin forest, sowing for two or three years, and then either leaving the field fallow for a year or so, or else letting it revert again to the bush. Next follows the sowing of the crops, and among some tribes, such as the Thonga, each native will sow some of each variety of seed in his garden. Then comes the hoeing and a double weeding of the seedlings, and then the protection of the crops from the ravages of birds, monkeys, baboons and wild pigs.[1] Next in order comes the harvesting of the various crops and the threshing and storing of the grain.

It will be seen, therefore, that the qualities demanded for this work are patience and endurance through long, and apparently uninteresting, tasks. Hoe culture is, perhaps, the most tedious form of cultivation known, and the constant clearing of new patches of the bush greatly increases the labour. Again, long months of work may be destroyed in a few weeks for want of rain, or in less than half an hour by the trampling of a herd of elephants. What then are the incentives that sustain the natives

---

[1] J. Shooter, op. cit., p. 19. Smith and Dale speak of constant re-hoeings necessary on account of the damage done by birds (op. cit., Vol. I, p. 137).

through this arduous type of labour ?   First and foremost, there is, of course, the direct stimulus of work to secure the staple food of the tribe.   Besides food also, the national beer is brewed from grain—a variety of intoxicating drinks prepared from mealies, millet, or sorghum.   In our own community we do not have to choose between eating our staple food or turning it into beer.   But in Bantu society this is so : and such is the longing for excitement after the monotony of village routine that many tribes go short of food in order to drink.   Thus the importance of beer in the social life of most Bantu peoples, either as the " favourite pastime "—to quote Junod—or as an essential accompaniment to religious rites such as burial or marriage, makes the supply of grain a great social asset.   The rich man can drink beer, and provide it for others, long after the store-houses of the poorer members of the community, the monogamists usually, are bare.

The fruits of agricultural labour therefore indirectly satisfy social ambition among the Bantu, although rank and leadership are not specifically correlated with the display of stores of vegetable produce as among the Melanesian and Polynesian peoples.   Nor should we say that the ownership of land is a function of social status. Land tenure among these people consists, as we have seen, of temporary rights of use rather than ownership in our own sense of the word.   Nor, where agricultural land consists of strips of bush temporarily cleared, sowed for a few seasons, and then left to revert to waste-ground, is there likely to be a strong personal sentiment attached to each field.   South African history does not furnish us with any example of important intertribal disputes or wars as to the possession of land, such disturbances always being due to theft or injury to cattle.[1]

---

[1] Land tenure is of course important in other parts of Africa such as Uganda and West Africa, but A. Kropf, *op. cit.*, p. 165, says that Kafir wars always concerned cattle, not land ; cf. also J. Barrow, *op. cit.*, Vol. I, p. 155.
Strong family sentiment attached to one particular strip of soil,

But besides the question of social status, agriculture seems to me to be the centre of another system of sentiments of quite a different order. Cultivation is the most seasonal of activities and provides the rhythm for the working year—a rhythm which I am inclined to believe acts as a sort of stimulus in itself under the monotonous conditions of primitive village life.

Writers on South African society speak as if only women were interested in agriculture, whereas all the thoughts of the men were centred on cattle. This is to a certain extent true, as we have seen, and in effect the women do the bulk of the work in the fields. But I think that in this respect the importance of the cattle cult has been slightly exaggerated, and that the agricultural cycle provides emotions nearly as intense, if not as dramatic.

I have noticed among the Babemba of North-Eastern Rhodesia—a purely agricultural and hunting people—that the feeling of general excitement and expectancy at the different epochs in the year is very marked. In the months before the rains come the heat is intense. The ground is hard and cannot be worked at all, and the country is blackened by forest fires. Food is beginning to be short, and the people are listless. The older people sleep a large part of the day, and even the children sit in the shade too tired to play. With the first heavy thunder showers this suspense is broken, and the people shout and sing. In a few days they shoulder their hoes and hurry out to dig the newly softened earth. An African spring is an unforgettable experience to the European, who watches a strip of blackened bush burst

such as we find among the Maori, Hopi Indians, or the peasants of modern Europe, does not appear to exist among the Bantu. Family sentiment is attached to the cattle, not to the soil (cf. R. Firth's account of the tremendous attachment of the Maori for forests, streams, and also agricultural land, *op. cit.*, pp. 361–6). Mrs. Barbara Aitken tells me that among the Tewe Indians of Arizona, the inheritance of land, and in particular the house, from mother to daughter, exerts a powerful influence on Hopi kinship sentiment. Among the Bantu, in cases where kraals are moved frequently and the population to each area is small, this feeling cannot exist.

suddenly, almost in a night-time, into vivid green. But the keen delight of the native and humming activity of his village during the sowing months is perhaps equally impressive. There is, moreover, a real sense of expectancy and interest in the beginning of tree-cutting preparatory to the making of the new gardens, and in the burning of the piled branches which serve to fertilize the fields, besides the joy in the time of harvest which must be universal among all agricultural peoples. I have been conscious throughout the year of the natives' relief and pleasure as each stage of the work is reached, even though the operations involved in cultivation seemed often dull and arduous in the extreme.

Now this is a very different type of society from those of the Zulu-Kafir group, but I should be surprised if, in spite of the great attachment of these people to their cattle, the same type of interest were not associated with the events in the agricultural year. Social status is correlated with the ownership of cattle, but it is for the most part the vegetation cycle that provides the names of the seasons and the months of the year.

Moreover, among most Bantu peoples the chief events of the agricultural year are marked by important religious festivals. Thus the natural rhythm of seasonal change is ceremonially emphasized. In the long suspense before the ending of the drought the chief must pray in public for rain. In many South African tribes also the ruler must bless the seeds before sowing, giving the people confidence to go forward on the next stage of their precarious task. The gathered harvest is celebrated almost universally by first-fruit rites which express the emotional attitude of the people at this time, and also enhance it. The native cannot get the same personal feeling of attachment to a field of grain as he can to a beloved animal, but at the same time he has watched the gradual ripening of the crops with keen emotions. The grain which has ripened after such long and patient endeavour must now be destroyed and consumed. The Corn King must be killed in order to be re-born—to use the phraseology made famous by Frazer in *The Golden Bough*. The harvest must therefore be a time of conflicting emotions. The resultant complex sentiments are expressed in various tribal first-fruit rites among the different Bantu peoples. All these reflect in varying degrees the thankfulness of the people for the return of plenty, their prayers for renewed blessing, and at the same time their fear and hesitation at beginning to consume the new grain.

Moreover, it is noteworthy that these rites take place on a tribal scale. In fact, all the national religious rites among the Southern Bantu are connected with the agricultural year rather than with the pastoral, and the men, although their interests are said to be entirely centred in their herds of cattle, play a prominent part at the *luma* or first-fruit rites and at the harvest ceremonies. It would seem as though the very arduous and tedious agricultural operations could not be carried through without the stimulus of the religious rite to encourage renewed effort and to provide solution for emotional conflict. " Religion sets its stamp on the culturally valuable attitude and enforces it by public enactment." [1] It is obvious also that these great gatherings, especially in a highly organized society such as that of the Zulu, were occasions of tremendous tribal excitement, feasting and dancing, and that in this way agricultural activities become associated with the sense of social cohesion, and the fellowship of the biggest group to which the native belongs.

It may be said in objection to this that it is the women who actually do the agricultural work in South Africa, whereas the men appear to play the prominent part in agricultural rites. This whole question is one which needs further investigation, and the part played by women in magico-religious ceremonies of fertility is not quite clear. The idea that the fertility of women and

[1] B. Malinowski, *Magic, Science and Religion*, p. 61.

the fertility of the crops are somehow associated finds expression in most primitive societies, as we shall see. In particular among the Matabele [1] the women perform a special rain ceremony of their own after the big tribal dance for the first-fruit rites, while a similar women's ceremony is the Shimunenga [2] Festival among the Ba-Ila. Miss Earthy says that among the Vachopi " the cycle of initiation rites for women seems to follow the cycle of the agricultural year ",[3] but the extent to which women are believed to influence the fertility of the land varies widely all over the South-Eastern area.

But besides the stimulus of the religious festival, joint labour and singing seems to provide an incentive to work among the women. Junod speaks of the *Djimo*, or organized working-parties, which sometimes assemble to do the hoeing, singing special *Djimo* songs.[4] Casalis says the Basuto women chant at their work—" singing an air which perfectly accords with the harmonious tinkling of the rings on their arms ". These songs, he says, " serve to invigorate the labourers and keep time in their movements ".[5] But the whole question of the incentives to female labour in a primitive society needs a good deal of further research. We want to know, for instance, the amount of emulation there is between different women on account of the success of their crops. Is industry and success in the fields a cause of jealousy among the women ? Are they associated with social prestige ? All such points need patient investigation if we are to understand the secondary values associated with food-getting activities among these people.

As to the forms of co-operation involved in agricultural labour, our information is again very meagre. Land we know is owned individually, allotted by the headman or the sub-chief, to be used during the lifetime of the owner

[1] L. Decle, *Three Years in Savage Africa*, 1898, pp. 156–60.
[2] Smith and Dale, *op. cit.*, Vol. II, p. 90.
[3] E. Dora Earthy, " Some Agricultural Rites of the Valenge and Vachopi ", *Bantu Studies*, Vol. II, No. 3, Dec. 1925, p. 194.
[4] Junod, *op. cit.*, Vol. II, p. 23.   [5] E. Casalis, *op. cit.*, pp. 143, 163.

and passed to his son.[1]   When not in use the land reverts
again to the bush, and may be distributed by the chief
to another claimant.   A man may leave a field in cultivation to his widows or son's wives, but it is clear that
with such a temporary form of land ownership, no definite
type of social grouping is associated.

The actual cultivation seems to have been carried out
by the family unit.   The man cleared the land of trees,
and the woman did the hoeing, the weeding, and bird-
scaring, with the help of her children.[2]   But beyond this
we have little information to go on.   It is my experience,
in a different type of society, that a woman rarely works
alone in the fields, and that such operations are carried
out by a whole system of mutual help within the kinship
group.   Now the women who usually combine in a
matrilocal society such as that of the Babemba, are the
mother, her married daughters, her own sisters, and to a
less extent her ortho-cousins.   In a patrilocal society like
that of the South-Eastern Bantu, the grouping must be
different, and there probably does not exist such a close
tie of relationship between the women members of the
village kraal.   It would be interesting to compare the
kinship obligations of the different types of society in
this respect.

Again there is the question of the support of the
widowed women, and the means by which those temporarily without assistance can work in the fields for the
payment of food.   Unmarried daughters may own fields
in their own right in some societies, but this is more
usually the prerogative of the married women only.

Also the organization of large-scale activities such as
harvesting, or some forms of hoeing, may call into being
further social groups.   Junod speaks of working-parties
of fifty strong giving their labour for the reward of beer.
Such parties may be on a clan or family scale, or may

---

[1] Junod, *op. cit.*, Vol. II, p. 6.
[2] Men also sowed their own patches in some societies (Smith and
Dale, *op. cit.*, Vol. I, p. 137 ; Junod, *op. cit.*, Vol. II, p. 23).

consist of all the women of one or more villages near by. The report of the 1883 Commission speaks of the Great Wife of a chief as organizing the agricultural work of the village, but this statement plainly needs substantiating by actual facts from different Zulu-Kafir tribes.[1]

Thus we see that agricultural operations in Bantu society are not so definitely correlated with social status as is the case with the complex of cattle-keeping activities. Possession of large supplies of grain is an attribute of wealth and a privilege of the older men of the community, usually polygamists. Authority, as we have seen, is correlated very generally in a primitive society with the power to provide food, and in this case the supply of the staple dish of porridge goes far towards a reputation for greatness. But vegetable supplies are not given and exchanged as a means of contracting legal relationships or carrying out social obligations, as they are in most Melanesian and Polynesian societies. It is the cattle that are exchanged for all principal legal transactions, such as marriage or inheritance, and which thus emphasize legal contracts and bind together the members of the community in a network of credit and debt.

But although less important in this latter respect, agricultural activities are plainly the centre of another system of human sentiments and desires Since their success depends on national religious ceremonies and the control of tribal deities, they contribute very largely to the power of the sub-chief or chief; and strengthen the cohesion of the tribe itself. Since agricultural activities mark the yearly rhythm, they become associated with deep changes in the people's emotional life and daily habits, and with the presence or absence of plenty of food. Moreover, the co-operation necessitated by different types of garden work calls into being new social groups : differentiates in particular between the men and the women of the community ; and stresses the importance of the individual household as an economic unit.

[1] *C.N.L.C.*, Minute 1960.

4. HUNTING

The part played by hunting in the whole economic organization of the Southern Bantu is very difficult to estimate exactly under present-day conditions. Hunting is in a transitional stage at the moment, owing to the introduction of European game laws over most of Southern and Eastern Africa. Thus, while on the one hand, the young men are free from the menace of war and able to indulge in hunting, on the other, they are prohibited from killing a number of animals which would otherwise have been available.

Writing in 1800, J. Barrow says of the Kafirs that the greater part of their time was spent in hunting,[1] but this would obviously be very far from the mark nowadays. Meat food is certainly most eagerly sought for. In some Bantu languages there is a special term denoting " meat hunger ".[2] It is the relish *par excellence* to be eaten with porridge, and it is devoured avidly, even when in a fairly advanced stage of decay. But game is merely a welcome addition to the daily diet ; compared to the importance of vegetable produce, it cannot be described as in any way a staple food.

As regards the activity itself, hunting is a more or less sporadic occupation, following no yearly routine as in the case of the cultivation of crops. It is confined in some areas to those periods when the grass has been burnt, and the animals can be clearly seen : in all, it is pursued with greater energy in the time of growth when the grain is short. Kropf says that in the old days the months of August to December, when the food supplies were running low, were the great hunting days.[3]

Game is secured by three chief methods among the South-Eastern Bantu. First, pursuit by individual hunters, armed with spears, or bows and arrows, tracking their quarry with the aid of dogs, and often spending

---

[1] J. Barrow, *op. cit.*, Vol. I, p. 162.
[2] Smith and Dale, *op. cit.*, Vol. I, p. 144 ; A. Kropf, *op. cit.*, p. 99.
[3] A. Kropf, *op. cit.*, p. 101.

hours, and even days, in the chase. With the inadequate weapons available, this form of chase is often exceedingly dangerous, especially in the case of the eland, the elephant, the rhinoceros, and hippopotamus, the latter being harpooned in mid-stream and brought ashore with a rope. Longer expeditions after the larger animals often lasted anything from one to six months.[1]

Second, traps may be set for various types of large buck—success in this case depending rather on luck and skill than individual daring.

Last, and perhaps the most successful method of obtaining game, is by driving the quarry either into enclosures, as among the Thonga, or into swampy ground where it cannot easily escape.[2] Such drives are almost necessitated when the short-length Zulu spear is used, and often result in a very large slaughter of game.

The values which centre round hunting activities are thus of a very different nature from those connected with agricultural pursuits. Hunting is an amusing, though sometimes dangerous activity. Earlier writers agree that the chase was formerly the greatest pleasure and excitement in the lives of the natives. The clan drives meant large gatherings of men and boys—times of delight and merriment which broke the monotony of the daily routine. Casalis says that the Basuto chiefs found in hunting " an element of power which they are careful not to neglect ", since the drives were much liked by their subjects, as occasions for excitement, boasting of individual exploits, and the giving of meat to the less affluent who did not own herds of cattle.[3] On the return of the hunters to their villages " the women and children shout for joy ". The element of hazard always involved in hunting, and the chance of displaying individual skill, make the pursuit itself of passionate interest, besides the unexpected supply of meat, snatched—so to speak

---

[1] Smith and Dale, *op. cit.*, Vol. I, p. 153 ; Junod, *op. cit.*, Vol. II, pp. 54, 59, 60.

[2] Junod, *op. cit.*, Vol. I, p. 58 ; J. Y. Gibson, *op. cit.*, p. 9.

[3] E. Casalis, *op. cit.*, pp. 170–1, 175 ; also A. Kropf, *op. cit.*, p. 111.

—from the environment, without any of the long routine of labour which agricultural work, and to a lesser extent pastoral activities, involve.

Co-operation in hunting activities among these peoples is exceedingly interesting, since it requires large-scale activities and transcends the usual family or village group. The communal battues of game used evidently to number as many as 500 men or more.[1] These were summoned by the chief of the tribe, and it was he who directed activities, and adjudicated the game. Kidd states that the clan was the basic unit in such an organization among the AmaMpondo, and that each was mustered separately and called by its *sibongo* name, performing a mimic dance of the animal with which it was associated.[2] Gibson describes a game drive among the Zulus in which " the men and boys assemble in little companies, into which they had been formed by relationship or proximity of dwellings, and each, following some recognized head, or captain, saluted the master of the hunt on arrival by dancing before him ".[3] It is difficult to be clear from these accounts as to whether a definite clan-grouping is meant, or some loosely organized band depending on chance association or propinquity.

In the setting of game-pits, Junod again states that the members of a clan united to build the larger enclosures or pits into which animals are driven.[4] But the smaller snares are probably owned by individuals, or the members of one family, and we have no account of the legal rules governing their use, or of any system of co-operation in setting.

As to individual hunting, a Thonga will apparently summon his fellow-clansmen to his aid, either if he cannot carry the quarry alone, or if he expects it to escape. In this case he will shout the clan rallying cry, " This is intended to exclude men of other clans and to

[1] D. Kidd, *The Essential Kafir*, p. 315 ; W. J. Burchell, *Travels into the Interior of Africa*, 1822, Vol. II, p. 320.
[2] D. Kidd, *Kafir Socialism*, p. 15 ; *The Essential Kafir*, p. 316.
[3] J. Y. Gibson, *op. cit.*, p. 9. [4] Junod, *op. cit.*, Vol. II, p. 58.

prevent fighting or any dispute about the possession of the animal." [1] Now Junod usually means a territorial unit when he speaks of the clan, although the mention of a clan rallying cry sounds more like a totemic kinship group. It is difficult to be clear what is meant in this case.

Hunting in former times seems to have been associated with political authority or prestige, but it is doubtful whether this could be said nowadays. " To be first in war or in the hunting field ", says an earlier writer, describing the Fingos, " was the crowning honour of life." [2] At the present time status depends more largely, as we have shown, on the possession of herds of cattle and well-filled grain-bins. But special prestige is apparently still attached to the hunters of dangerous game. Junod speaks of the *maphisa*—specialist hunters—" a kind of superior caste . . . very proud of their name ". These hunters, who are exceedingly jealous of each other, pursue only dangerous animals, such as the elephant and rhinoceros, and derive their reputation in society from exploits in the field. The *batimba*, or the hippopotamus hunters of the old days, were also an organized caste, handing on their knowledge from father to son living in special villages of their own, and bound by a complicated series of hunting taboos. [3] But beyond these specialist hunters we cannot say that the chase as a food-producing activity is definitely correlated with social status among the South-Eastern Bantu. It is a romantic and pleasurable pursuit, and the constant subject of folk-lore and myth. It unites the members of a tribe in common enjoyment, but has not the same sociological importance as agricultural or pastoral activities.

---

[1] Junod, *op. cit.*, Vol. II, p. 56.

[2] J. Ayliffe and J. Whiteside, *History of the Abambo, generally known as the Fingo*, Historical Tracts, 1912, p. 2 ; cf. also D. Campbell, *In the Heart of Bantuland*, 1922, pp. 36, 55, for an account of chieftainship given among the Central Bantu tribes according to skill in hunting.

[3] Junod, *op. cit.*, Vol. II, pp. 59 *et seq.* Prof. Seligman tells me that among the Dinka there are special groups of marsh-dwellers with few cattle, living almost entirely by fishing and hunting hippos.

5. FISHING

Fishing is a somewhat similar activity, though undertaken more sporadically among these people, and involving less danger and excitement in the pursuit. Fish is not a staple food, though it is a welcome addition to the diet during seasons when the grain supply is short, and is often an important article of trade between the villages on the river banks and those inland.

Fishing among the Southern Bantu also requires co-operative effort, although the exact combination of individual ownership and joint endeavour is not very easy to ascertain. Junod mentions three types of "collective" fishing. The *nhangu*, or triangular enclosure made of sticks stuck in the sand of the river bed, appears to need relatively complicated preparations, but individual ownership is evidently recognized in this case. The right to build a *nhangu* is obtained by paying a tax to the chief of the country, but the form of co-operation necessary for its construction is not clear. The *shibaba* is another form of "communal" fishing, its setting being regulated by laws and attended by taboos. It consists of a reed trap set on the river bank; and here again an individual owner is mentioned as cutting the first reed, but we do not know whether his helpers are members of his family, his clan, or merely the village as a whole. The *Tjeba* fishing is more interesting since it seems definitely to involve co-operation on a tribal scale. *Ku tjeba* means "to kill fish in company" in lakes which are drying up, and Junod states that every male member of the tribe must answer the summons of his chief to go to the shore. The expedition must be blessed by a descendant of the family which originally inhabited the shore, and tribute of one fish each must be levied to the chief. The type of leadership in such an enterprise would be interesting to study, since the chief himself is apparently not necessarily present.[1]

[1] Junod, *op. cit.*, Vol. II, pp. 85-8.

Besides these communal forms of fishing there are evidently individual fishermen, owners of smaller traps such as the *mono*, or cone-shaped trap of reeds common among Bantu peoples, or anglers with a hook. The study of fishing rights and the laws governing the owner-ship of boats and traps, is an important subject for further research in the field.

We see, then, that fishing, like hunting, can be carried out individually, or else on a village, clan, or even tribal scale. Like hunting also, success in fishing is not associa-ted with any definite social status. Its supply is too irregular to be a means of measuring wealth, although there is, as I have stated, some inter-village exchange of fish, and in some cases the dues of the chief are paid in this way. The pursuit does not require individual bravery, and success is rather the result of skill and luck than hardihood and daring. A man may acquire a reputation as a lucky fisherman and have power to sell his fishing magic, but I have never heard of cases in which this success was definitely associated with social status. Finally, there is less romance attached to fishing than hunting, but it is in itself a pleasurable pursuit.

6.   Conclusion

In conclusion, then, we have become clear that in order to analyse the nutritional relationships of a prim-itive society, we have to demand a new and more exacting type of observation in the field. First we have to study the nature of each food-producing activity in the tribe, its appeal to the native, and the incentives that drive him to work. We must make the imaginative effort to feel as he feels, whether driving his cattle into the kraal at nightfall, or weeding and hoeing his fields. We must examine the magic or religious rites which surround his economic activities, giving him confidence in difficult or hazardous undertakings, or impressing upon him from youth upwards the right cultural attitude towards the work he has to do. Even from the scanty material available, we have seen how the Bantu cultivator is spurred by emulation, the stimulus of joint working-parties, and by the desire to obtain a reputation for hospitality and wealth. The hunter desires to excel his fellows in luck and daring, and is animated also to a large extent by the excitement of the chase itself. The owner of cattle is trying to pile up wealth in the form of capital as he adds to his herd. He wants the prestige that go with ownership, as well as the supply of meat. In all these economic activities we have shown clearly that possession of food resources, knowledge and skill in technical activities, or the power to approach the right supernatural forces, are definitely correlated with social status in the group.

Next, the most important task of the field-worker is to draw up a calendar of economic routine.[1] Although it is rare to find a primitive people subsisting entirely upon one type of diet, yet the economic organization of most Bantu peoples is unusually complex from this point of view, the combination of agricultural, pastoral, and hunting activities forming a most diversified annual routine. Now for such a calendar we need, not only a bare account of the succession of the major agricultural operations—hoeing, sowing, weeding, and harvest—but a careful description of the passage of everyday life, such as can only be compiled from a day-to-day diary kept on the spot. No work is so irksome and apparently unrewarding to the field-worker as the constant noting down of trivial events in economic life. Yet I believe that to get a knowledge of the whole tempo of primitive society, we must understand, not only what task the people are engaged on, but the time they take to do it, how often it must be repeated, and the number of people

[1] From a theoretical point of view an excellent calendar of this description has been compiled by Dr. Firth in his analysis of Maori economics (*op. cit.*, Chaps. II, III, IV, and VII). His whole treatment of the question of economic incentives in primitive society has been very stimulating to me.

so engaged. Such apparently obvious facts are very rarely given by workers in the field.

We want also to compare the time spent on food-producing activities with that given to other primary needs, such as shelter or clothing, and also the effort expended in satisfying the savage man's æsthetic sense. We must estimate the effect of different occupations on the way that the subsequent leisure is used. To get such detailed information it is necessary to make out a series of daily time-tables, as well as the main calendar of seasonal events.

To complete the scheme of activities, we want an account of the changes in the weather and in the face of the country during the different months of the year, the emotions and anticipations which herald the coming of rain or sun, and the myths associated with weather lore.[1] We cannot study the secondary values centred round food production unless we know the emotional attitude of the people to such events.

Again the field-worker must supply the fullest descriptions of the seasonal alterations in diet, and in the actual amount of food consumed. Savage societies vary far more widely than do our own in this respect, and their rhythm of life changes accordingly. Instead of our regular three meals a day, the Bantu eats in general one large meal of cooked cereals, with meat or vegetable sauce, and two meals when he can. In the lean months of the year he may be reduced to forest fruits, caterpillars, mushrooms or the like. At some seasons the children seem to be nibbling extras—pumpkin, cucumber or the like—all day long. At others they definitely go short. So also beer is drunk in large quantities when grain is available, but all feasting or festivity is reduced during the hunger months. The seasonal rhythm of savage society depends therefore very definitely on the nature of its food.

Lastly, we have to return to the system of grouping

[1] Cf. Radcliffe-Brown's suggestive analysis of seasonal changes and the myths associated with them in the Andaman Islands.

which food production makes necessary, whether to regulate the ownership of raw materials, to provide for inheritance, the economic partnership formed by marriage, leadership in economic activities, or the co-operative undertaking itself. For instance, we have seen from the scanty material available, that among the Southern Bantu, agriculture is based on the work of the individual householder, owning his own fields, and working on a definite system of co-operation with his wife and near kinsmen. But the part played by the chief in agricultural leadership, and the national rites for the production of rain, makes of the tribe a composite economic group. Similarly, hunting and fishing can be carried out individually, but the clan, and sometimes the tribe, co-operate in the large game drives under the chief's directions, or in certain collective forms of catching fish. Herds of cattle are owned individually, and even the beasts allotted to the separate wives of one man are kept apart in the common herd. But the whole graze together under the supervision of the head of a patrilineal kinship group, and are subject also to certain rights on the part of the tribal chief himself.

By this network of legal relationships each food producer is bound. It is for this reason that I have tried to analyse the nutritional system of these particular tribes. Hunger is not the only want that shapes human groupings, but it is a very fundamental one ; and the isolation of nutritive institutions enables us to see the structure of a primitive society from a new point of view. It enables us, moreover, to examine the kinship sentiments of adult life, for we have now to return to our biographical study where we left it, at the moment when the adolescent boy was ready to assume his new duties as a food-producing member of the tribe. We have to watch his kinship attitudes as they are shaped and twisted in the light of the new economic interests and ambitions, to which, as an active member of society, he now becomes subject.

CHAPTER V

KINSHIP SENTIMENT AND ECONOMIC ORGANIZATION

1. TERMINOLOGY

WE suggested in the first part of this work that the primary extension of family sentiment to members of the wider kinship group largely depended upon the share the latter took in fulfilling the original family functions of distributing and consuming food. We showed that on occasion the households of the father's brothers, and to some extent those of the mother's family, might provide food for the growing child. Certain special foods, such as meat, are also divided between both sides of the family, portions being allotted to the father's brothers, his father, and those to whom he is united by marriage. Lastly, we described the laws of Bantu hospitality, by which the sharing of food by members of the household may have to be extended to distant members of the family or the clan. All these functions I have included under the description of the *primary* extension of nutritive ties.

Now our task in these succeeding pages is to examine the *secondary* extension of these early family sentiments to other members of the local group or tribe, according as these individuals become linked together in economic operations on a wider scale. We have to show how the emotional bonds of early childhood are modified, as the family household assumes new functions as a unit for the direct production of food. Economic organization necessitates new forms of leadership. Rivalries and ambitions as to the control of food resources puts kinship

sentiment to a new strain.   Besides its original function
of sharing and consuming the daily meals, the primitive
family becomes linked to others in a definitely economic
scheme.   This modification of early attitudes and their
later extension beyond the limits of the family, I have
called the *secondary* extension of nutritive relationships.

The introduction of such a nomenclature as *primary*
and *secondary* extensions might seem to imply a clear-
cut regularity in the growth of social sentiments, which
in actual fact does not exist.   Human emotions, which are
from their very nature passionate, complex, and infinitely
various, rebel against the scientist's classifying hand.
The field-worker cannot expect naturally to find such
arbitrary distinctions written large over the face of the
society he is studying.   On the other hand, the kinship
group performs so many specific social functions, economic, legal, or religious, in a primitive society, that there
actually is something like a standard attitude towards
the different members who have to play their part in
the scheme.   One is surprised to find that even a child
in a primitive society is prepared to tell you what such
stereotyped emotional attitudes should be.   He may
explain, if he has been brought up in a matrilineal tribe,
that he is afraid of his maternal uncles, whereas his
father's brothers may be treated with less respect.   To
ask the same question of a child in our own society
would produce no immediate kind of response.   Human
relationships in a primitive culture do actually fall into
patterns of a certain order, and such terms as *primary*
and *secondary* extension may well be used to facilitate
the description of their growth.

What, then, are the kinship groups we have to study ?
It is well to define what we mean by the terms.   By
family I have referred to the household unit, the group
composed by the father, mother and children.   In the
case of the polygamous Bantu household several such
families exist side by side as discrete units linked under
one patriarchal head.

But each child at birth becomes a member of two families, that of his father and of his mother respectively. However unilateral may be the kinship emphasis in his society, whether to the patrilineal or the matrilineal side, the members of both sides of the family have their rôle to play in his childhood, and are inevitably linked by legal and economic ties. This group, composed of the brothers and sisters of both father and mother, with their respective wives and children, the grandparents and the near relatives of their generation, I have called the *Kinship* group. It is not a household group as is the German *Gross familie*, but is a *bilateral* group composed of the near relatives united by marriage, acting as a legal unit on many occasions of family life, such as the birth of the child, marriage or death. It is to be distinguished from the *Clan*, which, according to the current anthropological definition, is a *unilateral* group comprising the relatives of the father or the mother only, and stretching to such wide limits that actual relationship is often impossible to trace. It will be seen that the Kinship group may in some cases coincide with the territorial unit or village, where a great deal of intermarriage is the custom. While in some of the small kraals of the Zulus and Thongas, it is the polygamous family itself that composes the local group. The patriarchal head may live with his wives and younger children, while his older sons have left the kraal to build villages of their own.

The larger territorial grouping is of course the *tribe*, a unit no longer bound by ties of relationship, but comprising all those individuals who occupy one stretch of country, speak a common language, and observe common customs, and perhaps the rule of a single chief. Local groupings of clan members such as are found in some societies, I shall refer to as *sub-tribes*.

Having now described the most important social groupings of our society, we must proceed to study the way in which they are linked together by nutritive ties, starting first from the bonds of the family and kinship group as these are modified by economic interests; turning next to the kinship horizon of the individual as it is changed by marriage; and considering lastly the economic ties of the clan and tribe.

2.   PATRILINEAL AND MATRILINEAL SENTIMENT

The most distinctive characteristic of the kinship sentiment of primitive peoples is the marked difference in attitude towards the relatives of the paternal and maternal line.   Such individuals are often distinguished linguistically by special kinship terms, and in actual life by the behaviour patterns the individual must observe towards them.   Among the patrilineal Thonga, for instance, we are told that a man's feelings towards his father's relatives are those of respect, restraint, and even fear : while the mother's people, " the group which I call my mother's home ", are treated with freedom and affection—the maternal uncles in particular being expected to act towards their uterine nephews and nieces with the utmost indulgence.[1]

Such a situation is, in the main, characteristic of a society of the patrilineal type.   In a matrilineal community the position is, in a sense, reversed, since the young man's attitude towards his maternal uncle, and his mother's family in general, is in this case one of respect, while his father is treated in a friendly and affectionate way.   Those societies in which the balance between the patrilineal and matrilineal principle is more evenly held, as, for instance, among the Bantu tribes of Northern Rhodesia, give evidence, as we should expect, of a smaller distinction in kinship sentiment between the two.

[1] Junod, *op. cit.*, Vol. I, pp. 232–4.   The acts of ritual freedom between uncle and uterine nephew to which Junod refers, are not, of course, universal, although they have been reported from other parts of South Africa (cf. A. R. Radcliffe-Brown, " The Mother's Brother in South Africa ", *S.A.J.S.*, Vol. XXI, November 1924, pp. 542–55).

The formation of such typical emotional attitudes towards the relatives of both parents has recently become of great importance in the study of primitive kinship. The old division of societies under the headings of Father-right and Mother-right was based on the fact that one line or other seems invariably to be predominant in determining such factors as succession, inheritance, authority or descent. But this classification ignored, not only the real bilateral nature of primitive kinship systems, but the strong emotional reactions of the individual to such necessary legal over-emphasis of the privileges of one side of the family as against the other. The importance of the human sentiments which underlie the legal systems of primitive kinship has only recently been stressed. Thus, to take only one example, Malinowski has pointed out that among the Trobriand Islanders, descent is matrilineal, according to the legal system of the tribe, but these matrilineal laws of inheritance are often in such dramatic conflict with the father's natural affection for his own sons that he tries, when he can, to evade them. In a patrilineal society, the emotional conflict is of a different type, but equally pronounced, as we shall see.[1]

Now recently, largely under the influence, I believe, of psycho-analysis, anthropologists have attempted to explain these distinctive patrilineal and matrilineal sentiments in terms of the early psychological reactions of the child. According to Freud, the child is influenced in its subsequent relationships, both by the behaviour of its parents towards it, and also by their attitude towards each other. Therefore, in a type of culture in which there are definite patterns of behaviour towards the different relatives on each side of the family, it is tempting to extend Freud's hypothesis to account for

---

[1] B. Malinowski, *The Father in Primitive Psychology*, Psyche Miniature, 1927, also *vide supra*. The same stress on the emotional attitudes underlying the bilateral organization of primitive kinship is evident in the work of Professor Radcliffe-Brown (cf. " A Further Note on the Ambrym ", *Man*, Vol. XXIX, March 1925).

the distinctive attitudes of the individual towards his paternal and maternal kinsmen as a whole.

This attempt has in fact been made by Professor Radcliffe-Brown, precisely in the case of those particular tribes with which we are dealing. To describe his theory briefly in his own words, he states that :

> " The pattern of behaviour towards the mother, which is developed in the family by reason of the nature of the family group and its social life, is extended, with suitable modifications, to the mother's sisters and to mother's brother, then to the group of maternal kindred as a whole, and finally to the maternal gods, the ancestors of the mother's group, who are, of course, members of that group of a special kind.   In the same way, the pattern of behaviour towards the father is extended to the father's brothers and sisters, and to the whole of the father's group (or rather to all the older members of it, the principle of age making important modifications necessary), and finally to the paternal gods."

The indulgent attitude of the mother to her baby is thus made to account for the special ritual licence which exists among the Thonga tribe between maternal uncle and nephew. The child's attitude to its mother is extended to the *malume*, or maternal uncle. Similarly, the fear and respect the child is taught to give to the father is extended to the paternal relatives and paternal gods.[1]

Malinowski has studied the formation of these typical attitudes towards the paternal and maternal relatives in Trobriand society, he being the first anthropologist actually to test psycho-analytical theories in the field. He shows that in his typically matrilineal tribe the boy has an attitude of respect with repressed hostility towards his maternal uncle—imitating his mother's reverent and submissive attitude to the latter—while rebelling against his authority in daily and economic life. The so-called

[1] A. R. Radcliffe-Brown, " The Mother's Brother in South Africa ", *S.A.J.S.*, Vol. XXI, November 1924, p. 553.

Œdipus complex is in fact transferred from the father to the maternal uncle in matrilineal cultures of this type.[1]

Evans-Pritchard recently tried to reduce such observations to a general principle, expressed in diagrammatic form, adding the rider that the child, through imitating its parents' behaviour to its relatives, tends to have " an ambivalent attitude towards any person about whom its relatives have very different and pronounced feelings ", the maternal uncle being the typical case in most primitive societies, whether patrilineal or matrilineal.[2]

Such brilliant and suggestive theories will probably revolutionize the conventional type of kinship study based on pseudo-historical explanations of kinship usages as the survivals of a previous matriarchal, or even group-marriage stages. But this process of extension of childish attitudes from the parents to the other adult members of the group must always be considered with the caveat, constantly voiced by Malinowski, and implied in his theory of social function, that the child's family sentiments must not be considered apart from the context of the social life in which they were formed. Kinship sentiment must not be analysed *in vacuo*, but only in relation to the social needs the ties of relationship exist to fulfil, and it is for this reason that the economic aspect of kinship is so important to my mind.

Let us consider, for instance, Radcliffe-Brown's theory that the attitude of the child to the maternal relatives is an echo of its tender feelings towards its own mother. Such a process of extension, if it can be considered apart from the actual kinship organization of each tribe, would be an absolutely universal phenomenon. The tender bonds between mother and child are, after all, invariable

---

[1] Cf. B. Malinowski, *Sex and Repression in Savage Society*. Note that Radcliffe-Brown states that the boy extends his *own* attitude towards his mother to the maternal uncle and the members of the mother's group. Malinowski, on the other hand, observes that the boy imitates the behaviour of his mother towards her brother, and follows the general tradition of his tribe, rather than extends his own.

[2] E. E. Evans-Pritchard. " The Study of Kinship in Primitive Society ", *Man*, November 1929, Vol. XXIX, p. 193.

in any type of society, but the attitude of the individual to his maternal relatives differs profoundly from culture to culture. The hypothesis cannot be extended to other societies, unless we realize that it is the mother's social status in the kinship group that is the determining factor. This was our chief aim in examining the customs of suckling and feeding the savage child. The nutritive dependence of the infant on the mother is the common feature, but the gradual shaping or transformation of this tie according to the social attributes of maternity provides the distinctive features of filial sentiment in that particular tribe. The infant's early affections are profoundly modified by the particular functions performed by the women in the domestic and economic life of the society.

So also in the case of the patrilineal and matrilineal sentiment characteristic of the primitive kinship group : we cannot merely speak of the transference of filial attitudes to the men and women of the paternal or maternal lines, as though each family existed, static, isolated in space. We have to consider the groups united by marriage as part of a complex social scheme. In a primitive society where the family is the chief unit of food-production, marriage forms a definite unit in the whole economic system. The two families are bound together by complicated, and often arduous, legal obligations for the upbringing of the children, and the transfer of property to the next generation. Where such a system of obligations exists, strains and rivalries must ensue. The child is certainly influenced in its attitude towards its paternal and maternal kinsmen, by observing the respective behaviour of its parents towards the same individuals. But this very behaviour is itself dictated by the nature of the marriage contract which binds together both groups. The feelings of the father and mother towards their relations-in-law depend on whether their interests clash or coincide. Freud's hypothesis is of the utmost importance to the anthropologist, but only if it stimulates a comparative study of the social attributes of paternity and maternity in different primitive tribes. The differences in patrilineal and matrilineal sentiment can only be explained on the basis of a thorough knowledge of the nature of the marriage contract, the economic obligations involved in matrimony, and the scheme of co-operation by which the two sides of the family are bound.

So also in the case of the subsequent modification of kinship sentiment in later adult life. The individual in a primitive society does not merely acquire in childhood an affectionate attitude towards one set of relatives, or an ambivalent feeling towards the other, through the medium of parental influence or the sharing of a common life. He is, from adolescence onwards, definitely placed in circumstances in which his interests coincide with those of some members of his family and clash with those of others : and the more fundamental the human desires which are regulated by kinship systems, the more pronounced and distinctive will such emotional attitudes be. In a community in which starvation is the chief peril, the production of food the most important activity, and its accumulation the measure of wealth, nutritive needs and wider economic interests must be the determining factors in the shaping of the kinship sentiment of the adult.

It is for this reason that we have first to study the legal obligations of marriage in Bantu society, with the conflicting economic interests at issue between the two family groups. This will enable us to understand the kinship sentiment towards the patrilineal and matrilineal relatives with whom the child grows up.

Next we shall turn to the functions of the two groups in the food-producing scheme. We shall see how these early childish sentiments are modified as the individual grows up, and comes himself to share the interests and ambitions of the wider economic life. We shall understand his attitude to those relatives with whom he is linked by his own marriage tie. By this means we can begin to get some sort of insight into the process of secondary extension of nutritive ties.

3. Marriage as an Economic Contract

The essential element of the marriage contract among the Southern Bantu is the transfer of *lobola*—usually in the form of cattle—between the relatives of the bridegroom and those of the bride.   This transaction not only forms public evidence of the legal obligations undertaken in marriage, but acts to a large extent as a guarantee of their fulfilment, as the *lobola* can be returned if the contract is broken.   The two groups united by marriage enter into a permanent contract by this means.

Now the chief obligation of the woman's family is to provide the man with a child-bearing wife.   In the case of desertion by the woman or of failure to bear a child, her father is forced to return the *lobola*, or to provide a new wife.   Sterility on the part of the woman is a cause for divorce among the Kafirs, Zulus, Basuto, Matabele, and Thonga, as well as a number of other Bantu tribes.[1]   And the only alternative to divorce and the return of the *lobola* is the replacement of the wife by some other woman of the family.[2]

But the family of the wife are under contract not only to produce a child-bearing wife, but to surrender their own claims on the woman's unborn children, who would otherwise belong to her own clan.   It is clear from the evidence, not only that the father acquires in marriage the sole right over the children,[3] but that this right is acquired through the *lobola* transaction itself.   " The delivery of lobolo," says Posselt of Zulu marriage, " *is not an essential part of a valid native marriage, but it is the very essence of the transfer of the custody of the children to their father :* all other considerations, rights or obligations

---

[1] Cf. J. Shooter, *op. cit.*, p. 85 ; Casalis, *op. cit.*, p. 184 ; Junod, *op. cit.*, Vol. I, p. 190 ; *C.N.L.C.*, Minute 481 ; J. T. Brown, *op. cit.*, p. 62 ; L. Decle, *op. cit.*, p. 158 ; L. Grout, *op. cit.*, p. 165 ; Smith and Dale, *op. cit.*, Vol. I, p. 227.

[2] Smith and Dale, *op. cit.*, Vol. II, p. 51 ; J. Maclean, *op. cit.*, p. 115 ; D. Kidd, *The Essential Kafir*, p. 215 ; also E. Torday's comprehensive summary of evidence in " The Principles of Bantu Marriage ", *Africa*, 1929, Vol. II, No. 3, p. 275.

[3] A. Kropf, *op. cit.*, p. 163.

are only ancillary." [1] Among the Bechuana, as long as no *Bogadi*, or bride price, is given, the woman and her offspring remain the property of her family and clan. [2] The same appears to be true of the Matabele, among whom the *lobola* is stated to be a consideration paid by the father for control over the children " without which the *Malume* would claim them ". [3] Among the Thonga, also, legitimacy is secured only by the payment of *lobola*. A child born out of wedlock can be legitimatized by the subsequent payment of *lobola*, and conversely, the return of the *lobola* at divorce would necessitate incorporating the children among the mother's clan. [4] Faye describes the *lobola* as " the purchase price of the bride's prospective progeny from the maternal clan to which it rightly belongs ". [5]

In Bantu marriage, therefore, the husband secures the right, not only to the sexual quality of the wife, but also to the sole possession of the children. And this contract is made by the passage of goods between the husband's family and the wife's. The *lobola* is not a payment made once and for all, but, according to a number of competent observers of African society, a species of mutual guarantee for the fulfilment of the contract between both parties. As Major Orde Brown says of the Eastern group of the Bantu :

> "On the one side, it ensures fair treatment by the husband, who might otherwise be called upon to set free his wife with the loss of dowry in addition, while on the other side, it tends to ensure good behaviour on the part of the woman, since her relations are all interested in her faithfulness, lack of which might entail upon them return of the dowry to the aggrieved husband." [6]

[1] F. W. T. Posselt, "Native Marriage", *Nada*, 1926, No. 4, p. 52.
[2] J. T. Brown, *op. cit.*, pp. 53, 62.
[3] H. M. G. Jackson, *Nada*, Dec. 1927, No. 5, pp. 11–12.
[4] Junod, *op. cit.*, Vol. I, p. 120.
[5] Faye, *Zulu References*, p. 102. Gutmann says the same of Chagga marriage payments, i.e. that the children have to be redeemed from the mother's clan (*Das Recht der Dschagga*, p. 135). C. Dundas adds that a woman divorced and remarried need not be paid for until she has born a child (*Kilimanjaro and its Inhabitants*, p. 251).
[6] G. St. J. Orde Brown, *The Vanishing Tribes of Kenya*, 1925, p. 74.

Casalis would also seem to support this theory when he states that divorce is frequent where the *lobola* price is small,[1] and Colenso when he speaks of the *lobola* as a " deposit " to ensure the good treatment of the wife.

But it is important for us to realize that the nature of this guarantee is of a very particular character, when the *lobola* is paid in the form of cattle—still the orthodox transaction over large areas of South Africa, in spite of the introduction of European currency. The tremendous value and sentiment attached to cattle among these people gives a peculiar importance to the nature of the marriage contract, and it was for this reason we discussed the subject at such length. A large head of stock is, as we have seen, the summit of all ambition to the African, and marriage is the chief occasion on which cattle change hands. The payment of the so-called " Bride-price " in the form of oxen therefore sets up a particular relationship between the two groups united by marriage. The *lobola* cattle or even their offspring are rarely sold,[2] and must usually be replaced if they die during the first year of marriage.[3] They are kept in the herd distinct before the eyes of all, giving a very tangible reality to the nature of the permanent legal contract between the two families.

Even the transaction itself is a ceremonial event. Kidd speaks of a public review of the marriage oxen at a Pondo wedding, and Casalis says the Basuto are anxious to have as many witnesses as possible of the event, representatives of the two families sitting down opposite each other in the centre of the kraal " while the animals pass one after the other between the two groups "—animals which, it must be remembered, are more like members of the

---

[1] E. Casalis, *op. cit.*, p. 184 ; J. Colenso, *op. cit.*, p. 138. Evidence from the Eastern area emphasizes this point. Dundas states that neither the Chagga husband nor wife risk breaking their marriage contract for fear of the return of the *lobola* ; Gutmann adds that the bride's relatives are in no hurry to get the dowry as they wish to prolong the husband's dependence on them, and their guardianship of the wife (C. Dundas, " Native Laws of some Bantu Tribes ", *J.R.A.I.*, Vol. LI, p. 256 ; Gutmann, *op. cit.*, p. 133).

[2] Smith and Dale, *op. cit.*, Vol. I, p. 51.

[3] D. Leslie, *op. cit.*, p. 141 ; D. Kidd, *The Essential Kafir*, p. 215.

family than like stock in our sense.[1]   Kinship sentiment in a community in which the acquisition of cattle is so large a source of ambition and jealousy, is bound to be affected profoundly by such a public type of transaction.[2]

The importance of the contract is further increased by the number of people who are party to it.   As a general rule, the greater the number of kinsmen who contribute to the *lobola*, or who share in receiving it, the greater is the security of marriage.   This statement implies both to the actual transfer of *lobola* cattle, and to the oxen slain at the marriage feast.   The Commission of 1883 speak of the *lobola* as " the bond of alliance between two families ".[3]   Among the Basuto, all the father's family contribute to the *lobola*, and this is true of many Kafir tribes.[4]   The Bechuana *bogadi* is " from the common stock, with additions from the maternal uncle ".   Among the Ba-Ila we are told that all the members of the clan may have to contribute to a man's *chiko*.[5]

The cattle received by the bride's family are also distributed among her near relatives, among all the South African tribes according to the numerous witnesses to the Commission on Native Law and Custom.[6]   Among the Thonga and Basuto, the maternal uncle receive their share.   " The cattle paid for the bride are divided amongst her male relations, and are considered by law to be held in trust for the benefit of herself and children, should she be left a widow.   She can accordingly legally demand assistance from any of those who have partaken of her dowry, and her children can apply to them on the same

---

[1] D. Kidd, *op. cit.*, p. 213 ; E. Casalis, *op. cit.*, p. 182.   Among the Akamba bride-price cattle are branded specially (C. Dundas, *J.R.A.I.*, Vol. LI, 1921, p. 256).

[2] It would be interesting to make a comparative study of the nature of kinship feeling and obligations in cultures in which the marriage payments differ widely in character, varying from the payment of cattle—an increasing and permanent form of wealth—to the annual delivery of consumable garden produce as in Melanesia, or the payment of a lump sum of money in discharge of all obligations in the future.

[3] *C.N.L.C.*, Min. 469.

[4] E. Casalis, *op. cit.*, p. 186 ; *C.N.L.C.*, p. 779.

[5] J. T. Brown, *op. cit.*, p. 48; Smith and Dale, *op. cit.*, Vol. II, p. 50.

[6] *C.N.L.C.*, Appendix C.

ground for something to begin the world with." [1] The girl knows who have contributed to her " bride-price " and teaches her children on whom they may claim in time of need. [2]

The division of oxen on the occasion of the marriage feast provides a similar guarantee for the fulfilment of the legal obligations of kinship, and assumes a complex form among these peoples. The essence of the ceremony is again the public avowal of the contract undertaken. Among the Fingo, we are told, marriage is not legal without the slaughter of cattle, which " is the making known, the publication of the marriage ceremony to the whole country ". [3] Shooter mentions that besides the *lobola* cattle, the bridegroom's father must give the *ukutu*, or the " cow for the girl's mother ", and sometimes an ox for her father. The bride's father must supply in return beasts to be slain at the feast, and also the *amadhlozi* or " ox of the house " to be given to the girl ; also the " ox which has a surplus " for the bridegroom himself, or the " ox for opening the cattle fold ". [4] It is thus clear that cattle are not only transferred from one party to the other, but they are also exchanged.

Marriage among the Bantu peoples of South Africa is therefore a complex legal transaction, involving a wide group of relatives and centred in the transfer of cattle—the most valued economic possession of the tribe and objects of personal affection. Besides the feelings of suspicion, or even masked hostility which usually exist between a man and his relations-in-law, there is the tension produced by the passage of stock, usually loved and treasured as friends, from one group to another.

This tension assumes its most complex form among the Zulu-Kafir tribes owing to the custom named by Bryant *lobolelana*. [5] By this usage, the cattle received for

---

[1] J. Maclean, *op. cit.*, p. 55 ; W. Shaw, *op. cit.*, p. 424 ; A. Kropf, *op. cit.*, p. 140.

[2] *C.N.L.C.*, Mins. 1420, 1763, 1644.   [3] *Ibid.*, Min. 5072.

[4] J. Shooter, *op. cit.*, p. 72 ; J. Maclean, *op. cit.*, p. 52.

[5] A. T. Bryant, *Zulu-English Dictionary*, p. 360.

a man's daughter are used to secure a wife for his son. The marriages of the boy and his sister are therefore to a large extent dependent on each other. So much is this the prescribed arrangement, that if a woman bears no daughter, her brother, as the representative of her family, must give the bride-price to buy a wife for her eldest son, because, as the latter claims, " the oxen which my father remitted to my *malume* for his sister ought to have provided our family with a woman capable of giving birth to girls as well as to boys ".[1]

This form of the *lobola* transaction is definitely correlated among the Khaha-Pedi peoples with preferential marriage of the cross-cousin type. The girl is the prescribed mate for her *malume's* son, and one cow is set aside from the *lobola* cattle which bought her mother to provide milk for her in youth, because she is the girl " begotten by the oxen ", i.e. the cattle which bought her mother made possible the marriage of her maternal uncle. When grown, the *malume's* son may claim this cow and offspring and they will form the nucleus of the herd he pays for his cousin. If he does not get his cousin in marriage, he may claim this cow and all the oxen given for his mother years ago in marriage.[2]

Junod gives many instances of the *lobolelana* usage among the Thonga, and accounts for the great respect of a man towards his wife's brother, and his still greater respect, and even avoidance of, the latter's wife—the *Great Mukōnwana*—largely on these grounds. " This woman," he says, " has been acquired by the oxen paid by the man to obtain his wife, and this explains the uneasiness which characterizes their relation." [3]

This special relationship of fear and distrust between

[1] Junod, *op. cit.*, Vol. I, p. 306.
[2] Junod, *op. cit.*, Vol. I, p. 293. Such cross-cousin marriage is found among the Pedi, Thonga, Venda, and some of the Bechuana tribes (cf. Junod, *op. cit.*, Vol. I, pp. 99, 247, 303, and J. T. Brown, *op. cit.*, p. 59).
[3] Junod, *op. cit.*, Vol. I, p. 243. Should the man acquire the right to the return of his *lobola*—through the desertion or childlessness of his wife—the great *mukōnwana* may have to satisfy the claim in person, since his oxen have gone to make possible her marriage to the brother-in-law.

a man and his wife's brother and the latter's wife is extended to a certain degree to the whole group of *Bakonwana,* or wife's male relatives. All are, in a sense, party to his marriage agreement and regarded with some anxiety on this account. When a man goes *bukonwanen* or to visit the village of his wife's family, he meets " the persons whom he fears most in the world ". These will include not only the elder male relatives of the wife, her brother and his wife, the *Great Mukōnwana,* but the mother-in-law and her sisters. In their village a man would not be free to enter a hut without permission. In particular, he would not be able to join them at meals, especially if his mother-in-law were to be present. " If I find my *Great Mukōnwana* eating, she will abandon her meal and leave the spot." [1]

The sharp contrast in the emotional attitude of the husband towards his own and his wife's people is paralleled, therefore, by distinctive forms of behaviour in daily life. The woman is in a similar position towards her relatives-in-law, as the *hlonipa* customs among the Zulu tribes show. The avoidance observed by a woman on eating or holding intercourse with her husband's family has been graphically described by Bryant, and are characteristic of these peoples : so also the special taboos which forbid the use of *amasi* or curded milk in the village of the relatives-in-law [2] (cf. Chapter IV). I do not maintain that these regulations and ritual prohibitions are due entirely to the nature of the whole *lobola* transaction. Mother- and father-in-law taboos are of course common in every type of primitive society. But I do believe that the conditions of economic tension between the two groups produced by the transfer and exchange of cattle are to a great extent reflected in such usages, and that the inclusion of the wife's brother and

---

[1] Junod, *op. cit.,* Vol. I, p. 291. Among the Zulus a man would never eat with his mother-in-law, while among the Khosa tribes or some Thonga clans, food can be shared only after a gift has been presented by the son-in-law (cf. also J. Shooter, *op. cit.,* p. 54 ; Smith and Dale, *op. cit.,* Vol. I, p. 341).

[2] A. T. Bryant, *Zulu-English Dictionary,* pp. 255–6.

most of her near male relatives in the general feeling of uneasiness, is due to the number of people who are party to the *lobola* transaction, and the special nature of the *lobolelana* tie.[1]

We have come, then, to the conclusion that, among the Southern Bantu peoples, the two groups united in marriage are bound by a permanent legal contract, which regulates the behaviour of husband and wife, and the ownership and upbringing of the children. To this contract a number of relatives on both sides of the family stand party, bound, if the conditions of the marriage are broken, to forfeit their gauge. Now this gauge, as we have seen, is usually reckoned in terms of head of stock. The slaughter of cattle at the marriage feast gives public witness to the legal transaction : the transfer of the *lobola* cattle determines the social status of the wife and legitimacy of the children ; and, since these cattle are used to buy a wife for the woman's brother, yet a third family of relatives is united in the same tie.

But our study of the pastoral cult among these people has shown us that cattle cannot be considered as an ordinary object of economic exchange. We have seen that the whole ambitions and emotions of the Zulu or Kafir are centred in a ceaseless endeavour to build up his herd. The transfer of *lobola* cattle at marriage, therefore, subjects the two groups of relatives to perpetual strains.[2] Each is anxiously watching to see that its side of the bargain is fulfilled. Jealousies and subjects of

[1] Junod points out that a further reason for the circumspect behaviour of a man with his *bakonwana*, is that he has certain legal claims to marry some of the women of their group. The *tinamu* are those of his wife's female relations who may one day become his wives or whose children call him " father ". To obtain one of these women to wife, he must treat the male *bakonwana* with respect (Junod, *op. cit.*, Vol. I, pp. 245–8).

[2] The number of cattle contributed to the *lobola* varies from tribe to tribe. From the data collected by Herskovits (*op. cit.*, p. 371) 25 head would be an average *lobola* among the Zulu or Vandau. Shaw gives 3–10 head for a commoner and 10–50 for a chief (*op. cit.*, p. 424) ; Colenso says 8 or 9 cows will buy a " common wife " but 150 are needed for a chief's daughter (*op. cit.*, p. 26) ; Casalis gives 25–30 as the usual *lobola* among the Basuto (*op. cit.*, p. 182) ; J. Shooter 12 in Natal (*op. cit.*, p. 50).

conflict constantly occur. A large proportion of the time and energies of the cattle-owning Bantu appears to be given to the endless discussion and debate of *lobola* quarrels, whether of present transactions, or unfulfilled obligations in the past.

It is in this atmosphere the child grows up. He realizes that his father's and his mother's people form sharply divided groups. In his early days these individuals have different obligations towards him in daily life (cf. Chapter I). Later, the distinctions are expressed dramatically by the observation of a series of ritual taboos on their common intercourse. As he grows up, he himself comes to understand the sources of economic conflict between the two. He shares the same ambitions to which they are due, and his own attitude towards the paternal and maternal kinsmen assumes its final pattern, as he finds, through experience, with which party his lot is cast. It is this last problem which we have to consider now.

4. THE ECONOMIC FUNCTIONS OF THE FAMILY AND KINSHIP GROUP

To complete our study of patrilineal and matrilineal sentiment among the Southern Bantu peoples, we have to describe the secondary extensions of nutritive relationships to the family or kinship group. First, how does the individual family function as an economic unit ? Next, in the wider scheme of co-operation among relatives, to which group are the boy's interests bound ? Does he side with paternal or maternal relatives as regards economic co-operation or inheritance of food resources ?

The family, as we have seen, is the primary economic unit, whether in agricultural or pastoral activities. The father is the actual owner of the gardens which his wife tills, and she and her unmarried daughters provide the family grain supply from these fields.[1] The man has full

---

[1] I do not know whether the sons have any obligation to help their mothers in the clearing of the fields—specifically man's work in some tribes.

powers to dispose of the granaries when full. The patriarchal head is also the possessor of the kraal cattle : he regulates their departure to and fro from new grazing-grounds ; and selects beasts for slaughter and for exchange. In all these functions he may be helped by his brothers, who may still be members of his kraal, and grazing their cattle with his : or alternatively, by his elder sons.

In the case of both fields and cattle, it is the father who can perform the sacrifice to the ancestral spirits to procure a blessing on the crops or the herds. It is he who kills the beast at any ceremonial event. The eldest member of the family is thus in a position of supreme control, because on him the general success of pastoral and agricultural activities depends. It will be a very long time before the young man is able to approach the supernatural guardians of prosperity on his own.

As regards hunting and fishing activities, it is almost impossible to make any definite statement. The teaching of hunting lore to boys, the setting of traps, or the planning of game drives, are all operations which require leadership and definite rules of co-operation, but we do not know, from the material collected, whether the family is the important unit in this case or not.

But where agricultural or pastoral activities are concerned, it is clear that the group of relatives with which the young man co-operates is the paternal side of the family. He has to accept his father's authority in the organization of economic activities, and works with his brothers and half-brothers—both before and after marriage—and with the paternal uncles, if these have not already kraals of their own.

Further, in a pastoral community, the young men are dependent on their elders for the necessary beasts in order to start a herd of their own. Unlike the agricultural activities of a primitive society, it is impossible in the case of cattle-raising to build up a fortune with industry and a tract of land alone. Unless the boy is able to earn money under white employment, he is absolutely dependent on his kinsmen for his marriage cattle, and for the first step towards an economic life of his own. Now among these Southern Bantu, it is the father who is legally bound to provide beasts for his son's *lobola*, even if only for the eldest son.[1] The binding nature of this obligation seems to have impressed many observers of native custom, and the witnesses examined by the 1883 Commission refer to this parental obligation again and again.[2] Kropf states particularly that Basuto boys make no effort to provide their own *lobola* payment, but lead an idle life, while the fathers arrange the transaction and provide the beasts.[3] They are of course assisted in fulfilling this duty by their brothers, or the other adult members of the kinship group, and also, as we have seen, by their eldest sons in some cases. But no contributions to the *lobola* are made, as far as I am aware, by the male relatives of the maternal line.

The last question that affects our problem is the rule of inheritance of food resources—among these tribes in particular the division of the dead man's herd, since land property is subject not so much to permanent ownership as to a temporary right of use.

Inheritance follows invariably the patrilineal line, but among the male relatives of the father there is a considerable field for choice. The dead man's property goes, either to his brothers or to his sons, and Junod states that Thonga society is rent by these two principles : viz. the rights of the brothers of a man's own generation, and those of his sons, and tremendous rivalry and tension is produced in this way.[4]

Again, there is a considerable field for dispute even among the sons of any given kraal. Polygamy was prac-

---

[1] Among some tribes—for instance the Venda—the father is only obliged to buy a wife for his eldest son, the latter being responsible for the marriage of his younger brothers.

[2] *C.N.L.C.*, Rec. 67, p. 29.   [3] A. Kropf, *op. cit.*, p. 124.

[4] E. Casalis mentions a case of the paternal uncles combining with some of their nephews to oust the one who had been selected as the heir (*op. cit.*, pp. 215–16 ; cf. also Lichtenstein, *op. cit.*, Vol. I, p. 288).

tised on a very considerable scale among the Zulu-Kafir peoples, and the number of possible claimants to a succession was large.   While the son of the chief wife was the probable heir, it was possible in some cases to disinherit him for bad behaviour.[1]   In some tribes it was the custom for the chief always to choose his own successor.[2]   In others the right devolved upon the eldest son of the Great Wife.   Casalis says that in a Basuto household it was the eldest son who could divide the inheritance as he willed among the remaining brothers, and that his power was thus so great, that the father often had to consult him in life, so that there was always " a sad rivalry " between them.   The power of the *malume*, or maternal uncle, was considerable in a polygamous kraal, he explains, just for the reason that inter-kraal jealousy was so great.[3]   Bryant says that a Great Wife was not chosen until a man had reached the age of fifty or so, so that the sons should not be ready to succeed his father too soon.[4]   In this case the older sons of less important households had to be subject to the authority of a younger man, since the eldest son of a Great Wife had some rights of authority over the marriages contracted by members of less houses, and the power to dispose of their cattle to a certain extent.[5]

Perhaps the best commentary on fraternal sentiment among these Southern Bantu is Bryant's statement that among the Zulu, the son of one wife—the *isizinda*—was specially appointed to judge disputes between his father's heirs.   During life he was the least important of all : after death he became the *ieYisa*, " the father of the family ".   He has " absolutely no rights nor property of any kind (save that of his own hut) and has no concern with the estate and liabilities left by the father ".   His

[1] H. M. G. Jackson, *Nada*, " Matabele Customary Law ", 1926, No. 4, p. 33.
[2] J. Shooter, *op. cit.*, p. 108 ; *C.N.L.C.*, Min. 801.   Except where the Great Wife has been bought with the cattle of the tribe.
[3] E. Casalis, *op. cit.*, pp. 179, 181 ; Junod, *op. cit.*, Vol. I, p. 304.
[4] A. T. Bryant, " The Zulu Family and State Organization ", *Bantu Studies*, Vol. II, No. 1, p. 49 ; also J. Shooter, *op. cit.*, p. 107.
[5] *C.N.L.C.*, Mins. 779–81, Q. 1974–6, 797 ; A. Kropf, *op. cit.*, p. 161.

sole function was to act as a disinterested arbiter in disputes which were considered inevitable.[1] Mourning ceremonies were occasions when the tension of family feeling
was particularly likely to explode, and Smith and Dale
describe an incident at a Ba-Ila funeral when emotions
ran so high that at the adjudication of the inheritance
" the young men lost all control of themselves and
attempted to drive off as many of the cattle as they could
by force ".[2]

The relations of a man to his paternal kinsmen are
therefore complex. As a child he has been brought up
with the boys of the kraal—his brothers, half-brothers,
and paternal cousins. Although there is a certain amount
of rivalry between the children of co-wives (cf. Chapter I),
it is clear that the boys co-operate together in foraging
expeditions and other games, and all unite together in
mock fights with the boys of other kraals.[3]

But in early adolescence, economic activities and
rivalries begin to set up new conditions of strain. The
functions of the elder brother becomes more pronounced.
He has definite authority over his brothers in joint work,
such as herding the cattle, or bringing them home to be
milked.

Later still, the question of marriage causes difficulties.
The eldest brother, among most Kafir peoples, is legally
bound to support his brothers. He has usually also the
power to forbid, or to further, a desired match. Among
the Venda, the eldest brother must buy wives for his
juniors, even if he has to borrow cattle from his maternal
uncle for the *lobola* by pledging the person of any future
daughter he may have.[4]

During the father's lifetime the power of the elder
brother is therefore fairly complete. Further, in certain
circumstances he may perform the sacrifice to the ancestral
gods, and Junod recalls an instance of a man being forced

[1] A. T. Bryant, *Zulu-English Dictionary*, p. 730.
[2] Smith and Dale, *op. cit.*, Vol. I, p. 390.
[3] J. Y. Gibson, *op. cit.*, p. 10 ; E. Casalis, *op. cit.*, p. 195.
[4] Junod, *op. cit.*, Vol. I, p. 304.

to seek reconciliation with a brother with whom he had quarrelled, rather than be cut off from the benefits which the ancestral spirits could give. The younger brothers are legally dependent on their senior, while their father is alive, and hence live in conditions of perpetual strain and envy. At his death they must submit to the adjudication of the inheritance proposed by the eldest son.

Towards the male members of the older generation, the patrilineal sentiment is equally ambivalent. On the one hand the father, and to a less extent, the paternal uncles, are the source of all that life holds good. From childhood onwards, as we have seen, the authority of the father is associated with the possession and distribution of food, and the ownership of the cattle-herd. The young man is absolutely dependent on his paternal relatives for his subsistence, his marriage, and his start in life. Further, he is bound to them by the tie of the common clan. He is taught from childhood up that he is a member of his father's group through the whole *lobola* transaction. If he plays in his mother's village he is rebuked. " You are stupid," they would say, " you have your own village ; you go to the village of your *bakonwana* to increase it ! This is true folly. Has not your mother been bought with money ? The children she bore belong to your father, just like the calves of her cows." [1]

On the other hand, the father is the leader in economic life, with all the feelings of jealousy and rebellion that this involves. From the time when he first begins to help in the herding of goats and cattle, the boy is subject to his father's control. To a lesser extent, also, he is bound to respect and fear his paternal uncles, who share with the father in maintaining authority in the group. With the latter also he is a rival for the inheritance of the father's property when he is dead.

In other words, the boy identifies himself in all his economic ambitions with the members of his father's group, but this very identification of legal interests makes

[1] Junod, *op. cit.*, Vol. I, p. 231.

for conditions of tension, suspicion, and rebellion against authority—all these sources of conduct becoming prominent in adult life.

Turning now to the maternal relatives, we find that the conditions are reversed. The boy has no legal rights to inherit from his maternal uncles, except for his personal property and chattels. He does not co-operate with his mother's people in carrying out economic pursuits. In childhood he received great indulgence from his maternal grandparent, who would say if the small boy did damage, " That is no business of mine. Let the father of the child scold him, as he does harm to his property. I have nothing to do with their affairs. It is not my village." [1] Besides this general attitude of indulgence on the part of the maternal kinsmen, the *malume*, or maternal uncle, treats the boy with special affection and freedom. Among a number of South African tribes there is a relationship of ritual licence between a man and his uterine nephew. Among the Thonga the nephew may go to his uncle's village with his comrades when he expects a good meal is towards, and steals the food which has been prepared. For this he cannot even be rebuked, unless the sons of the *malume* in exasperation drive him from the kraal. The uterine niece has similar rights of freedom with her uncle, who is the natural guardian of the mother, and whose marriage was made possible by her own.

Now the affectionate feelings of the child towards his maternal relatives are able to remain unchanged in after life. Although his sentiments towards his father's people becomes strained, as he comes to join with them in economic undertakings, he has no such duties to perform towards the maternal group. There is no secondary modification of his first nutritive ties. He receives no great material advantage from his mother's people, but on the other hand they do not compete with him in his ambitions. Junod records a case of a chief calling in his mother's family to help him in a difficulty. These men

[1] Junod, *op. cit.*, Vol. I, p. 232.

had no legal obligation to aid him, but they would also have no right to claim the inheritance once won ! This puts the crux of the matter very clearly. The legal over-emphasis of the rights of one side of the family results in emotional reactions to the other side.

5. CONCLUSION

To conclude then, we have observed through the study of Bantu economic organization, that kinship sentiment is determined very largely by nutritive needs, as much in adult life as in the early childish days. The character-istic patrilineal and matrilineal sentiments of primitive kinship cannot be analysed, unless we study the functions of the two groups in fulfilling man's chief biological needs. Of these fundamental wants, nutrition is the chief. The groups united in marriage have to carry out certain definite food-producing activities. The marriage con-tract is itself a regulation of the handing on to the next generation of the control of food supplies. We have seen that in Bantu society the most important feature of this transaction is the transfer of cattle from group to group, and the rules of its transfer from generation to generation. The passionate longing for cattle among these peoples leads to feelings of high emotional tension between the two groups. Such attitudes between his paternal and maternal relatives modify and shape the boy's early family ties.

Later, the same question of cattle ownership puts him in a position of permanent rivalry with the members of the group to which he legally belongs. By the time he has reached full tribal status, his patrilineal and matri-lineal sentiments have assumed their final shape, and he has linked himself to other groups by marriage, with the same ties of union and discord to form. We thus see that the whole institution of marriage acquires new mean-ing, when we consider its place in the Nutritive System as a whole. We have now to examine Chieftainship in a primitive community from the same point of view.

CHAPTER VI

ECONOMIC FUNCTIONS OF THE CLAN AND TRIBE

1. THE CLAN AMONG THE SOUTH-EASTERN BANTU

THE study of the unilateral kinship emphasis leads us directly to consider the structure of the clan itself—since the latter, according to recent anthropological definition, is also a unilateral group. To the older anthropologists, such as Morgan and Bachofen, the clan was the primary unit, and the monogamous family a later product of evolution. More recently, however, Lowie, Malinowski and others have pointed out that the clan is in reality an outgrowth of the family and the kinship group—an extension on one side of the family, matrilineal or patrilineal, which defines descent and succession, and makes possible large-scale undertakings in economic or military life.[1] In other words, the clan came into being in order to fulfil certain functions in tribal life, and its structure can only be understood with reference to these functions. The part played by the clan in the whole nutritional system we are now considering, is one of the most important of these factors.

It is therefore our task to discover how far the economic functions of the kinship group have been extended to a

---

[1] Cf. R. Lowie, *Primitive Society*, 1921, Chap. VII, especially his references to Swanton's work on the North American area : " virtually all the ruder Indian cultures lacked the sib scheme ; while the sib appeared among tribes with a far richer, economic, industrial, ceremonial and political equipment " (" Social Organization of American Tribes ", *The American Anthropologist*, 1905, Vol. VII, p. 663). *Cf.* also B. Malinowski, *Encyclopædia Britannica*, 14th ed., article on " Kinship ". Malinowski also considers the laws of clan exogamy to be an extension of the family incest rules.

unilateral body of the clan type, or, in the last instance, to the tribe itself. To what extent are the ties of clan or tribal cohesion dependent on the joint activities of their members in the food quest ?

In discussing this question we are confronted with the problem of terminology. Those writers on South African society from whom we have drawn most of our material, use the term *clan* indiscriminately to describe a *tribe*, the members of a *kinship group*, a local unit, or a unilateral body of the type we have defined above. Kidd, whose whole thesis is a glorification of the " clan system ", never once explains exactly what he means by a *clan*. Gibson, Casalis, and Kropf leave us in similar doubts, and it is often difficult to decide from their accounts of the functioning of the clan on different occasions, which unit of tribal organization is actually meant. Junod, on the other hand, definitely uses the term in a different sense to our own, since he speaks, not of a unilateral kinship group, but of a sub-division of a tribe occupying a certain territorial area and using a special dialect.[1]

We must remember, too, that the history of the Zulu-Xosa peoples is a long series of migrations, cattle-raids, and organized conquests, which led from the earliest days to a quick growth and dissolution of the various social units. These circumstances did not favour the cohesion of larger groups, such as the clan or the tribe. The family kraal remained the basic unit of Kafir organization, and even the inmates of the kraal, as we have seen, showed a constant tendency to split—to " hive off " is the word frequently used by writers of South African history.[2] The acquisition of cattle and dependents led to the segregation of new households and the building of new kraals. The village of Cetshwayo, one of the biggest Zulu despots, apparently numbered no more than 69 huts,[3] and large kraals such as are found in parts of Bechuanaland did not

[1] Junod, *op. cit.*, Vol. I, p. 14.
[2] J. T. Brown, *op. cit.*, p. 26 ; W. Shaw, *op. cit.*, p. 436 ; J. Maclean, *op. cit.*, p. 12.
[3] D. Leslie, *op. cit.*, p. 9.

exist. Zulu society was characterized, in fact, by the perpetual growth and disruption of family units, and the main body of the tribe itself showed a similar tendency to split into sub-tribes, or even smaller territorial groups.

In these circumstances it is difficult to decide whether the South African clan was ever a strongly knit unit with important legal and economic functions ; and it is still harder to describe the part which it plays in native society to-day. Barrow, writing in 1806, and Shooter in 1851,[1] mention certain tribes of Zululand and Natal, in which groups of men were prohibited from eating different animals such as the eland, zebra, monkey, hyena, etc., but they do not tell us whether these are totemic taboos of the type associated with a definite clan structure in many North American and Melanesian societies. Brown speaks of a form of totemism associated with food taboos among the Bechuana natives, but it seems clear that the totemic animal in South Africa is rather a name loosely applied to a sub-tribe or a clan, or a praise title of the type of the *sibongo* of the Bechuana or Basuto, than an integral part of an organized clan cult such as we find in other parts of the world.[2] Junod gives an interesting analysis of the different forms of so-called " totemism " in Portuguese East Africa, applying such tests as the use of animal names in salutation, mimetic dances representing the chosen animal, taboos on its use as food. But his study only goes to show how difficult it is to dogmatize on the question of clan organization in the case of South Africa, since in earlier days the word clan was used without any exact definition, and at the present many typical marks of clan structure are falling into disuse.[3]

Moreover, the military system of the Zulu tribes, initiated by Chaka, cut across the older clan organization,

---

[1] J. Barrow, *op. cit.*, Vol. I, p. 164 ; J. Shooter, *op. cit.*, p. 215.
[2] J. T. Brown, *op. cit.*, pp. 20, 27, 34.
[3] Junod, *Le Totémism chez les Thongas, les Pédis et les Vendas*, Société de Géographie de Genève, Vol. LXIII, 1924.

as Gibson shows.   Chaka's army has been figured at from
twelve to fifteen thousand men, and the division of these
troops into different regiments, housed in barracks after
the manner of a modern standing army, superimposed a
new military grouping on the older kinship ties.   It was
also the Zulu practice for warriors to marry captured
women and to organize their children into new regiments.
Thus tribal as well as clan distinctions were swept aside
by Chaka's army rule, the influence of this Zulu system
being widely spread in South Africa.[1]

We can say in short, that among the Zulu-Xosa peoples
of to-day the distinctive clan grouping is not a pronounced feature of tribal organization.   Nor can we be
certain, owing to terminological confusion, whether the
clan had any important economic functions to perform
even in the earlier days.

Among the Ba-Ila, to take another area for comparison,
this is far from the case.   Clan members give their consent
to the marriage of a daughter of one of their members,
and contribute to the *chiko*, or bride-price, of the son.
They have to pay their fellow-clansmen's debts in cattle,
take the responsibility for their crimes, and refrain from
suing them for repayments of any sort.[2]   " The true clan
is that which appears when you are in trouble, when you
are bereaved or ill and a clansman comes to see you. . . .
Because they help you in all your troubles, they stand
by you to death and everything else that comes to you
—that is the great and true *mukoa*."   A man may
apparently claim relationship, and thus support, by calling
out the name of his clan.   " When a man is desperately
hungry he will say to another : ' My clansman, don't
you see that I need food ? ' "[3]

The clan, therefore, plays an important part in the
economic and legal life of a Ba-Ila tribe, which it cannot

---

[1] J. Gibson, *op. cit.*, p. 219 ; L. Grout, *op. cit.*, p. 73.
[2] Smith and Dale, *op. cit.*, Vol. I, Chap. XI, *passim* ; Vol. II, p. 50 ;
Vol. I, pp. 393, 417.
[3] Smith and Dale, *op. cit.*, Vol. I, p. 295.

be said to do among the South-Eastern group of the Bantu, unless there is a great deal of information missing from our material. There still remains, however, the tribal unit to be considered. Does the tribe function as an economic unit, either in the ownership of land or food resources, or as a body which co-operates in food-producing activities on a large scale?

2. The Economic Functions of the Chief

These questions can be best answered, I think, by an analysis of the economic functions of the tribal chief. The Bantu chief is the apex of a complex political structure, kraal linked to kraal under one sub-chief, and the sub-chiefs bound themselves under the authority of the paramount chief or king of the tribe. In Zulu society, in fact, before the days of Chaka, the tribe could be defined as a body which recognized the rule of a single chief. His authority was the strongest, and sometimes the only, link between the discrete units of the individual kraals, and the tribe could not act as a whole except at his decree. It is for this reason, I say, that the tribal functions only become apparent through the study of the part played by the chief in the economic scheme.

We have already shown that authority in Bantu society is correlated with the possession of food and the obligation to provide for dependents. The sub-chief and the chief in this way assume the functions of the patriarchal head of a family, transformed, and on a larger scale. They are addressed by the " father " term and become the object of a quasi-filial sentiment. Like the father, also, the chief is in control of food resources, organizes economic activities, and is alone able to make contact with the tribal ancestors, whose blessings are essential for the prosperity of agricultural and pastoral activities.

But to consider these questions in further detail—what economic powers does the chief actually possess? He is in the first place the theoretical owner of all tribal land —hunting, grazing or agricultural. " The nation is his, the people, the cattle, the lands—*everything*." [1] In this capacity he receives tribute of all produce so derived, stores which he has in many cases to redistribute to his people or to hold as reserves. Secondly, he is definitely responsible for organizing certain forms of economic activity, chiefly pastoral and hunting. Thirdly, he has usually very important magic functions as a producer of rain and as the officiant at the first-fruit rites.

(a) Land Tenure

To consider first the problem of land tenure. The chief owns all land in theory, to the extent that individuals cannot sell territory, and that the right of distribution is his alone. He gives large areas to his sub-chiefs, and they in turn to their individual headmen, who are also responsible for dividing out strips of ground among the inmates of a kraal. Land once allotted by a chief may be retained by the cultivator as long as he continues to work his fields, and the technical right of the chief to evict occupiers of the soil appears to be rarely exercised. It is a common arrangement for a chief to attract new sub-chiefs to his domain by the grant of fresh tracts of land. [2]

Grazing areas are in a somewhat different category, and remain under the authority of the chief. They are in essence tribal lands, although the chief may reserve lands for winter grazing among the Basuto. [3] A witness to the *Report on Native Laws and Customs* in 1883, summed up the question by saying, " according to native customs, the land occupied by a tribe is regarded theoretically as the property of the paramount chief : in relation to the tribe, he is a trustee, holding it for the

---

[1] L. Grout, *op. cit.*, p. 118.
[2] J. Maclean, *op. cit.*, p. 120 ; I. Schapera, *op. cit.*, p. 173 ; *C.N.L.C.*, p. 65 ; L. Grout, *op. cit.*, p. 96 ; E. Casalis, *op. cit.*, p. 159 ; A. Kropf, *op. cit.*, p. 166 ; D. Leslie, *op. cit.*, p. 163.
[3] E. Casalis, *op. cit.*, p. 160.

people, who occupy and use it, in subordination to him, on communistic principles ".   Hence his right of taxing his subjects—" He is the soil." [1]

In virtue of his theoretical ownership of tribal land, the chief has, therefore, rights of tribute from the soil. This tribute takes the form of statute labour, agricultural produce, and beer, the latter not a definite levy but a form of courtesy, or a substitute for hunting quarry.[2] Among the Zulu the chief has the right to call for work for public purposes, and the young men of the tribe between initiation and joining the army were definitely set apart for such service at the direction of the chief's council.[3] The Thonga chief has similar rights to call upon the young men of the tribe to clean his village square and repair his huts ; while it is the duty of the sub-chiefs to lead a party annually to till the Chief Wife's fields.[4]   Among the Basuto, young men between initiation and marriage " are considered as set apart for public service, and are expected to lead the flocks to graze without any remuneration, to carry messages, to furnish the fuel for the court where strangers are received, and to fetch building materials from a distance ".[5]   They assemble every year " to dig up and sow the fields appropriated for the personal maintenance of their chief and his first wife ".[5]   The exact rights of the Bantu chief to agricultural labour vary, of course, from tribe to tribe, from a definite institution of slavery in some of the Central African peoples, to the rights to free labour we have just described.   But I have not noted a single Bantu society in which authority was not formerly maintained by such a system, even if conditions have now been changed very much by the introduction of European methods of cultivation.

Tribute of agricultural produce is also a common

---

[1] *C.N.L.C.*, Appendix C, pp. 54, 65, 78, etc.
[2] Junod, *op. cit.*, Vol. I, p. 405.
[3] A. T. Bryant, *Zulu-English Dictionary*, p. 384 ; J. Shooter, *op. cit.*, p. 104 ; T. B. Jenkinson, *op. cit.*, p. 25.
[4] Junod, *op. cit.*, Vol. I, p. 406.
[5] Casalis, *op. cit.*, pp. 266, 162 ; also G. M. Theal, *The Yellow and Dark-skinned Peoples of South Africa*, 1910, p. 182.

prerogative of the chief among most Bantu societies. Such tribute may be delivered annually, either at harvest, or on the occasion of a surplus of certain types of food, such as an unusually good crop of wild fruits, or a plentiful supply of beer. For instance, the Thonga chief receives baskets of mealies from each village, and a certain quantity of beer when it is brewed for a feast.[1] Among the Vachopi each family will present the chief with a basket of mealies at the harvest rites.[2] Such tribute was formerly an essential element of the whole economic system, enabling the King to feed the statute labourers gathered for work. At the present day the exaction of labour dues is in some cases illegal under European rule, and the whole question of tribute is, therefore, in a state of transition. I have myself been constantly amazed that among the Babemba, tribute which was formerly exacted under threat of mutilation by enormously powerful chiefs, still survives to this day when the chiefs have no legal right, according to the British courts, to demand it at all. The status of a chief can still be gauged by the amount of tribute he gets, and the amount of food he gives his labourers—the one factor being necessarily dependent on the other. In former days it was one of the most essential attributes of chieftainship, both among these peoples and among the Southern Bantu.

(b) Rights over Cattle

The cattle herds of the tribe were also theoretically the property of the chief. Brown, describing Bechuana customs, says " the chief is nominally the owner of all the cattle of the tribe ", and his statement is born out by Grout and Kropf in their accounts of the Zulu and Basuto peoples.[3] In former days the actual ownership may have

---

[1] Junod, op. cit., Vol. I, p. 405 ; Holub, op. cit., Vol. II, p. 239.
[2] E. Dora Earthy, " Some Agricultural Rites of the Valenge and Vachopi ", B.S., Vol. II, No. 4, 1926, p. 265.
[3] J. T. Brown, op. cit., p. 48 ; L. Grout, op. cit., p. 118 ; A. Kropf, op. cit., p. 108 ; D. Leslie, op. cit., p. 85 ; W. Shaw, op. cit., p. 437.

lain with the chief as well, since Kropf says that all the bulls of the herd belonged to him, but nowadays individual ownership is of course recognized, although the chief's herd is still by far the biggest, numbering among the Zulu some thousands of head.[1]

The power of the chief now lies in the fact that he can control the movements of the cattle, and can loan out beasts to his sub-chiefs and favourites,[2] such loans placing the latter in a position of dependence on him.[3]   He also reserves the right of confiscating, or " eating up ", the cattle of a too-powerful rival, whose herd bids fair to surpass his own.[4]   In times of stress too he can levy cattle to strengthen his depleted herd—such cattle among the Matabele serving to supply the oxen for a big feast, and giving the King a national, as well as a personal herd.[5] Formerly, theft of cattle was definitely considered as a crime against the chief, who thereby instituted measures of revenge on behalf of the individual owner.   Last, and perhaps most interesting of all, the Great Wife of the chief was purchased by cattle supplied by the whole tribe, her son deriving from this transaction his right to sit on the tribal throne.   There is at least one instance of the son of a chief's Great Wife, begotten by a lover after the death of her husband, and yet being chosen as heir to the chieftainship.   The son of the second wife, although born in the lifetime of the chief, had less good a claim to succeed, since his mother's *lobola* had been furnished from the King's personal herd alone.[6]

It is thus clear that while individual ownership of cattle existed among the Zulu-Kafir peoples, yet the chief retained considerable powers over the accumulation of

---

[1] L. Grout, *op. cit.*, p. 96.

[2] J. T. Brown, *op. cit.*, pp. 98, 166 ;   J. Y. Gibson, *op. cit.*, p. 7.

[3] J. Shooter, *op. cit.*, p. 28.

[4] J. Maclean, *op. cit.*, pp. 58, 73, 74 ;   A. W. Cole, *op. cit.*, p. 191 ; J. Colenso, *op. cit.*, pp. 28, 61 ;   Holub, *op. cit.*, Vol. II, p. 160 ;   F. Fleming, *Kafraria*, p. 115.

[5] L. Decle, *op. cit.*, pp. 157, 162 ;   W. Shaw, *op. cit.*, p. 443.

[6] A. Kropf, *op. cit.*, p. 135 ;   Holub, *op. cit.*, Vol. II, p. 159 ;   Vol. I, p. 383.

stock by his subjects, and the right to levy tribute on pastoral wealth as well as agricultural. Among a cattle-loving people such as the Southern Bantu such privileges formed a powerful sanction for his authority.

(c) *The Chief and the Hunt*

But besides his leadership in pastoral activities, the chief had also an important position in the organization of the hunt. Hunting, as we have already seen, involved in many cases large-scale operations, and the tribal drives of game were almost universally under the direction of the chief among the Southern Bantu. Burchell describes such an organization of the hunt among the Batlapin, while according to Holub, the preparations for such a battue occupied months, and sometimes involved the mustering of as many as 800 men.[1] The chief was also clearly the man in authority in the big Basuto game drives described by Kidd, and those of the Thonga too. Gibson's graphic account of the assembling of the Zulus for a hunt, each group of men and boys saluting the master of the ceremonies with a special dance, gives one some idea of the excitement that must have attended these events, and the way in which the chief's authority must have been enhanced by the dramatic scene itself, and also by his power of distributing the quarry. We have already suggested in the biographical chapters of this book that the boy's first sense of tribal cohesion dates from his participation in economic activities on a large scale. I think even the scanty data available from this area serves to prove this point. The young man on such occasions probably meets for the first time his more distant relatives or the members of his clan. He sees them at a time of pleasurable excitement and engaged in a common food-producing activity. He observes that the chief is in the position of supreme authority, either directing operations, or else distributing game. It is for such reasons that I

---

[1] W. J. Burchell, *op. cit.*, Vol. II, pp. 420, 545 ; Holub, *op. cit.*, Vol. II, p. 242.

believe that the chief's authority in Bantu society is so largely dependent on his position in the whole economic scheme, and that tribal ties as well as those of the family are, in a sense, also nutritive bonds.

On individual expeditions, also, tribute of hunting quarry is due to the Bantu chief in virtue of his ownership of the soil. Junod says definitely that this tribute was given because " the general idea is that he must receive that part of the body which was in contact with the soil, because the chief is the owner of the soil ".[1] In practice, however, a different adjudication of parts was made. The Basutos give the first victim and the heads of the other animals ; the Batlapin the breast of all game killed. In general, the levée amounted to a quarter of the game killed.[2]

Among the Thonga certain special animals were also subject to tribute—wild bull, eland, giraffe and antelope —while the skin of a lion and the tusk of an elephant were also the chief's prerogative. A hippopotamus and crocodile might not even be cut up and opened without the presence of the chief or his courtiers. So important was this function of chieftainship that in some cases the seizing of a portion of the animal became symbolic of chiefly power. For instance, H. Franklin's dramatic account of the murder of a chief among the Mtasa of the Umtali district gives evidence of the importance of this rule of meat division. Since the chief always received the heart of an animal killed in the hunt, his murderer would claim succession by shouting from the roof of the dead man's house : " I have killed my meat from the top of a near-by hill. . . . Meat has been killed, but I reserve the heart for myself. I claim the chieftainship, as I killed this man." [3]

We see thus that the chief has actually considerable economic power among these Bantu societies. He is the

[1] Junod, *op. cit.*, Vol. II, p. 57.
[2] E. Casalis, *op. cit.*, p. 172 ; W. J. Burchell, *op. cit.*, Vol. II, p. 348.
[3] H. Franklin, " A Selection from Notes on Manyika Customs ", *Nada*, No. 5, 1927, p. 56.

biggest owner of cattle, and has the right not only to prevent others from rivalling his herd, but also to levy tribute of stock on others if he needs. He has the prerogative of distributing agricultural land to his subjects, and of reserving grazing rights for his own herd. He organizes and directs economic activities, particularly hunting and cattle-raising, and he receives tribute of the products of these activities from every local group. The system of collecting tribute through the headmen and sub-chief strengthens and cements the whole system of political government too, and the actual possession of the foodstuff so accumulated, gives to the chief that prestige he needs in order to enable him to enforce his decrees.

3. The Chief as a Provider of Food

But there is this further point to be considered. The advantage is not all to one side. Firth has shown very clearly in his analysis of Maori culture that there is economic advantage to a primitive community in the circulation of wealth, such as is produced by the giving of tribute to the chief in the form of food and his redistribution of supplies in the form of feasts, and payment given to subjects working for him. Malinowski has described the accumulation of large supplies of food, yams and the like, in the chief's store-houses as a kind of communal bank, since this food must be distributed, in time of need, to those villagers who are in distress. Now this aspect of the economic functions of the Bantu chief provides an extraordinarily interesting field of research for future field-workers, especially in view of the altering status of the native rulers under European government.

It is clear that in the old days the chief was considered as the food provider, not only in complimentary songs, but also in actual fact. " Such is, in fact, the great social bond of these tribes ; the sovereigns, instead of being supported by the community, are the chief supporters of it . . ." says Casalis of the Basutos, adding, " they must, with the produce of their flocks, feed the poor, furnish the warriors with arms, supply the troops in the field ".[1] He points out that even in his day the ability to earn money under European service diminished the power of the Basuto chief—a process which has proceeded to a still greater length to-day. Of the Zulu chief Grout says, " The nation is his, the people, the cattle, the lands—everything ; but then he must provide for all, protect all, govern all." [2] In the case of famine it was the chief to come to the rescue of the people, and Schapera maintains that " if a man's crops failed, he would look to the chief for assistance ; the chief gave out his cattle to the poorer members of his tribe to tend for him, and allowed them to use the milk ".[3]

Besides this general duty of support of his people, the chief distributed large quantities of food in the form of big tribal feasts, and the payment of those engaged in statute labour for him. Casalis uses the significant phrase that on these occasions " it is taken for granted that the donee immediately becomes the donor in his turn ".[4] This sums up the point exactly. The chief receives food in the form of tribute but he redistributes it at national assemblies and in payment for services.

Such services included the agricultural work done by the mass of the people and the assistance of headmen and sub-chiefs who sometimes resided at the court for as long as four to five months of the year to aid the king in the administration of justice.[5] Also, among the Zulu peoples

---

[1] E. Casalis, op. cit., pp. 155, 216.   [2] L. Grout, op. cit., p. 118.
[3] I. Schapera, op. cit., p. 174. It must be remembered that chieftainship among most South African tribes is an entirely different institution from that found among the conquering races further north ruling over slave or subject peoples. The Southern Bantu chief could be removed from his office if he failed to support his people, while among the Lacustrian peoples the chief is definitely a ruler over a subject population, and can exact tribute in vegetable produce and labour from them. The old Babemba chiefs of the Tanganyika plateau similarly exacted tribute from the conquered Ba-Bisa, BaNsenga, BaMambwe and similar tribes.
[4] E. Casalis, op. cit., pp. 221, 222.
[5] J. Shooter, op. cit., p. 99 ; Junod, op. cit., Vol. I, pp. 404-7 ; J. Maclean, op. cit., p. 77 ; G. M. Theal, op. cit., p. 182.

the warrior bands, for the army was entirely dependent on the chief for food. A Zulu soldier told Leslie that in the old days " one day we hungered, and another we feasted, just as the King happened to give us beer and beef ".[1] Gardiner says that Dingana fed his regiments every evening with beef, and as these armies sometimes reached as many as 900 men, the amount of food distributed must have been immense.[2]

It is thus clear that a certain proportion of each tribe was actually dependent on the chief for his daily bread, either permanently or during his period of statute labour. The rest were conscious of the chief's obligation to support them in time of need. The fact that it was generally understood that the chief was in possession of food, and could be relied upon to give it if wanted, contributed powerfully to his people's belief in him. I do not maintain that we find among the Bantu the same display of food by chiefs that is recorded among many Oceanic peoples. The possession of large herds of cattle gave more kudos to the Southern Bantu chief than the sight of large store-houses of vegetable crops.[3] But I do believe that the common knowledge that he was constantly receiving and accumulating supplies in the capital, contributed, not only to his own power, but to the sense of tribal cohesion and well-being as a whole.

The Bantu chief therefore performs an active and practical function in the direction of economic operations and in the distribution and accumulation of food. He is the organizer and the banker of the communal economic undertakings, and maintains the circulation of wealth.

There remains yet a very important sphere of his influence to consider—his magic powers over the fertility of crops and cattle, or his right of access to the tribal gods.

[1] D. Leslie, op. cit., p. 278.
[2] A. F. Gardiner, Narrative of a Journey to the Zoolu Country, 1836, p. 55 ; cf. also D. Kidd, The Essential Kafir, p. 44.
[3] When Dingana wanted to impress Gardiner with his magnificence he left the corpses of newly killed oxen at the gate of his village and displayed his army in the act of eating beef (A. F. Gardiner, op. cit., pp. 30, 71).

To this question, then, we must now turn, both in order to study the functions of Bantu chieftainship, and also to gauge the nature and strength of the ties which bind together the members of the tribe

4. ECONOMIC WELFARE AND THE ANCESTRAL GODS

To begin from familiar ground, the father, the headman, and the chief have each their functions to perform in the economic structure of the tribe, functions that are analagous but not identical. Each wields authority in his own sphere of economic activities, and provides and distributes supplies to his dependents, the chief having additional attributes in that he is the theoretical owner of all sources of food supplies, and receives in consequence tribute from his people, which the father as a rule does not.

Now the same hierarchical organization can be observed in the case of those ancestral spirits who are believed to be responsible for the general welfare and prosperity of the people. Just as the father's right of access to the family ancestors is one of the sources of his authority in the kinship group, so the chief's privilege of approaching the tribal deities is one of the most essential functions of his leadership, and fixes his whole position in the economic scheme.

The immediate family ancestors perform quasi-paternal functions, since they bless their own descendants with prosperity—increase of cattle, fruit trees, and crops—and protect them from sickness. Like the father, these personal ancestors are members of one definite family, either paternal or maternal, and are responsible only for their own descendants. An individual belonging to a different family group cannot, of course, expect to receive any privileges from them, and their shrine is definitely associated with one particular homestead or kraal.[1] They play

[1] The Gandjelo, or Thonga ancestral shrine, placed at the right-hand side of the entry of the village (Junod, *op. cit.*, Vol. II, p. 388; also Lindblom, *op. cit.*, pp. 218, 219).

a part in all specifically family ceremonies, such as birth marriage, or death—expecting, like the living chief, to receive tribute of all food supplies owned by their descendants.

But these family ancestors, like the patriarchal head of the family himself, are, of course, members of a wider social organization. The same system of grouping holds in the spiritual world as on earth, and the ancestral spirits may be divided into family ancestors, and village or tribal deities,[1] and, the functions of these tribal spirits are of the utmost importance in the understanding of the economic organization of the people.

The national gods are worshipped at the most important crises of economic life—" For such public benefits as victory, rain, fertility of lands and herds, salvation from epidemics and ravaging beasts, and often for successful hunting and fishing "—to use Willoughby's description.[2]

We can now distinguish yet a further element in the economic power of the chief. The communal ancestors are, for the most part, the individual ancestors of the chief. This is particularly the case where a definite ruling dynasty exists, as among the Bechuana tribes. Willoughby says that the paramount chief sacrifices to the national gods in his capacity as the priest of his ancestral line. " He is the son of the gods, not only their protégé ", says Junod also, describing the Thonga chief.[3]

The tribal deities are also associated with a definite tract of land—the territory of which the chief is, as we have seen, the theoretical owner. Ancestors remain associated with a given area for a very long time, even after the original occupiers of the land have moved elsewhere. Mr. Smith speaks of the " spiritual ownership "

---

[1] Junod, *op. cit.*, Vol. II, p. 374 ; W. C. Willoughby, *The Soul of the Bantu*, 1928, p. 179 ; Smith and Dale, *op. cit.*, Vol. II, p. 180. Mr. Smith uses the terms " geni ", " divinities ", and " demi-gods ", to describe these three classes of spirits. The village *mizhimo* or ancestral spirits are, of course, more important in the case of the larger Ba-Ila kraals than is the case among the South-Eastern Bantu.

[2] Willoughby, *op. cit.*, p. 179.

[3] Willoughby, *op. cit.*, p. 179 ; Junod, *op. cit.*, Vol. I, p. 405.

of land or water, recording an instance in which a victorious tribe in possession of a good fishing-pool was yet obliged to induce the only surviving member of the family of the conquered owners to live at the spot, and to make offerings to his ancestors in order that fishing might be propitious.[1] The chief's authority similarly rests upon his succession to a given line of ancestors who have lived and died on the soil. The gods of the country are those of the ruling dynasty.

Chief as Rainmaker.—But the most crying need of the native toiling on the parched plains of Southern Africa is some security as to the supply of rain. The tribal deities among most of these peoples are responsible for the annual rainfall, or can, at any rate, be solicited to produce it. Now the chief, among the majority of the Southern Bantu, is himself the rain priest. " The fundamental glory of the old Bechuana chiefs was their ability to make rain "—constantly referred to in the *dithoko* or praise songs of the Basuto and Bechuana chiefs.[2] The great Zulu kings Panda and Dingana are described as holding sacrifices for rain. " Dingana, are you still the rain-maker ? Are you still the greatest of living men ? "[3] Umbadine, a Swazi chief, apparently kept a special herd of rain cattle to be sacrificed for the benefit of tribes far to the north and south.[4] And in these ceremonies the chief seems to have acted, not as a magician, but as an intermediary with the tribal gods. " I also say that God gives the rain," explained an Amambala chief to Shaw. " I ask rain from the spirits."[5]

---

[1] Smith and Dale, *op. cit.*, Vol. I, p. 389.

[2] S. S. Dornan, " Rain-making in South Africa ", *B.S.*, Vol. III, No. 2, 1928.

[3] J. Y. Gibson, *op. cit.*, p. 91 ; cf. also J. T. Brown, *op. cit.*, p. 128 ; D. Kidd, *The Essential Kafir*, p. 114 ; Holub, *op. cit.*, Vol. I, pp. 329-30, 336 ; H. Callaway, *op. cit.*, p. 59 ; W. Shaw, *op. cit.*, p. 461.

[4] D. Kidd, *The Essential Kafir*, p. 115.

[5] W. Shaw, *op. cit.*, p. 461. It is true that in some cases the High God is believed to be the giver of rain, as is Leza the rain-giver of Northern Rhodesian tribes such as the Ba-Ila, Babemba, but I do not know of any case in which the High God has been directly approached in time of need for rain.

In the exceptionally interesting harvest ceremony recorded by Willoughby among the Bechuana we find mentioned the offering of a special tribute, *dikgahela*, or " things which indicate gratitude to the chief who has nourished the corn with his rain ". At this ceremony every woman carries a portion of her Kafir corn to the village assembly, whence it is taken to the chief's place. The women, marching procession and carrying corn on their heads, raise the cry of " Rain ! Rain ! Rain ! " as they go. From these tithes beer is made, and taken in large pots to the chief's place, again with further cries of " Rain ! " Next day the people assemble for a public drinking of the beer, dancing and shouting with ululation cries of " Rain ! " [1]

Moreover, besides his own powers as rain-producer, the chief can usually command the services of other rain-doctors or magicians. Either special diviners were attached to the court,[2] or the chief would pay for the doctor called.[3] In some cases the success of the latter was such that their power bid fair to rival that of the chief himself, and we find Chaka declaring himself to be *the* rain-maker of the Zulus,[4] to the exclusion of others. The supreme control over the food resources is allied, as in every other case we have mentioned, with authority in other spheres of social organization.

5. FIRST-FRUIT RITES

But the tribal ancestors have yet another function to perform. They give increase to the crops ; and here again we find once more that at the ceremonies of the sowing of the seed and the annual first-fruit rites it is the chief who takes the essential part. The ceremony of

---

[1] Willoughby, *op. cit.*, p. 251.
[2] E. Casalis, *op. cit.*, p. 284.
[3] J. Colenso, *op. cit.*, p. 142 ; L. Decle, *op. cit.*, p. 154 ; J. Maclean, *op. cit.*, p. 104 ; D. E. Ellenberger and J. C. McGregor, *History of the Basuto*, 1912, p. 265 ; Lichtenstein, *op. cit.*, Vol. I, p. 256 ; A. Kropf, *op. cit.*, p. 195.
[4] D. Kidd, *The Essential Kafir*, p. 114.

the first-fruits among the Zulu Kafir peoples is specially characteristic. The rites appear to have a double function —the public and ritual exercise of prerogative throughout the community, and the removal of danger believed to be inherent in the eating of the new crops.

Casalis calls the Basuto first-fruits a " rite of primogeniture ", since the year's supplies must be tested in order of rank—first the Gods, then the chief, the headmen, and the family heads. The eldest son of the reigning house must divide the pumpkins in order of age between his brothers, and heralds then bear round the remaining portions to the bystanders in definite precedence.[1] Junod says of the Thonga rite, " the Gods must be the first to enjoy the produce of the New Year ", then the chief, the sub-chiefs, the counsellors, the headmen, then the younger brothers in order of age. There is a stringent taboo directed against the person who precedes his superiors in the enjoyment of the first-fruit. From which he concludes that " the religious meaning of the rite is clear ; the Gods, if deprived of the rights they possess by virtue of their hierarchical position, would avenge themselves by threatening the harvest ; so they must be given their share first ".[2]

The first-fruit rites of these South-Eastern Bantu are thus on a tribal scale. The distinctive features of the rites include the breaking of calabashes by the chief, the spattering of the assembled tribesmen with the first-fruits or with cooked food, the prayer to the ancestral spirits and the ritual tasting of the corn. Without the performance of this rite it is absolutely forbidden to taste the new grain, and Grout records the imposition of the death sentence for the breaking of this taboo. Supernatural penalties are also expected to fall, and the idea of defence against danger is definitely to be found in these rites.

[1] E. Casalis, *op. cit.*, p. 215.
[2] Junod, *op. cit.*, Vol. II, pp. 403–4.

6. Conclusion

I have only had space in these pages to deal with the two chief rites connected with economic activities, and these perforce in a very summary way. But even from this cursory study the two main points emerge.

First, that the annual performance of the rain sacrifices and the First-fruit rites are believed to be absolutely essential for the prosperity of the crops and for the safe enjoyment of the new harvest: and that in these rites the chief or King is the central or only officiant. Without him, in some cases, rain will not fall. Unless he blesses the crops it is forbidden to begin the year's supply of food. His power as a chief might well depend on these functions alone.[1]

Second, these great annual rites are on a tribal scale. The people muster together from a wide area, bound by the authority of a common chief. The events have, therefore, a secondary function besides that of securing supernatural blessings on the fertility of the crops. Willoughby points out that the annual ceremonies to the communal ancestors are as important as affirmation of "politico-religious" solidarity as from any other point of view.[2] We have just noted the dramatic expressions of the scale of social rank in the society by the ritual tasting in order of preference of the new crops of the year.

We see thus that a double process is at work. The people look for the fulfilment of their greatest need—a successful harvest—to the intercession of the highest authority they see on earth, their chief or King. Their confidence is maintained through the disappointments and endurances of their agricultural work, by the thought

---

[1] The situation was complicated among the Zulu after the days of Chaka, by the superposition of a military ceremonial on the older harvest rite. Grout says that the old soldiers retired and the new enlisted at the time of the First-fruit ceremony and the warriors were then entitled to a huge feast of meat (L. Grout, *op. cit.*, p. 161 ; see also J. Shooter, *op. cit.*, p. 26 ; A. F. Gardiner, *op. cit.*, p. 96).

[2] Willoughby, *op. cit.*, p. 180.

H.W.S.T.   M

that he has pleaded on their behalf with the supernatural powers.

Conversely, the political power of the chief himself is derived very largely from the functions he performs in the economic sphere, these attributes being publicly demonstrated at the annual feasts. On this the sense of tribal cohesion depends. The muster of tribesmen for the First-fruit ceremony is itself a witness to the power of the chief. The young men assembled realize, perhaps for the first time, what sort of unit their tribe really is. In our biographical study we should include such gatherings under the heading of the *secondary* extension of kinship ties to a tribal scale, and I think it is clear from the nature of the rites that these bonds must be described as nutritive in the widest sense.

To conclude, then, our examination of the economic functions of the clan and tribe. We showed that the clan as a unilateral kinship group does not appear to be an actively functioning unit in the nutritive complex among the Southern Bantu, its place being taken by the kinship group. This may be due to the constantly disruptive tendencies of the Zulu society, or to the lack of accurate information in our material and to the careless use of the term " clan ".

The tribe, on the other hand, is definitely an economic unit among the South-Eastern Bantu. It owns grazing and hunting-ground in common, and even the cattle may be in a sense referred to as tribal stock from the rights of overlordship of the tribal chief. The King also organizes and synchronizes tribal economic activities—pastoral, hunting and agricultural, and regulates, in however primitive a fashion, the accumulation and distribution of tribal food supplies. Lastly, the tribe itself must assemble at the two great events of the food-producing year—the prayers for rain and the blessing of the harvest.[1] When we consider how difficult is a national assembly under

---

[1] Among some tribes also the blessing of the seeds (cf. E. Dora Earthy, *op. cit.*, *B.S.*, Vol. II, No. 3, p. 195).

primitive conditions of communication and transport, this is a very important fact. It is a public expression of the hierarchic organization of the whole nutritional system. Tribal, as well as family and household ties, depend on man's primary biological need for food. As a member of his household group the child shared and received food from certain individuals whom he recognized as members of his family and kinship group. As an adult he reaches full economic status as a food-producer when he joins for the first time the great tribal activities, the communal hunt, or the national ceremonies for first-fruits and rain.

CHAPTER VII

FOOD AS A SYMBOL

1. THE SACRALIZATION OF FOOD

WE have now completed the biographical study on which we set out in the first part of this work. We have shown that the emotional bonds of human kinship are intimately dependent on the whole complex of institutions by which food is distributed, shared, and produced in any particular community. The ties which bind the child to the members of his family and household group are determined, to a very large extent, by the strength and variety of his alimentary needs. Clan is linked to clan, and subject to chief, by a common system of obligations in the food-producing scheme.

But we must turn now to another aspect of the problem. We have to consider the secondary values which food itself acquires, as the source of so many human emotions, and the centre of such complex social ties. In almost every primitive community foodstuffs themselves—and the acts of eating, exchanging, or producing food—come to possess symbolic value in the ceremonial life of the tribe. In fact, one of the most prominent and universal features of primitive ritual is what has been called the *sacralization* of food.

In his religious and legal ceremonies the savage is constantly handling food, offering it ritually to his God, or to other members of his group, eating it, dividing it, or exchanging it. Moreover, he tends to select certain types of food, whether plant or animal, as objects of special religious cults : or to believe that eating itself, and in particular the eating of certain specified foodstuffs, has a definite magic effect upon him, working moral or physical changes, or giving him access to new sources of power.

Now the whole problem of the sacralization of food is beyond the scope of this work.   To give any adequate idea of the question we should have to range from the complex ceremonial of eating and preparing food, both in ritual or in daily life ; to the whole phenomenon of the food taboo ; totemism, and the various cults of different animals and plants used for food ; the sacrifice in primitive ritual ; and lastly, all the ceremonies connected with the ritual exchange of food.   Such a wide survey would be impossible here, but we must, I think, distinguish the essential elements in this process of sacralization in order to deal effectively with the special problem we are considering—the use of food to symbolize social relationships in a primitive tribe.   The first of these factors is concerned with the physiology of nutrition ; the second with what might be called its sociology ; and the third involves a knowledge of the nature of the food itself—the characteristics of the animal or plant, and the way it strikes the imagination of the native.   Let us then deal with these briefly one by one.

We have not yet considered the physiological sensations connected with the alimentary system, being chiefly concerned in this work with what I might call the social significance of food.   But we must realize that the digestive system gives rise to some of the strongest sensations which the savage experiences, and we cannot, therefore, entirely omit the values which food thus acquires.   Such sensations include not only hunger and repletion, which occur first to our minds, but the whole range of affects to which the alimentary tract gives rise.   To list only the most prominent, there is the taste of different foods in the mouth, and the sensation produced by certain substances such as strong alcohol, peppermint, mustard, or pepper,

both in the mouth and in the stomach.[1]   Different nar-
cotics and stimulants may give rise, not only to sensations
in the stomach, but also to general changes in the whole
feeling tone of the body.   The need for food provides also
a variety of sensations, from the vague discomfort pre-
monitory to hunger, to the sharp pangs of gastric con-
traction, incomplete satisfaction, over-repletion, digestive
pains, or the languor and pronounced psychic phenomena,
such as mental dissociation, which prolonged starvation
brings.

Now this whole range of feeling tones bulks very largely
in the psychology of the primitive man.   The diet of the
savage may seem monotonous to us, accustomed as we
are to a wide variety of foodstuffs, but we have to remember two important facts.   First we must recognize that
the native notices changes in the taste and texture of foods
which are not apparent to us.   I have heard Africans
dispute hotly as to the cooking of basketfuls of porridge
which appeared to the Englishman not only identical, but
also entirely uninteresting.   In the same way Boas was
able to collect from the Kwakiutl Indians of North-West
America, a whole volume of cooking receipts, of which the
sole ingredients were salted fish washed down with crude
oil.   To the white man the diet seemed not only repug-
nant, but also monotonous in the extreme.   To the Indian
it was evidently of the strongest interest and raised the
most important problems of social etiquette.[2]

In the second place, the diet of the savage, though
monotonous during any one season, is subject to the most
drastic changes in the course of the year.   Those of us
who are accustomed to a regular, if varied, supply of
food throughout the year, cannot easily picture the
changes so produced in the whole feeling-tone of the community.   We have already spoken of the alternating
seasons of plenty and shortage which are usual in savage

[1] Cf. E. G. Boring, " The Sensations of the Alimentary Canal ",
American Journal of Psychology, Vol. XXVI, Jan. 1915.
[2] Franz Boas, *Ethnology of the Kwakiutl*, Bureau of American Ethnology, 35th Report, Part I, 1921.

society, and the altered social rhythm so produced. But we have not yet considered the physiological changes produced by such altered diet. In my experience, the native may well eat twice, or even three times as much food in the harvest season as he does in the time of scarcity. He passes through the whole range of sensations from inanition to repletion in a way which is rare among civilized men.

Moreover, the change is not only one of quantity, but also one of quality. In our own case modern transport systems have made it possible for us to maintain our diatetic values fairly constant throughout the year. But the Andaman Islander, on the other hand, may live for a period on honey and wild fruits, next upon pork, and next upon fish.[1] The African may eat porridge and dried peas and beans for one season, mushrooms and wild fruits for another, and then a great quantity of vegetables such as cucumbers and marrows later on. The effect of such changes in diet on the health of the savage has never yet been studied adequately from the medical point of view, and digestive disturbances are more frequent among primitive people than is usually imagined. But the anthropologist has long been aware that such changing food values affect not only the general energy and feeling-tone of the native, but actually cause profound digestive disturbances—recognized and accepted philosophically by the natives themselves. In North-Eastern Rhodesia, when the first mealies ripen after the hunger months, the people will roast them, and bolt seven or eight at a time. I have seen them rocking to and fro with indigestion, saying in defence of their greed, " It is because we are glad that the new food has come." Junod speaks of the colic pains common among the Thonga when the Bukanye fruit and the new mealies ripen, and Malinowski describes the outbreak of dysentery in the Trobriands following the eating of unripe yams.[2] Natives living chiefly on vege-

[1] A. R. Brown, *The Andaman Islanders*, pp. 36–40.
[2] Junod, *op. cit.*, Vol. II, p. 17 ; B. Malinowski, *Argonauts of the Western Pacific*, p. 77. The word *luma* used for First-fruit rites among

tarian food also appear much the worse for the enormous meals of meat they manage to consume at a sitting when such luck comes their way.   Such facts must be common in all types of primitive society.

We can see, therefore, that the savage experiences more violent changes of alimentary sensation than we do, and he experiences them usually in common with all the rest of his fellows, which rarely happens to the civilized man. In many cases also the native distinguishes these affects with greater terminological exactitude than we do, or at any rate describes his sensations in more concrete terms. " We shall be glad, we shall eat till we vomit," says the Trobriand Islander, in anticipating a feast.   " We shall eat until our bellies swell out and we can no longer stand," is the Kafir expression.[1]   Moreover, primitive languages often contain separate terms defining such states as over-repletion, satisfaction, inadequate satisfaction, or the various degrees of hunger ;   and in some cases ritual taboos enjoin such particular states on a man at different stages of his life.   For instance, a Kwakiutl woman may eat when her husband is out on a hunting expedition, but she may not eat to the point of repletion, and there is a special word *ts ! egwelk*,—to be made " short inside "— which describes this condition of semi-satisfaction.   Other taboos among these Indians of North-West America refer to special foods which make the eater sleepy, nauseated, thirsty, or produce coughing fits.   These digestive sensations are evidently so well recognized as to be the subject of ritual restrictions of diet.[2]

But the primitive man may recognize the sensations he experiences without an accurate knowledge of their causes.   Malinowski states that the Trobriand Islanders

the Thonga means " to bite " or to cause violent colic pains.   The meat orgy following the killing of a large animal such as the elephant might have similar results, and it is noteworthy that *luma* rites only follow the killing of such big animals.

[1] B. Malinowski, *Argonauts of the Western Pacific*, p. 171 ;   A. Kropf, *op. cit.*, p. 88.

[2] F. Boas, *The Ethnology of the Kwakiutl*, American Bureau of Ethnology, 35th Report, Part I, p. 640.

enjoy the act of eating without any knowledge of the physiological function of nutrition, just as they enjoy sexual pleasure without being aware of the physiological nature of paternity. This was not so with the natives among whom I worked, but I noticed that the sensations connected with the alimentary or sexual functions were reckoned on a par with what we should describe as emotional conditions, such as anger or sorrow. It must be remembered here that visceral sensations actually are produced through the action of the involuntary nervous system under the strain of strong emotions such as fear or rage. The savage recognizes that eating, sexual satisfaction, pregnancy, as well as a number of emotions, may all be responsible for physiological sensations which are, in many respects, similar. What wonder that he concludes sometimes that their cause is similar ? " When I drink beer I feel hot inside, as I do when I am angry," a Mubemba said to me ; and a man who has just had sexual intercourse is also described as " hot ". Radcliffe-Brown points out that the word *kimil* is used by the Andaman Islander to describe heat, the condition of a man after eating and also after slaying an enemy. It is well known, too, that among some primitive tribes pregnancy is supposed to be a result of eating some special food recognized by the first attack of sickness that the woman experiences.[1] The Malayan speaks of the *hantu* or the spirit of the forest, together with the *hantu* that make people gamble, smoke opium, dispute, or those that produce stomach-ache or headache, as though all these could be traced to a similar cause.[2] In fact, as Mr. Smith sums up the situation among the *Ba-ila :* " The parts they assign to the organs in the economy of the body are psychical rather than physiological, i.e. they regard them more as the seats of emotions than of vital processes." [3]

[1] A. R. Brown, " Beliefs concerning Childbirth in some Australian Tribes ", *Man*, 1912, No. 96, p. 181.

[2] A. Hale, " On the Sakais ", *J.A.I.*, 1886, Vol. XV, p. 300.

[3] Smith and Dale, *op. cit.*, Vol. I, p. 224.

I think we must recognize, therefore, that the strong affects associated with the physiological function of nutrition account for the primitive man's belief that eating itself is, to a certain extent, a magic act. It is certainly one which changes his state and sometimes makes him feel as though he were possessed by new powers. Moreover, the savage, with his rich experience of the psychical changes produced by such physical conditions as starvation, satiety, and the swallowing of certain substances, reproduces these alimentary states purposely throughout his religious life in order that he may experience their mental correlates. Fasting is a case in point, and the studies of professional fasting men such as Succi and others have given us a great deal of knowledge on this point. Since, therefore, starvation brings about a process of mental dissociation and a new spiritual vision, fasting is used universally in almost every type of religion known in order to produce the sensation of contact with the supernatural.[1] Among some North American tribes such as the Navaho, ritual fasts play such a prominent part in the organized religion that social status may depend on the success of an individual in experiencing a fast-dream. While even among the Zulu, where fatness is a sign of wealth, a thin Diviner is preferred, since " the continually stuffed body cannot see secret things ".[2] Certain drugs are also used in primitive ritual in a similar way because they are known to produce trance conditions that allow of prophecy or divination.

But we have to remember also that digestive disturbances of various sorts may also be reproduced artificially for ritual reasons. Thus purges and emetics are used in many primitive rites either to make the user feel he is being rid of some undesirable moral quality or else to mark

---

[1] There are, of course, many elements in the psychology of fasting. Westermarck distinguishes between fasting as a means of access to spiritual powers, before a ceremony, before some dangerous undertaking, as a penance, or on the occasion of some unnatural event such as an eclipse (*Origin and Development of Moral Ideas*, Vol. II, Chap. XXXVII), and the list could be multiplied still further.

[2] H. Callaway, *op. cit.*, p. 387.

his passage from one state to another. The Jewish psalmist, weighed down with guilt, begs that he may be purged from his sins ; but in many more primitive religions the purging is actual, and not metaphorical. At their initiation ceremonies the Nandi boys and girls must be purged as marking their passage from youth to adult life, and the same is also true of the boys' initiation ceremonies in Bartle Bay. So also the divorced woman of Gilbert Island must drink an emetic before she is free to marry a new husband, otherwise she would still remain associated with her late husband's family. Among the Thonga, the whole army used formerly to be treated ritually with emetics in order that fear might be thrown up and valour remain.[1]

The ritual use of ginger or other burning substances is another example of the reproduction of a physical sensation in order to produce its supposed mental correlate. Ginger root is chewed ceremonially throughout Melanesia because of its burning taste. It will give valour to the young man setting out on a courting expedition, deadly aim when rubbed on gun cartridges, or the destruction of an enemy who has been cursed with the root. Warm foods are likewise believed to have magical properties, as distinct from those which are eaten cold. Frazer gives many instances where hot foods are tabooed during certain magic states. In our own area the Thonga are forbidden to eat hot meals after they have killed a man—" because they are hot themselves, they are defiled (*ba na nsila*) ".[2]

Such examples could, in fact, be multiplied indefinitely, but we cannot do more here than indicate an enormous field of research on this question of the physiological basis of the ritual use of food. Suffice it to say that the primitive man acquires his belief as to the nature of eating on

[1] A. C. Hollis, *The Nandi*, 1909, pp. 53, 60 ; C. G. Seligman, *The Melanesians of B. New Guinea*, 1910, p. 496 ; A. Grimble, " From Birth to Death in Gilbert Islands ", *J.R.A.I.*, Vol. LI, 1921, p. 33 ; Junod, *op. cit.*, Vol. I, p. 467.

[2] Cf. R. W. Williamson, *The Ways of the South Sea Savage*, 1911, p. 122 ; C. G. Seligman, *op. cit.*, p. 179 ; G. Brown, *Melanesians and Polynesians*, 1910, pp. 76, 89 ; Junod, *op. cit.*, Vol. I, p. 479.

the basis of the rich variety of sensations so aroused, these sensations playing a more prominent part in his psychology than in our own. These beliefs are expressed in all sorts of taboos and restrictions on eating, and by the reproduction of different parts of the digestive process in ritual life. In fact, we cannot analyse the whole system of values centred round food in a primitive tribe unless we bear in mind the physiological nature of nutrition and the native theory of digestion current in that particular society.

The second aspect of sacralization depends, I think, on the nature of the food supply itself. The primitive man, unlike the civilized town-dweller, gets his food direct from the environment itself. The flesh which he cooks and eats is also the animal or fish which he has watched with keen excitement, and captured, perhaps after long hours of difficulty and danger. His dish of porridge or vegetable sauce has also its previous history of work, anxiety and co-operative effort. Thus each object of diet is the centre of a double sentiment in a way which it is difficult for us fully to understand. The savage may want a certain type of food to satisfy the pangs of hunger and yet be reluctant to eat the object of so many complex emotional sensations. The resultant conflict usually finds solution in some form of sacralization of the particular food—some ritual act by which tradition prescribes that the food may be safely eaten.

In the case of the cattle-loving peoples of South Africa, this conflict is, of course, particularly acute, and a beast cannot be killed for meat without destroying what is, in effect, a personal friend. Evans-Pritchard tells me that among the Nuer a man will only eat his favourite bullock if it has died naturally, and then with conflicting feelings. He would say, " The eye and the heart are mournful ; but the stomach is glad ", adding that his stomach had prayed independently to God to ask him to kill a bullock, while at the same time his heart begged God not to strike down a treasured friend. This expresses very clearly the central element in all those rites which surround the killing of cattle among most Bantu peoples, varying from refusal to kill cattle, to sacrificial slaughter on occasions like the birth, marriage or death of an individual, and the ritual division of the animal killed.

In the case of game, another set of factors seems to be involved. The animals and birds of his neighbourhood excite the primitive man's interest and admiration. He knows their habits and characteristics, tracks them through the forest, and ascribes to them almost human qualities in his fables and legends, sometimes even identifying himself with one particular species of animal in a form of totemic cult. The slaying or eating of a wild animal may therefore cut across a complex sentiment in his mind, and we find every variety of ritual act surrounding this occasion, from the typical totemic taboo kept by the members of a special clan, to ritual apologies to the slain animal, ceremonies purifying the hunter from his dangerous deed, or rites to lay the ghost of the victim.

The difficulties and dangers of the chase must also be borne in mind, and it is noteworthy that the majority of hunting rites centre round the pursuit of specially dangerous animals. Among most Bantu tribes the killing of hippos and elephants involve special precautionary ceremonies before the animal may be eaten, and any collection of food taboos will show us the extraordinary number which refer to dangerous animals of prey. The psychology is, perhaps, best expressed in Boas's account of the Kwakiutl, who throw away a devil fish if they have cooked it by accident, saying, " They are afraid to eat it, because it kills people and it is a sea-monster ".[1]

Vegetable produce is, of course, also the object of this, same double sentiment. The joy in the new supply of food—often after long periods of scarcity—conflicts with

---

[1] F. Boas, op. cit., Part I, p. 615. It must be remembered that the Thonga believe that only the large and dangerous animals have a *nuru* or avenging spirit returning to harm the hunter after their death, and only to be set at rest by the *lurula* rite (cf. Junod, op. cit., Vol. II, p. 77 ; also Smith and Dale, op. cit., Vol. I, p. 167).

the sense of sacrilege at the consumption of the fruits of so much toil.   We have spoken already of the First-fruit rites necessary among many peoples before the new harvest may be eaten.   We have also to consider the phenomenon of the cult of special plants in primitive religions, such as the plantain used so frequently in religious rites among the Baganda, the corn ceremonies among some North American Indians, and the rice ceremonies in Japan.

Lastly we must include under this aspect of food sacralization, the whole phenomenon of the Sympathetic food taboo, since these restrictions *par excellence* depend on the appearance and qualities of the living animals or plants used for food.   All these regulations come under the heading of what Marett terms *negative magic*.   The pregnant woman must refuse to eat an animal with an unpleasant appearance for fear her child should be born resembling it.   The betrothed avoids honey or such slippery substances for fear his bride should slip away from him.   The warrior may not eat the flesh of hares or other timid animals lest he acquire this contemptible quality.   Frazer has collected an enormous number of such sympathetic food taboos, and we can do no more than mention the subject here as showing the primitive man's keen interest in the habits and aspect of the plants and animals he eats, and the fact that he makes no sharp cleavage in his associations between his daily food as such, and the living objects of the environment which produce it.

In conclusion, we must now turn to the sociological aspect of the question and consider nutrition as a process demanding the co-operative effort of the group.   Eating in a primitive community is hardly ever an act which concerns the individual member of the society alone.   To the savage the objects of his daily diet are the centre of a whole nexus of personal values, as well as those which are based on the physiological nature of eating or the characteristics of the food itself.   The food of each meal is the property of one member of the kinship group, and the chief form of possession which differentiates him from other members of the community. It has probably been produced by a series of co-operative undertakings by other kinsmen. It will have to be shared according to fixed rules, either in the household, between subject and chief, stranger or host, or by persons bound in some special legal relation to each other. Thus we find that all these nutritive customs acquire symbolic value themselves, just as do the actual physical processes of tasting, eating, and digesting. We cannot separate the one aspect of the subject from the other. The acts of preparing, consuming and sharing food, having become associated with certain deep sentiments in the family setting, are used to symbolize analogous emotional attitudes in the wider ceremonial life of the tribe, and customs performed initially as part of the etiquette and duties of the household group, come to figure in primitive rites and legal transactions as a means of symbolizing such human ties and giving public expression to them. It is a study of the ritual use of eating as a means of contracting such social relationships in a primitive community that I want now to undertake.

We have to realize, in fact, a paradoxical situation. On the one hand, the savage marches more nearly on his belly than we do, his interests and emotions more closely centred on his immediate physiological needs than are our own. On the other hand, food is the source of some of his most intense emotions, provides the basis for some of his most abstract ideas, and the metaphors of his religious life. Even the writer of the Beatitudes, trying to express his reverence for a certain state of spiritual exaltation, exclaims, " Blessed are those that hunger and thirst after righteousness ", because these words most nearly convey what he thinks he feels.

Moreover, since food is always given, shared and handled in a primitive society according to fixed rules of relationship, the objects of the savage diet are never considered simply and solely as food itself—as something with which the stomach has to be filled.   We discuss and contemplate food less often perhaps than does the native, but we consider it chiefly something which we intend to eat, whereas to the primitive man it may come to symbolize some of his highest spiritual experiences, and express his most significant social ties.

It is these sacramental values of food with which we now have to deal, concentrating chiefly on the sociological aspect of the problem, as distinct from the physiological, since our study has been mainly concerned with the nutritive relationships of primitive tribes.   For this purpose I shall start first with the question of the common meal and all the ritual taboos which surround the sharing of food—a phenomenon to which Robertson Smith and Crawley have given the name *Commensualism* in primitive rites.

2.   COMMENSUALISM

In every primitive society we find a complicated series of rules by which the common eating of food is prescribed on special ceremonial occasions ; or, conversely, tabooed —whether according to the occasion, the magic state of the participants, or the relationship in which they stand.

Thus commensual regulations fall under two main headings : *positive* rules prescribing the ritual sharing of food when two or more individuals desire to commit an act of union, or to express their feelings of cohesion on some public occasion ; and *negative* commands prohibiting from eating or drinking together those who are, for some special reason, at enmity, or in a state which would be magically dangerous to the other.

Such commensual taboos cover a very wide field, and extend from the sphere of the purely magical to the daily intercourse of everyday life.   Indeed, it is not always possible to distinguish between the two.   The magic acts connected with eating have appeared of more importance to the theoretical anthropologist than the ordinary course of household etiquette, and observers in the field have followed, for the most part, their line of interest.   For this reason, we are often obliged to study a series of food taboos in any particular community without forming any clear idea of the normal routine by which food is eaten in that group.   The actual line of division between the magic act and the daily custom may be thus impossible to ascertain.   A man may desire to eat alone because he is afraid of the magic power of his fellows, but he may equally well do so for a variety of reasons bound up with his general code of etiquette.   Until we know the whole attitude of his society towards food, and his code of etiquette in daily life, we cannot hope to understand the ritual restrictions which surround it.

Now this information has so far been lacking in the best ethnological material available.   Tylor and Westermarck, for instance, who have collected together a mass of comparative data as to the nature of commensual taboos, have never been able to describe these regulations in their setting of normal tribal activities.   It is for this reason that the whole problem of Commensualism has been lifted on to the plane of the specifically sacred, and has been considered in relation to general theories of religion and magic rather than to the facts of everyday life.   A brief examination of the chief of these theories will enable us to put this question to the test in the case of those Bantu tribes we have been studying.

Eating taboos have been made the basis of several important conceptions of primitive magic.   These ritual customs appear to have struck the imagination of early observers of primitive society and to have been easily recorded.   Commensual regulations have thus provided the bulk of the material on which such writers as Crawley and Frazer have constructed their general theories as to the nature of primitive psychology.

The work of Frazer is concerned chiefly with the negative aspect of commensual regulations—the imposition of taboos on the sharing of food between different individuals of the primitive community on certain specified occasions. These observances he regards as a form of negative magic, either sympathetic or contagious. A man is prohibited from eating with his fellows either permanently, or on some special occasion, in order to guard himself against the supernatural perils which surround him at different epochs of his life. Should he eat in the presence of others, they may cast their baneful influence upon him. Were he to open his mouth to swallow, his volatile soul might escape through his lips or be charmed away by magic skill. Viewed by an inferior person while at meals, his magic power or *mana* may be profaned. In contact with persons in a tabooed state—mourners, warriors, manslayers, women during childbirth or menstruation— their influence might affect him adversely, should he allow them to share his food. To guard himself, therefore, from these dangers, the primitive man takes special precautions of a magic nature. He eats in solitude, behind locked doors, or with a cloth held up to his face. He prays or performs lustrations according to given rules.[1]

Frazer's attitude to the positive type of commensual regulations depends also on his conception of the principle of contagion of magic properties. The ritual sharing of food is performed, according to him, in order that the eaters may acquire certain properties of the object eaten —the strength or vitality of the God, or the totem of the group. The common meal is thus an individual act performed in unison to promote a definite magic end.

Turning now to the theories of Crawley, we see that his analysis of eating customs is similarly based on one comprehensive conception of the nature of primitive magic. By this hypothesis he attempts to explain a wide variety of codes governing the sharing of food in savage society. We have ourselves classed the function of nutrition with such fundamental physiological processes as sex, and procreation, as being the bases of com-

[1] Frazer, *The Golden Bough*, abridged ed., 1925, pp. 198, 199, etc.

plex emotional systems in man. Crawley was perhaps the first to call attention to the importance of these dim innate tendencies—" psycho-physiological thoughts " as he terms them—in giving us an understanding of the nature of magico-religious beliefs. But his theory is based, I believe, on a misconception of these biological processes, and is expressed in a language so mystical as to be misleading to the psychologist.

To put it briefly, Crawley explains the whole phenomenon of *Commensualism* by the assumption that man inherits a biological disposition to carry out the chief biological functions—such as eating, copulation, excretion, etc.—in solitude, believing that he is thus able to " secure in some way the safety of such important functions ". He is afraid to satisfy these physical needs in public for fear of arousing the disgust of others whose desire cannot be so satisfied.[1] Thus rationalizing his instinctive desire to eat in solitude, he convinces himself that he is subject during mealtimes to possession by evil spirits, the contagious influence of hostile personalities, and, in particular, to the dangers of contact with the other sex. He therefore surrounds his daily meals with magic precautions to ensure his safety at a time of such peril.

In order to support his theory Crawley lists together a series of eating customs collected from every part of the world. He cites instances of savage tribes where eating actually is performed in secret ; others where food is taken in silence, or where prayers are raised before the meal. He adds further the numerous instances where rank or caste forms a barrier to sharing food with inferiors, and also the precautions taken to avoid poison when eating with others, deleterious matter in food, dirty

---

[1] Crawley, *The Mystic Rose*, 2nd ed., Vol. I., p. 175 ; *The Tree of Life*, 1905, p. 211. Crawley's theory appears to be based on a too sweeping generalization as to animal psychology. Practically nothing is known as to the habits of herd animals when eating, and while most animals behave differently when eating or copulating in the presence of their fellows, it seems unnecessary to postulate that those acts are invariably performed in solitude. In the case of the anthropoid apes this is specifically not the case.

cooking vessels, or waste matter left over from the meal. Such a theory illustrates to my mind the danger of attempting to explain on one hypothesis the whole complex series of values which become centred in human society round the act of eating and round food itself. Crawley does not explain the beliefs he cites in relation to the eating customs of each particular tribe. He merely starts from the general assumption that the phenomenon of the food taboo is due to an innate biological tendency to safeguard the physiological functions of the body, and thence proceeds to account in this manner for every variety of eating custom which could be conceived to have a precautionary significance at all. Like Frazer, he groups together a wide range of prohibitions under the name of " taboo " and postulates a single concept of the nature of magic to account for the whole.

With regard to the positive observances of Commensualism, Crawley's view is of a similar mystical type. Food is exchanged between men to signify union, he says. This " goes back to the animal expression of sympathy by contact and by a gift of food . . . food produces flesh, and flesh is connected with blood ", so that " eating food together produces identity of substance, of flesh, and thereby introduces the mutual responsibility resulting from eating what is part of the other, and giving the other what is part of oneself to eat ".[1] By this theory, therefore, the sharing of food is a ritual expression of union to the savage because he is somehow mysteriously and unconsciously aware that food makes flesh, and also, apparently, that common flesh forms a tie.

Here, again, we must differ very strongly from Crawley. He appears to assume, on slight enough grounds, that man inherits from his animal ancestors a tendency both to eat alone, and also to make gifts of food—both of these traits being expressed by the primitive man in the form of commensal rules. Moreover, he, like Frazer, considers eating solely as an individual physiological process affect-

[1] Crawley, *The Mystic Rose*, Vol. II, p. 121.

ing the psychology of the eater alone. Neither of these writers touch on the sociological aspect of nutrition, the point which we have been stressing so largely here.

Robertson Smith, in his account of the rôle of sacrifice in Semitic religions, comes nearer to our point of view. This writer concentrates chiefly on the positive aspects of Commensualism, and describes the function of the ritual meal as an expression of group life. He was, in fact, the first to point out, in a brilliant piece of pioneer work, that eating in a primitive society is a social act, performed between members of a group and expressing the obligations of that membership. "The act of eating and drinking together is the solemn and stated expression of the fact that all who share the meal are brethren, and that the duties of friendship and brotherhood are implicitly acknowledged in their common act." [1] Such duties among the Semites consist chiefly of the rights of blood-brotherships, blood-revenge, and hospitality, and " those who sit at meat together ", he says, " are united for all social effects : those who do not eat together are aliens to one another, without fellowship in religion, and without reciprocal social duties ".[2] This brings us to the root of the matter at once. The savage does not usually eat with his fellows unless he be on terms of close kinship with them. Hence a ritual act of eating in common is believed to initiate just such a relationship. It gives it ceremonial expression, and binds each party to behaviour of the type expected between close friends. So also the sacrifice in primitive ritual is " an act of social fellowship between the deity and his worshippers ", which thereby binds the god in certain obligations to his living kinsmen. " The bond of food is valid in itself ", through the obligations it usually implies. " The essence of the thing lies in the physical act of eating together." [3]

This conception marked a very important advance in anthropological theory, but here again we have criticism

[1] W. Robertson Smith, *The Religion of the Semites*, 1894, p. 265.
[2] W. Robertson Smith, *op. cit.*, p. 269.   [3] *Ibid.*, p. 271.

to level.   Robertson Smith considered that the sacrificial repast or the covenant of peace originated, not in the common meal of the household, but in the public feast of the clan itself.   " Kinship is an older thing than family life," he states.   " In such a society there is hardly any family life, and there can be no sacred household meal." [1]

These statements are of course in direct contradiction to the actually observed facts.   The view that the clan precedes the family in tribal evolution has been abandoned in the light of modern anthropological research.   The theories of Robertson Smith, Morgan, and more recently Rivers, have been refuted again and again in the work of Westermarck, Lowie, Kroeber, Malinowski and others.[2] The clan grows out of the family, and not the family out of the clan, and no society has yet been discovered in which it could be said that " there is hardly any family life at all ".   Field-observation has again forced a modification of earlier anthropological theories, and to my mind it is the sentiments formed in the intimate circle of the family hearth which are reflected in the sacrificial meal of primitive ritual.   These sentiments can obviously only be understood through a first-hand observation of the daily life of the tribe.

It is for want of this concrete data that Durkheim and his followers of the French sociological school have given a misleading account of this question.   Like Robertson Smith, they have emphasized that eating is a social activity, rather than an individual physiological process, but in their hands this sociological aspect of nutrition has developed into a positive apotheosis of the ceremonial meal.   The ritual sharing of food is, to them, not the act of a specific unit of the tribe, whether of family, age-group, or village, but a kind of mystic and religious communion of the society at large.   The sacrifice as

[1] W. Robertson Smith, *op. cit.*, pp. 279, 277, 289.
[2] B. Malinowski, " Kinship ", *Man*, Feb. 1930, for a summary of this controversy.

described by Hubert and Mauss is the means by which man puts himself into communion with the world of the sacred, through the victim specially consecrated and offered to the God. It is when he is gathered together with his fellows that the savage feels most conscious of the strength of his whole society. He becomes uplifted by a mystic sense of power—the spirit of his group or his God. Thus the repetition of the sacrifice constantly strengthens his social consciousness :—" *elle alimente les forces sociales . . . en rappelant fréquemment aux consciences particulières la présence des forces collectives entretient précisément leur existence idéale* ".[1] The ceremonial meal is thus considered by the Durkheimian school as an expression of social cohesion in general, rather than of the ties uniting the actual units of a primitive society.

The most interesting development of this theory is, of course, Radcliffe-Brown's conception of the " social value " of food, which he describes with a wealth of suggestive detail in his volume on the Andaman Islands. Food is the source of the chief pleasures and anxieties of the Andaman Islander. " It is particularly in connection with food that he is made to feel that he is a member of the community, sharing with others their joys and sorrows, taking part in a common activity, often dependent upon others for the satisfaction of his hunger, and obliged by custom to share with those others what he himself obtains." [2] Food is thus the object above all others which most frequently calls the social sentiments into action. It becomes symbolic of the mystic force of society, and acquires some of the attributes of the society itself—its dangerous yet protective power. It has, in other words, *social value*, and hence must be surrounded by a series of rites and taboos. " Since the greater part of social life is the getting and eating of food, to place a person outside the social life would be to forbid him from

---

[1] H. Hubert et M. Mauss, " Essai sur le Sacrifice ", *L'Année Sociologique*, Vol. II, 1898, p. 137.
[2] A. R. Brown, *op. cit.*, 1922, p. 270.

partaking of the food that is obtained by the society and consumed by it." [1]   Radcliffe-Brown thus accounts for the negative rules of Commensualism, the regulations and precautions which surround the sharing of food, as well as its positive aspect as a symbol of union between different individuals, in terms entirely of the *social value* of food. Such a theory is exceedingly suggestive, but can have no meaning unless it is based on a thorough study of the eating customs of the Andaman Islanders themselves.   If the whole community does eat in common, the theory may hold true in that particular society, but Radcliffe-Brown does not give us any information on this point. Observations on different Bantu tribes have shown us, on the contrary, that the members of each community eat in separate groups, and we have already stressed the segregation of the different units in each village at the time of the daily meal.   The family household, in the typical Bantu kraal, is the centre of a series of smaller sex and age groups which are dependent upon it for the supply of their food.   The common meal is, therefore, associated with intimate relationships and interests on a family basis, rather than with general feelings of cohesion between the members of the clan or the society at large.   It is for this reason that the problems of Commensualism in a primitive society can only be elucidated by means of a biographical study of the eating customs of each tribe.   Such a rite as the sacrifice must be explained in terms of the social organization of the particular group by which it is practised.

3.   THE SACRIFICE IN BANTU WORSHIP

The typical Bantu sacrifice consists in the offering of flour or beer to the ancestral spirits, or else the killing of an animal, and its division among the people according to fixed rules.   In the latter case the ceremony is essentially a ritual act of Commensualism, and I want there-

---

[1] A. R. Brown, *op. cit.*, 1922, p. 279.

fore to test, by means of concrete examples, our theory that the sacrifice is based on the sentiments formed round the family meal in early childhood, rather than on a mystical sense of clan or tribal cohesion.

To begin with, we see at once that the whole core of ancestor worship among these peoples is centred in the cult of the immediate family Gods. The ceremonies offered to the village or tribal deities grow out of the family rites and are, in a sense, a replica of them. In this, as in other aspects of ancestor worship, there is a remarkable similarity in the rites and beliefs of Bantu tribes throughout the length and breadth of Africa, as appears from the study of such comparative works as Willoughby's *The Soul of the Bantu*. I shall, therefore, in this section, take examples from a wider cultural area than in the first part of this work.

The ancestral spirits in a primitive cult have to be considered as members of the social organization to which they belonged on earth, as Robertson Smith pointed out.[1] Now the basis of this organization is, of course, the family group. The Gods are therefore grouped definitely in patrilineal and matrilineal lines, watching the interests of their own descendants only, and bearing their part in the whole scheme of legal obligations by which the family organization holds together. A man belongs to a different clan to his wife in most primitive societies, and in many cases it is an offence for a man to offer sacrifice to the ancestors of his wife, or for her to appeal to his. The welfare of the children is definitely in the hands of one line of ancestors—the paternal Gods in the case of the patrilineal peoples of South Africa—although the maternal spirits may receive offerings through the maternal uncle in the case of the sickness of a child, and

---

[1] W. Robertson Smith, *op. cit.*, p. 29. " The circle into which a man was born was not simply a group of kinsfolk and fellow-citizens, but embraced also certain divine beings, the gods of the family and of the state, which to the ancient mind were as much a part of the particular community with which they stood connected as the human members of the social circle."

among the Thonga the maternal uncle is specially pledged to intercede for his uterine nephews.[1]

It is thus that the Bantu sacrifice in its most fundamental aspects is an emphasis of the family obligations of the immediate ancestral gods. The ancestral cult takes its root and being, first of all, in the ordinary occasions of family life. Food is thrown to the family spirits before the eating and cooking of the daily meal, the drinking of water in some cases, or before the beginning of a feast of beer.[2] Further, an animal is sacrificed at all the chief family rites, the birth and naming of the child, initiation, marriage, death or the adjudication of the inheritance. Offerings are also made at the sickness of one of the inmates of the household, or to ensure luck in the hunting-field—all events which affect the individual family group.[3]

Secondly, the family ancestors are, among most Bantu tribes, definitely associated with a special household shrine, and remain attached to the home in which they lived. Among the Kafirs a special space—the *Unsamo*—was reserved at the back of the hut for the spirit of the paternal grandfather, and on this offerings to the gods were usually made.[4] Among the Thonga, libations are poured into the *gandjela*, or altar, placed at the right side of the kraal entrance, or under a tree designated by the divining bones.[5] The sacred spots in a Mwila's hut are the foot of the *musemo*, the central post of the hut, and either side of the main entrance—the right side being associated with the husband's ancestors and the

---

[1] Smith and Dale, *op. cit.*, Vol. II, p. 166; Junod, *op. cit.*, Vol. I, p. 268, Vol. II, pp. 362, 367–8; cf. also A. R. Radcliffe-Brown, " The Mother's Brother in South Africa ", *S.A.J.S.*, Vol. XXI, Nov. 1924, pp. 542–55.

[2] Junod, *op. cit.*, Vol. II, p. 390; Smith and Dale, *op. cit.*, Vol. II, p. 123; F. W. Melland, *In Witch-Bound Africa*, 1923, p. 170; C. Hobley, *Bantu Beliefs and Magic*, 1922, p. 52.

[3] Cf. Willoughby's analysis of the family rites of ancestor worship (*op. cit.*, Chap. III); also D. Kidd, *Savage Childhood*, Chap. I; Junod, *op. cit.*, Vol. I, Part I; Smith and Dale, *op. cit.*, Vol. II, p. 156; etc., etc.

[4] D. Kidd, *Savage Childhood*, p. 26.

[5] Junod, *op. cit.*, Vol. II, p. 388.

left with the wife's.[1] At these spots it is the family
spirits only who are invoked, and the members of the
family only who receive blessings. " We do not know
why he should regard others besides us ; he will regard
us only ", explained a Basuto to Casalis.[2]

Lastly, the very nature of the sacrifice shows that
the ritual meal among most Bantu peoples is not a mere
expression of vague group feeling, but a definite repre-
sentation of the complicated legal obligations of family
life. Concrete demands are made of the spirits, to which
the sacrifice pledges them to accede.

For example, the father's functions on earth have to
be performed by the God's above. A Basuto whose
father has died " worships his father praying him to
look on him continually, and give him all that he wishes,
and give him cattle, corn,—everything ".[3] All those
benefits, in fact, for which the son depended on his
father on earth, the spirit is pledged to give to his
descendants by the sacrifice he receives.

The marriage contract, which involves complicated
legal obligations on the part of the living relatives,
similarly demands the co-operation of the family spirits.
The sacrifice to the ancestors on the occasion of marriage
binds them to observe this tie. Without the offering of
a sacrifice from the relatives of the bride to the spirits
of the bridegroom's family, the marriage is in some cases
incomplete. In the rites of the Natal Kafirs, a special
ox is given by the bride's father to be sacrificed to the
bridegroom's ancestors. The killing of this—the *umdado*
beast—is " an imperative marriage rite " for the Chief
Wife of the bridegroom. Among the Pondo the girl,
on her marriage, receives a cow from her father, which
is the cow of her ancestors, and whose calves can not
be sold.[4] The Thonga father offers a goat to his clan

---

[1] Smith and Dale, *op. cit.*, Vol. II, p. 173. It will be remembered
that membership of the clan follows matrilineal descent among the
Ba-Ila, while the society is patrilineal in other respects.
[2] E. Casalis, *op. cit.*, p. 145.   [3] Willoughby, *op. cit.*, p. 187.
[4] D. Kidd, *The Essential Kafir*, pp. 201–16.

ancestors when his daughter is married. " Look at her," he says, " accompany her where she will live. May she also found a village, may she have many children." [1]

The gods have therefore to fulfil not only the general obligations of the human father to succour and provide for his family, but they are, as he is, parties to the marriage contract of their earthly children, and can revenge the violation of this tie. The sacrifice binds them publicly to fulfil such duties, and the sacrifice in itself is a public meal. It is, in fact, a replica of the family meal—in a sense, a meal shared by god and worshippers alike. " The evoked spirit and his ghostly kinsmen feed upon the victim, and the sacrificer and his living relatives share the feast with their unseen guests." [2] The Thonga calls to his ancestral spirits, " Let us eat in peace together, father and mother ; give me life, me and my children, that we may live together without cough, here, at home." [3] The Zulus exposed meat in a special hut in order that the spirits might eat, and by eating be pledged to help. [4] It is the partaking of the meal which lays them under the obligation. Just as the man who shares food on earth, receives it from those members of his family to whom he is bound by legal obligation, so the act of eating is held to bind the unseen members of the family group.

Moreover, the dead observe the same eating etiquette as those on earth. They have to share food with their fellow-spirits. The Thonga headman sacrificing at a funeral calls to the deceased and bids him summon the other dead relatives by name, just as he would invite them to an earthly feast. The ghostly guests, once summoned, appear to behave much as they might do on earth, watching jealously to see that they receive their right portions of the sacrifice. [5]

[1] Junod, *op. cit.*, Vol. I, p. 111.
[2] Willoughby, *op. cit.*, p. 355.
[3] Junod quoted Willoughby, *op. cit.*, p. 58.
[4] L. Grout, *op. cit.*, p. 143 ; Callaway, *op. cit.*, p. 11.
[5] Junod, *op. cit.*, Vol. II, p. 396 ; also Callaway, *op. cit.*, Part II.

From yet another point of view, too, we can see that the sacrificial meal is a replica of the ordinary arrangements which govern the consumption of food in the daily routine of the village. The principal offerings to the gods consist of slaughtered oxen, or goats, or sheep. Wild animals are never offered as sacrifices, and this is an important point to remember, knowing as we do what complex personal values centre round domestic animals in the Bantu kinship scheme.[1] Now the animal sacrificed is shared by the family descendants, but it must be divided with the utmost care according to the fixed kinship rules. The beast is cut into separate portions, and these are then taken away and cooked and eaten by each household on its own hearth. Communal cooking does not exist among these societies, as far as I am aware, and the sacrifice is never a communal meal, in the sense of a group of the whole society round one board.

Thus the Durkheimian conception of a society uplifted by a sense of mystic tribal union in a common sacrificial feast is a picture which does not exist in actual life. Kinship bonds are expressly emphasized in the ancestral sacrifices of the Bantu peoples, rather than the merging of family sentiment in a wider tie. The spirits appealed to in daily life are the ancestors of the family group. The ritual meal binds the living and the dead to fulfil their part in this complex scheme of family obligations. It expresses the tie of child to father, father to child, and that of the man and his relatives. All share in the general sense of rejoicing and delight in the feast of meat, but each is keenly aware by whom the beasts have been provided, according to what scheme they have been divided, and what obligation they lay on a particular ancestral group. The sacrificial meal is a symbol based on the eating customs of the people in daily life, and the legal concepts which govern their kinship rules. It is not the result of philosophic concept, or behaviour carried out in a state of mystic exaltation.

[1] Willoughby, *op. cit.*, pp. 343–7.

According to our theory also the tribal ceremonies of sacrifice to the national gods should bear the imprint of the family pattern in the same way. Such sacrifices of course exist almost universally among the Bantu tribes. They take place in times of drought, at the season of First-fruits,[1] during the sowing of the seed, harvest, and formerly in time of war. The procedure in these cases is hard to ascertain. The psychology of the public feast or sacrifice in Bantu society remains yet to be analysed. Callaway describes a black ox ceremony for rain, formerly carried out among the Zulu, in which oxen, sheep and rams were sacrificed to the tribal ancestors. It was no common meal, his informant added, and each man present received a portion in both hands and burst into song as all carried the food to their mouths.[2] But as we have seen, Willoughby was told of a similar rite among the Bamangwato tribes in which a black bull was killed. " Of this sacrificial meat the chief was the first to partake, and after him, in strict order of procedure, each man, woman, and child in the throng had a meal." [3] Such descriptions do not give us a clear idea of the relevant facts, i.e. who contributed the oxen for the sacrifices, and what " the strict order of procedure " entailed. Willoughby states that " in all magico-religious celebrations the Becwana are careful to range the members of a family, and, when the celebration is shared by a larger group, the families in a clan, or the clans in a tribe, according to each one's status ".[4] It would appear then in this case that the social grouping of the tribe is again displayed. The individual families remain apart and distinct, although they are participating in an assembly on a national scale.

We come, in fact, to the conclusion that no general theory of the nature of sacrifice meets the case. There is, perhaps, more material available on this subject than

---

[1] Specially characteristic of the Southern Bantu group.
[2] Callaway, *op. cit.*, pp. 93, 94.
[3] Willoughby, *op. cit.*, p. 209.   [4] *Ibid.*, p. 227.

on any other aspect of primitive religion, probably owing to the importance of the sacrificial idea in the Christian and early Greek religions. Earlier German writers drew up a fairly complete classification of the different types of sacrifice met with, such as the Bittopfer, Dankopfer, Sühnopfer, etc. All these types of sacrifice obviously occur in primitive ritual, and even in the case of Bantu society we cannot pretend to have dealt with every aspect of the subject in these few pages. But the point we would stress is this ; any ritual act of eating in a primitive society must depend upon the nature of the values formed round food in that particular society, and these can only be analysed after a study of the whole nutritional system of the group. Historical explanations of the evolution of different types of sacrifice may help us, as well as knowledge of the spread of different customs by diffusion from tribe to tribe.[1] But such data can never be substituted for the knowledge of the nutritional habits of the tribe in question or the means by which these are impressed on the growing child. Thus we can agree with Robertson Smith that the act of eating is a significant tie of relationship, and that therefore the sacrifice is a ceremony binding God and man. But when we consider Bantu society this symbolic act appears to link the members of the individual family with the unseen world. It is not an expression of clan cohesion as a whole. It is binding because of the sentiment it evokes in the minds of the participants, and these sentiments are formed round the family hearth in early

[1] We have here omitted any reference to the psycho-analytic conception of the origin of the sacrifice in primitive ritual. Freud conceives the first " totemic meal " as the body of the patriarch of the primeval horde slain by his jealous but remorseful sons, and describes the sacrifice as " the repetition and commemoration of this memorable and criminal act,. with which began social organization, moral limitations, and religion " (*Totem and Taboo*, p. 190). Any theory which first invents an imaginary incident in pre-history, then postulates its inheritance through successive generations by a process of *Wiederholungzwang*, and finally accounts for all forms of social institution by this means is hardly likely to commend itself to the sociologist (cf. *The Meaning of Sacrifice*, R. Money-Kyrle, 1930, for a summary of this view).

life. The rite of sacrifice expresses actual social obligations and groupings and can only be explained in these terms.

4. FOOD AS A SYMBOL OF UNION

Apart from the question of sacrifice, among the Bantu, as almost universally in primitive society, the gift or sharing of food is a legal symbol of union. Smith and Dale say of the Ba-Ila, " Eating together means union in close relationship between equals ",[1] and refer to the making of a temporary covenant between two individuals by the exchange of food—a clanship of porridge—is the term given to such a relationship.[2] Sharing of food is the symbol of reconciliation after a fight. Junod describes the peace-making between two brothers who have quarrelled for some time. They say, " Let us eat out of the same spoon, drink out of the same cup, and be friends again." [3] Willoughby records the same rite among the Bechuana. A white ox is killed and the two men to be reconciled plunge their hands in the chyme of the stomach and eat some of the flesh.[4] It is also a common practice to remove the severe taboos between a man and his mother-in-law by a common sharing of food. In the Maputju clan of the Thonga a man will not eat with his mother-in-law until he has provided an " ox for communicating together " to share with her and his other relatives-in-law. Among the Xosa clan the son-in-law must bring his mother-in-law a plate of food with a gift on top.[5]

The symbolic sharing of food at marriage rites is also a common sign of union. Crawley recalls that the marriage of Confareatio in early Rome consisted of the

[1] Smith and Dale, op. cit., Vol. II, p. 59.
[2] Smith and Dale, op. cit., Vol. I, p. 308 ; Vol. II, p. 299.
[3] Junod, op. cit., Vol. II, p. 399.
[4] Willoughby, op. cit., p. 196 ; J. C. MacGregor and D. F. Ellenberger, op. cit., p. 258.
[5] Junod, op. cit., Vol. I, p. 240.

eating of the Panis Farreus in the presence of the Flamen Dialis and the Pontif ex Maximus.[1] Similar rites are to be found in Ancient Greece and among the peasantry of Europe, India, and Japan. Where the husband and wife do not eat together after marriage, as among the Bantu, this symbol is less common, but at the Ba-Ila wedding ceremony the bride and bridegroom eat ritually together as he gives her a new name. This is followed by the " eating of the bread " among relatives as a sign of aggregation to the new group.[2] The Bechuana marriage rite also includes the ritual eating of a slice of roast meat by the pair.[3] Among some of the Central Africans—Yao and Anyasa—the formal eating of porridge and a fowl by the parents of both parties constitutes the legal, binding ceremony of marriage.

But if we can state that a common meal signifies union in primitive ritual—and there seems little doubt that this is the case—the converse of the proposition is also true. Earlier anthropologists have all stressed the importance of the taboos prohibiting the sharing of food between different individuals in the community on occasions when such a procedure is considered dangerous or unsuitable. When the savage is conscious that he is at variance with one or more of his fellows, he will refrain from eating with them. As instances we may cite restrictions that apply to those relatives united by marriage, or to those who are believed to be passing through some magically dangerous crisis of their lives.

The taboo on the sharing of food between relatives-in-law is common throughout Bantu society. It applies sometimes to the whole group of relatives united by marriage, as in the case of the Ba-Ila or the Babemba ;[4] or between the husband and his mother-in-law and

---

[1] Crawley, *The Mystic Rose*, Vol. II, p. 127.
[2] Smith and Dale, *op. cit.*, Vol. II, p. 56. When the bride repudiates her marriage with an impotent man she will publicly refuse food from him (Vol. II, p. 71).
[3] Willoughby, *op. cit.*, p. 187.
[4] Smith and Dale, Vol. I, p. 341.

father-in-law, as among the Venda, Zulu, Thonga and
other South Bantu tribes ; also, though less commonly,
between the man and the wife of his wife's brother—
the Mukonwana.[1] These taboos usually last for some
stated interval, such as the birth of one or more children,
and are finally removed by a special ceremony. They
are somewhat similar to the custom of the Thonga of
refusing food in the village of the prospective bride or
bridegroom when on a betrothal visit. In the Maputju
country the bridegroom's friends must be given a pound
or ten shillings before they will consent to eat food in
the bride's village, while among the Ba-Ronga generally
they must be persuaded and solicited before they will
eat.[2] Among the Zulu, the bride may not eat food from
the bridegroom's kraal until the marriage gifts have
arrived, thus signifying her aggregation to the new group.[3]
All such taboos between the relatives united by marriage
probably serve a useful purpose during the preliminary
period in which each side of the family is inclined to
look upon the other with feelings of hostility and suspicion. In a primitive society a man is in contact with
very few other groups besides his own immediate relatives,
and the making of a new intimate relationship is difficult,
unless the awkward period is tided over by a prescribed
form of ceremonial behaviour—in this case avoidance of
meals and common intercourse. The bride in our own
community often feels just the same embarrassment on
settling down to live among her husband's relatives,
but she must rely on her own tact and resource, rather
than a ritual avoidance, to express the attitude of both
parties involved.

Other taboos on Commensualism apply to those who
are considered to be magically dangerous to their fellows
for one reason or another—men who have committed
some violent or extreme act, those who have been in
contact with some unusual or perturbing affair, or are

---

[1] Junod, *op. cit.*, Vol. I, p. 239, 290, 307.
[2] Junod, *op. cit.*, Vol. I, pp. 104, 113,
[3] J. Shooter, *op. cit.*, p. 54.

passing through a period of profound emotion, or a physiological crisis such as puberty, parturition, or death. Frazer, Westermarck and others have made an extensive collection of the food taboos binding on man-slayers, hunters of dangerous animals, mourners, or women during menstruation or childbirth, to give only a few examples. Among the Southern Bantu in particular, Bryant notes that the Zulu warrior must undergo a long period of purification before he may rejoin the household meals, while the absentee members of a Thonga family in which mourning has taken place may not join the common meal until a special rite—the *lumo milomo*—has been performed.[1] Hunters must also eat outside the village on certain occasions.

All such taboos serve to show us that the common meal in a primitive society is an event which unites the participants in certain ties of social relationship, only to be understood by knowledge of the kinship structure of that particular society. If therefore one member of the group commits a perturbing act or becomes in any alarming way out of the ordinary, the usual emotional attitude of his fellows towards him is disturbed, and the fixed types of behaviour pattern upon which social intercourse is so largely built in a primitive society, become impossible. For this reason the offender, or the unfortunate one, must be isolated from ordinary intercourse, and in particular from the daily meal; and it requires the prescribed ritual of purification with all the sanction of tradition behind it to restore the confidence of the community and make possible the resumption of the everyday rules of etiquette.

5. TABOOS ON SHARING SPECIAL FOODS

Another interesting aspect of Commensualism is the series of taboos in primitive ritual which centre round

[1] A. T. Bryant, *Zulu-English Dictionary*, p. 549; Junod, *op. cit.*, Vol. II, p. 397.

certain articles of diet which have become symbolic of the
life of the group. Among the Southern Bantu in particular there is a special significance attached to the
sharing of milk between two or more individuals. The
cattle belonging to a household are considered, in a
sense, members of that group itself, as we have seen,
and the transfer of stock from one family to another,
acts as a specially binding tie. So also the *amasi*, or
curded milk, among the Zulu-Xosa peoples acquires a
symbolic value in family transactions and rites. *Amasi*
may only be eaten by members of the household themselves. Strangers may not share the dish. Father Mayo
states that both *amasi* and *umcuba*—a grain dish—are
considered as specially the family foods, to be shared
by no outsider, and that a young bride entering the
household must abstain from these dishes for a year
after marriage.[1] Lichtenstein believes that it is the
drinking of milk from the bridegroom's cows that definitely
seals the bride's aggregation to the new group. The
husband's relatives hand her the milk, reminding her
that it comes from their herd, and as she drinks the
people shout : " She drinks the milk : she hath drunk
the milk." [2] From this moment the union of marriage
is concluded.

The taboos governing the use of the household milk-
sack among the Xosa peoples show similarly that milk
is considered particularly symbolic of the family group.
It was a cause for divorce for a woman to take milk
from her husband's sack without permission.[3] A man's
relatives would not eat *amasi* in the kraal of the wife's
family, and vice-versa—or as Junod puts it more con-
cisely, linking it up with exogamic rules—a man may not
drink milk in a village in which he may take a wife.[4]
Outside the family, too, the same symbolism is extended.

[1] F. Mayo, " The Zulu-Kafirs of Natal ", *Anthropos*, 1906, Vol. I,
pp. 467-8 ; also D. Leslie, *op. cit.*, p. 197.
[2] H. Lichtenstein, *op. cit.*, Vol. I, p. 262.
[3] A. Kropf, *op. cit.*, p. 155.
[4] Junod, *op. cit.*, Vol. I, p. 251.

Mrs. Hoernle says that among the Pondo it is tantamount to pledging blood-brotherhood with a man to drink milk from his herd : while Gardiner records the case of prisoners who refused to eat *amasi* made from the milk of another man's cows, " alleging that, as they were in disgrace, it was not proper for them to partake of it among their friends ".[1] The sentiments formed round milk among the cattle-owning Bantu are obviously so diverse as to call for a separate study.

Yet another series of taboos should be mentioned here as showing the extent to which the food owned and prepared by a certain household becomes symbolic of its social life. There is a very common belief in primitive society that the food of a dead man's store-house is impure, especially for his immediate relatives. The deceased toiled in his lifetime for the production of this supply of food and saw to its preservation. His use of it was regulated by the legal and moral rules of his society which protected the property from some members of the group and obliged him to bestow it on others. Its possession was the chief means by which his social status in the community was reckoned and his personality valuated. We see therefore that death, in most primitive societies, cuts across a very complex sentiment of personal ownership in the case of supplies of food. Its inheritance means in a sense the assumption of the legal status of the dead man, with the resultant conflicting emotions of desire and grief on the part of the descendants.[2]

These warring sentiments are sometimes expressed in rites of purification of the dead man's food supply before it is inherited, and sometimes even in its ritual destruction. Junod gives a graphic account of the *luma milomo* rite among the Thonga by which the food of the deceased

---

[1] Mrs. Hoernle, " The Sib in the Marriage Ceremonies of the S.E. Bantu ", *S.A.J.S.*, Vol. XXII, 1925, p. 481 ; A. F. Gardiner, *op. cit.*, p. 159.

[2] It is perhaps not irrelevant to recall that " to inherit " in the language of the Ba-Ila is " to eat the name ", and the same common Bantu root " kulya " is used often by the Babemba in the same sense.

is made free for his successor. Seeds of each kind of
cereal from the dead man's store-house—beans, maize,
or kafir-corn—must be cooked and poured into one of
his baskets. The *ntukula*, or uterine nephew or niece,
must then receive some of the cooked food between his
or her great toes in order to begin the *luma* rite. After
this the relatives are free to eat. " Other people may
very well eat from the deceased's store of food without
any harm, as its contamination is dangerous only to his
family." The gardens and other supplies of the dead
man must be purified in a similar way.[1]

I have only been able to mention here a few of the
taboos which restrict the sharing of special types of food between different members of a primitive society, but I have
tried by this means to show that it is not only the common
meal itself which acquires such complex emotional values
in a primitive tribe, but also the eating together of some
specified food which has come to signify the privileges
or obligations of a household or kinship group.

6. FOOD AND THE DAY'S ROUTINE

We have considered the act of eating as symbolic in
itself and must now turn to the problem of the preparation of food. The cooking and serving of meals are the
most recurrent household activities in any community,
and play a prominent part in the village life of a savage

---

[1] Junod, *op. cit.*, Vol. I, p. 147. I am indebted to the Trustees of the
late Mr. B. Deacon for permission to quote from his unpublished notes,
now being edited by Miss C. H. Wedgwood, an interesting expression of a similar psychology shown in a rite practised by the natives of
Malekula. A ceremonial exchange of food is here necessary after the
death of a relative. Each kinsman must take some food to a village
where he has no friends, and find an individual who will accept the
food. If the latter was a friend of the dead man he would refuse
indignantly, saying, " Why did you give to me, who was A's greatest
friend, one of his yams ? " implying that in former days he and A
always eat together, hence all things of his should go to strangers since
the days of eating together are now irrevocably gone. Cf. also
W. H. R. Rivers, *History of Melanesian Society*, Vol. I, p. 204. The
natives of Tikopia were tabooed from eating the food of a dead man
—his whole clan strictly coming under this category.

tribe. The sequence of meals is the day's essential routine. For the sake of convenience food must be taken at a more or less fixed time ; the cooking and the serving located in certain fixed areas in house or village ; and placed under the direction of different members of the community appointed to the task. Meals make the framework of the daily programme, and become fixed as the habit of household life.[1] They acquire a meaning apart from their purely pragmatic value. They become symbolic of domestic activities, the established and normal continuance of a well-ordered village existence.

The cooking and serving of food thus become the centre of complex emotional associations in the setting of everyday affairs. Primitive ritual expresses these sentiments and uses them as metaphors in ceremonial acts. The whole series of food-preparing activities is surrounded by magic precautions, ceremonially prescribed, or on occasions, ceremonially tabooed. The savage dietary is very limited, and the man who is tabooed from eating any one special food is, as we have seen, emphatically distinguished from the rest of the community by this fact. He is set apart, or even abnormal in some particular degree. So also the taboo on cooking, or the regular sequence of meals, is the most dramatic way of marking the fact that the whole communal life is transformed by unusual conditions, or in some way disturbed. There are occasions when the routine of life is broken, and disorderly emotions are let loose, particularly in the case of the death of an important member of the community, or in conditions of pestilence or war.

The primitive society faces this crisis by a ritual break in the daily course of life. The only activity shared by the whole community is the cooking and sharing of meals, and to a lesser degree also, the normal

[1] Even natural phenomena are associated by the savage with the sequence of his own domestic routine. The Basuto name for the Vesper star is *sefalaboho* or " Dish-cleaner " or *kopa-selalolo*—" Ask for supper " (E. Casalis, *op. cit.*, p. 143).

sex life. Thus to symbolize the disturbance of the village order these everyday activities are ritually brought to a sudden stop. Subsequently, to restore the confidence of the disorganized community, the preparation of food and the continuance of normal sex life must, after a given period, be ritually resumed. Such a step gives a similarly dramatic reassurance that the disturbing crisis is past.

This type of ritual is illustrated very clearly in the Bantu conception of the sacredness of Fire. The symbolism of fire is of course manifold both in primitive and in civilized religions. Fire is purging, burning, destroying, life-giving, and in some cases represents man's mastery of skilled crafts. Prometheus was bound because he stole fire from heaven to teach man the arts of the forge and other forms of technical skill.[1] But in Bantu cultures in general, apart from such organized Fire cults as we find among the Bergdama or Herero, the hearth appears to be symbolic of the communal life of the group. The cooking of food marks the household routine, and the lighting of the fire initiates domestic life in a new community. When the Thonga move a village, the lighting of fires is taboo during the period of building, and the inoculation of the new fire with a medicinal pill is one of the most important ritual acts which the headman carries out.[2] Among the Bechuana, the chief must light the fire ceremonially in the Place of Assembly, before a new township comes into existence. His sub-chiefs will then distribute the glowing cinders to the several families under their sway.[3] The Ba-Ila designate a fireless house

[1] Cf. Preface to Professor Gilbert Murray's translation of Aeschylus, *Prometheus Bound*, 1931.

[2] Junod, *op. cit.*, Vol. I, pp. 325–8 ; also H. Schintz, *Deutsch-Sud Afrika*, 1891, p. 166.

[3] Willoughby, *op. cit.*, p. 291. Cf. also Mackenzie's account of the institution of a chief's village among the Konde with the extinction of old fires and the lighting of new ones by the young chief (D. R. Mackenzie, *The Spirit-ridden Konde*, 1925, pp. 76, 171). The new Kamba village was not truly founded until the chief wife has cooked porridge in her new house, smeared its poles with the cooked food, and partaken of it ritually with her whole family (C. W. Hobley, *The Akamba*, p. 58).

by a special word *Kane-kezhi*, and the rite of the re-marriage of a widower necessitates the extinction and relighting of his fire " that fire is thus a new one and the woman becomes new ".[1]

Fire, therefore, as symbolic of the social life of the group, must be extinguished when the routine of village life is broken or interrupted, and ceremonially relit when the normal order of events is resumed. Cooking represents the usual course of domestic activities, and as such, is also forbidden when the society is in a state of disruption, or facing extraordinary or unusual events. The places where food is eaten may be likewise tabooed, to indicate that the household is temporarily disjointed or its members passing through some crisis.

Thus we find that village fires are commonly extinguished during mourning, and fasts may be kept or the cooking of food prohibited at such times. Barring war or pestilence, death constitutes the greatest possible disruption the small primitive group has to face. It means, especially in the case of a chief or headman, that work must be reorganized, kinship ties reshaped, and the inheritance distributed, usually according to very complex laws. In these conditions Kidd records that the people of a Kafir kraal which is unclean during mourning, may not cook during the first day, and for months after are tabooed the drinking of milk, or trading with other kraals. Hahn's account of the extinction of the tribal fires at the mortuary rites of an Ovambo chief in the South-Western area may also be cited here. Among the Akamba no cooking may take place for a day after a death has occurred.[2]

An interesting parallel to these taboos on cooking stands out in the case of those Melanesian and Polynesian communities in which there is such a marked distinction

---

[1] Smith and Dale, *op. cit.*, Vol. II, p. 60.
[2] D. Kidd, *The Essential Kafir*, p. 249 ; C. H. L. Hahn, *The Ovambo*, pp. 17–18 ; C. W. Hobley, *The Akamba*, p. 67. It is interesting to note that in all these cases the prohibition on fire-lighting or cooking is associated also with the rigid observance of communal sex taboos.

in ritual between the use of cooked and uncooked food. In an environment in which wild coconuts, edible roots and fruits exist in profusion, it is perfectly possible for a native to exist for a longish period on an uncooked diet. Thus we find that the cooked dishes as distinct from the raw foodstuffs appear to be symbolic in these communities of the normal social and domestic life. In the Solomon Isles we are told that a widow, after fasting completely for some days, must subsist on uncooked food for two months, while in the Aurora Island, the relatives of a dead man may have to live on wild breadfruit or coconuts for a considerable period after the death.[1]

Further than this, cooked food, besides representing the common or the ordinary, may come to be considered polluting in any sacred sphere of life. It is interesting that among the Maori where raw foodstuffs were stored in ornamental huts, admired, and handled with such delight, yet " cooked food was the most powerful agency of pollution ".[2] The work of Elsdon Best is crowded with references to the precautions observed by the Maori to guard against this danger. *Tamaoa* is the special term meaning " to deprive of *Tapu* by means of cooked food, the most soul destroying thing according to native ideas ". Cooked food may not be carried during hunting expeditions or in the *Whare-Matu*, the house set apart for the manufacture and repair of hunting implements.[3]

With the taboos on cooked foods may be considered also the special taboos laid in some communities on the

---

[1] C. E. Fox, *The Threshold of the Pacific*, 1924, p. 214 ; R. H. Codrington, *The Melanesians*, 1891, p. 281.

[2] G. H. L. Pitt-Rivers, " A Visit to a Maori Village ", *J.P.S.*, Vol. XXXIII, 1924, p. 56. Malinowski states that in the Trobriand Islands cooking-huts were built on the borders of the village in order that the store-houses of yams should not be polluted by the odour of cooking (*The Sexual Life of Savages*, p. 60).

[3] Elsdon Best, *Transactions of the New Zealand Institute*, 1909, pp. 435, 436, 441, 445 ; *J.P.S.*, Vol. X, 1901, p. 7. Also R. Firth, *Primitive Economics of the New Zealand Maori*, 1928, p. 140. Cooking may also be dangerous of course if the animal cooked is dangerous, and its spirit might avenge the injury done to the meat (G. Brown, *Melanesians and Polynesians*, 1910, p. 83 ; W. G. Ivens, *Melanesians of the S. E. Solomon Islands*, 1927, p. 203).

particular staple food of the group.   Staple foods seem also to represent the ordinary or the normal in primitive ritual ; prohibitions on eating the staple food of the community during mourning are also common in primitive societies.   Rivers states that mourning relatives abstain from coconuts, taro, yam and fish in Tikopia.[1]   The inhabitants of Dobu Island in the Trobriand group are tabooed from eating coconuts, other staple foods, and from participation in the normal routine of life—trading and the circulation of the Kula ring.[2]   Abstinence from eating the principal food of the tribe is an important mourning taboo among the tribe of Kariera described by Radcliffe-Brown—this food being formerly kangaroo, and now more usually mutton.[3]   Ivens describes a ceremony in the Solomon Islands by which the sacred rites opening the Bonito fishing are brought to an end by a ceremonial eating of areca nut by the priest.   This is described as the " making common " of the food of the community, since the chewing of areca nut is the common form of intercourse in daily life.[4]   It is interesting to note, too, that the mourners, tabooed from eating cooked food in the Solomon Islands, were perfectly free during this time to eat any dish of European origin, which was not the subject of such complex sentiments in tribal ritual.

A comparative analysis of the ritual significance of cooked or staple foods in different primitive societies demands a more searching examination than space permits.   We can only indicate here that the cooking and preparation of food in a savage community becomes, like the sharing of daily meals, the object of family sentiment and a part of the whole system of legal obligations in which the kinship system consists.   It signifies the routine of local group life.   Further observations in

---

[1] W. H. R. Rivers, *History of Melanesian Society*, Vol. I, p. 314.
[2] B. Malinowski, *Argonauts of the Western Pacific*, pp. 346, 489.
[3] A. R. Brown, " Three Tribes of Western Australia ", *J.R.A.I.*, Vol. XLIII, 1913, p. 169.
[4] W. G. Ivens, *op. cit.*, p. 320.

the field—particularly on the little touched problem of daily activities and the legal status of the woman in the primitive community—will make possible a closer estimate of the values centred round cooked food, as they are expressed in primitive ritual.

7. WOMAN AND THE SYMBOLISM OF FOOD

We cannot leave the subject of meals and home life without considering the part played by the woman in domestic activities. As we have seen, the Bantu woman is responsible for the production of vegetable supplies and the preparation of cooked food. This is an essential function of her marriage relationship, and from earliest childhood her desires and ambitions are centred in these pursuits. Her status as a member of the community is measured in terms of these activities.

There is, therefore, in Bantu society a continuous association of the rôle of both wife and mother with the control and provision of food in the family circle, and this intricate pattern of maternity is mirrored again and again in the legal codes that govern marriage obligations, and the ritual acts expressing inter-sex relations.

Myths of the origin of different primitive races commonly contain an account of the first ancestress of the tribe, who is depicted either as bringing fire to her descendants or, more commonly still, as inventing the cooking of food. The primæval ancestors of the Ba Ronga are *Likalahumba*—the man who brings the glowing cinder—and *Nsilambowa*—the woman who first grinds the vegetables.[1] Another Thonga myth describes the history of the Hlengwe tribe which first gathered strength from having eaten cooked food, stolen from the Sono tribe.

A typical legend told among the Basuto pictures the first men as living one side of a great river and subsisting on game, while the first women keep to the other bank

[1] Junod, *op. cit.*, Vol. I, p. 21.

and live by gathering grass seeds. One day when the hunters could not cook their meat because their fires had gone out, one of them crossed the river and met a woman who took him to her hut, and gave him porridge made of grass seeds for the first time. " He said it was very nice, and he further said, ' I will stay and sleep here '." His companions one by one followed his example, and the institution of marriage was thus founded by the recognized exchange of meat and cooked grain between man and woman.[1]

The connection of the woman with the fireside hearth is also emphasized in primitive ritual. Among the Bergdama, where the ceremonial of the sacred Fire is the centre of all religious and social life, it is the chief woman in the community—the wife of the headman— who is responsible for guarding the flames. Among the Herero the eldest daughter of the chief's Great Wife performs this function.[2] The royal fire of the Thonga is kept burning in the hut of the Great Wife of the chief, and the fuel for this fire is furnished by a special sub-clan—the Makeneta—and must be tended by the Great Wife herself, in whose custody is also the magic horn of the tribe. In daily life it is the headman's wife who must ceremonially light the new fire in a rebuilt village.[3] Among the Ba-Ila, so close is the association between the household fire and the status of the wife that a woman may be divorced if her fire-stick has been removed from the hut.[4]

Besides the connection of the woman with the household fire, the offering or sharing of food between man and woman comes to represent almost universally in

[1] S. S. Dornan, " The Bechuana ", *Proceedings of the Rhodesian Scientific Association*, Vol. VIII, Part I (1908), p. 79.

[2] H. Vedder, *Die Bergdama*, Vol. I, 1923, p. 25 ; E. Brauer, *Züge aus der Religion der Herero*, 1925, p. 66 ; J. Irle, *Die Herero*, 1906, Chap. V.

[3] Junod, *op. cit.*, Vol. I, p. 391.

[4] Smith and Dale, *op. cit.*, Vol. I, p. 142 ; H. S. Stannus states that among the Akamba " the fire may not be touched by male children, but is tended by the girls ". " Notes on some Tribes of British Central Africa ", *J.R.A.I.*, Vol. XL, p. 327.

primitive society the definite legal relationship between
the two.   The symbolism of marriage rites displays this
fact more fully.   The offering of food—usually cooked
food—may represent either a proposal of marriage, the
completion of the act of marriage, or the expression of
the legal obligation of the man or the woman throughout
married life.

The proposal of marriage by the offering of food is
exceedingly characteristic of some groups of Melanesian
societies.   In these communities strong prohibitions and
codes of etiquette prevent the boy and girl from eating
together before marriage, even in societies in which pre-
nuptial intercourse is a recognized feature of social life.
Among the Trobrianders the unmarried boys living in
the *bukumatula*, or lover's house, return to the parental
household in order to eat.   They will never share meals
with their lovers.   " We object ", says Malinowski, " to
an unmarried girl sharing a man's bed—the Trobriander
would object just as strongly to her sharing his meal." [1]
Among the Mafulu of New Guinea described by R. W.
Williamson, no girl who is not a near relative of a
bachelor may even see him eat. [2]   In such communities
the offering of food from the woman to the man signifies
a definite proposal of marriage, or at any rate an advance
made by one party or the other. [3]   The public sharing
of food between the man and woman may also constitute the final act of the long series of marriage nego-
tiations.   In the Trobriands the marriage preparations
are terminated by the girl simply leaving her parents'
home and beginning to cook her husband's meals during
the day.   " The word goes round : ' Isepuna is already
married to Kalogusa.'   Such proceedings constitute the
act of marriage." [4]   Where meals are taken in common

---

[1] B. Malinowski, *The Sexual Life of Savages*, p. 64.
[2] R. W. Williamson, *The Ways of the South Sea Savage*, p. 215.
[3] Cf. also W. G. Ivens, *op. cit.*, p. 87 ; R. Parkinson, *Dreissig Jahre
in der Südsee*, 1907, p. 65.
[4] B. Malinowski, *op. cit.*, p. 75 ; cf. also A. E. Hunt, " Ethnographic
Notes on the Murray Islands, Torres Straits ", *J.R.A.I.*, 1899, p. 10 ;
C. E. Fox, *op. cit.*, p. 204.

during married life, the first repast shared constitutes a legally binding act.[1]

In Bantu society the case is different. The unmarried boy and girl are not so rigidly tabooed from eating together, although in practice the two eat apart. But after marriage the husband and wife do not share meals, or indeed join in many co-operative undertakings. Therefore we should not expect to find that the first offering of food from the boy to the girl, or the girl to the boy, is so typically an act of marriage proposal. And this is in fact the case. But the gift of cooked food from woman to man *after* marriage symbolizes in many instances the relationship of matrimony throughout the wedded life of the pair. The Thonga wife's greeting to her husband on his return to the village after a long absence consists in an immediate and silent offering of a dish of cooked food to the man.[2] Roscoe records that at the court of the Baganda King this matrimonial obligation is ritually expressed daily. The Queen has to send her husband twelve baskets of cooked food every day, while the Queen Mother must also provide three baskets. The offering in this case is, of course, entirely symbolic, as the King has his own staff of cooks to prepare his meals.[3]

The wife's function as food preparer is also expressed in the metaphors of legal contract and terminology. At the temporary allotting of the widows of a dead Thonga to his heirs the act is completed by the phrase, " You so-and-so, you shall give food to so-and-so—(*phamela manyana*)." [4] Similarly, the counsellors who desire the

---

[1] Melanesian communities in which the men eat apart from the women after married life has begun, belong of course to a different category. Cf. Rivers' account of the men's association connected with the *Sukwe* in the Banks Islands (Rivers, *History of Melanesian Society*, Vol. I, p. 61 ; Codrington, *op. cit.*, p. 101, *et seq.*).

[2] J. Chalmers, *Work and Adventure in N. Guinea*, p. 105, describes exactly the same form of greeting among the Nameanumu of the Segeri district. The returning husbands say nothing to their wives until they have tested the latter's cooking. They may then come and sit with their wives. He says, " I have noticed that the wives are particularly happy when preparing this return food."

[3] J. Roscoe, *The Baganda*, 1911, p. 206.

[4] Junod, *op. cit.*, Vol. I, p. 203.

Thonga chief to take his Great Wife must address him formally thus: "Who do you suppose is going to feed you? Who will cook the meat? Who is going to brew the beer?" This speech being regardless of the fact that the chief has already probably a number of lesser wives who are already performing these functions for him.[1]

Men who act temporarily as cooks among the Bantu for some special ritual reason, are styled as women while they perform this task. For instance, the blacksmith among the Ba-Ila, who is under sex taboos while preparing the smelting furnaces, is obliged to select a man to cook for him during this time. The latter is invariably addressed *Mwinangu*, or my wife.[2]

As regards her agricultural duties the same ritual expression of the woman's function is commonly found. Among the Ba-Ila the man places a hoe on the woman's hearth after the consummation of the marriage.[3] At a Pondo wedding the bridegroom's party mimics the bride's new duties, carrying a calabash, firewood, thatching-grass, and cooking-pots to her kraal.[4] While the Zulu girl is given a broom, a grinding-stone, and a cooking-bowl.[5] At a Bechuana burial the corpse of a woman is "shown" a winnowing fan, a cook-pot, some Kafir-corn, a corn mortar, and cooking utensils, while a man's Great Wife is buried under the threshing-floor so that "she may hear the thud of the flails threshing out each new crop".[6]

This leads us to another aspect of the problem. Frazer has made famous the almost universal primitive belief that the fertility of the woman and the fertility of the crops are closely interlinked. This belief is expressed in an infinite variety of different primitive rites, whether those of classical Greece, or of the savage tribes now in existence. In some cases, sexual intercourse, ritual or

[1] Junod, *op. cit.*, Vol. I, p. 375.
[2] Smith and Dale, *op. cit.*, Vol. I, p. 207.
[3] *Ibid.*, *op. cit.*, Vol. II, p. 55.
[4] D. Kidd, *The Essential Kafir*, p. 219.
[5] A. F. Gardiner, *op. cit.*, p. 89.
[6] Willoughby, *op. cit.*, p. 57.

actual, is thought to confer fertility on the land, and is performed either at seasons of ritualized licence by all the vigorous members of the community, or by the King or magician on behalf of the whole community, or by the owner of the field and his wife. Very usually too pregnant women, mothers of large families, or of twins, are considered lucky in agricultural undertakings, and barren women the reverse.

The magic power of human fertility is perhaps most clearly evinced in the rites of such a tribe as the Kiwai Papuans of New Guinea, where each event in the agricultural year must be preceded by ritual intercourse between the owner of each field and his wife, on the ground which is about to be cultivated.[1] But in Bantu society we find facts of the same kind. Women in general are able to bless fields, whereas their influence on cattle is, on the whole, baneful. Chaka's mother was mourned as " the Great Mother of earth and corn "—" the over-ruling spirit of vegetation " and cultivation was declared to be tabooed for a year after her death.[2] Willoughby says that among the Bechuana a man must sleep ritually with each wife before she sows her field. An ordinary woman's milk is a charm of fertility among some South African tribes, whereas the milk from the breast of a woman who has lost a child will hurt the gardens or storehouses.

In those agricultural societies where female initiation ceremonies are practised, this connection between the fertility of the woman and that of the vegetable world is also emphasized ritually. In the girl's Chisungu ceremonies I witnessed among the Babemba, the ceremonial planting of one of each of the different kinds of seeds sown

---

[1] Cf. Gunnar Landtmann, *The Kiwai Papuans of British New Guinea*, pp. 75–80, etc.; also W. E. Armstrong, " Government Report on the Suau-Tawala ", I, 1917–1922, p. 18.

[2] Willoughby, *op. cit.*, to p. 231; D. Kidd, *Savage Childhood*, p. 40; D. Leslie, *op. cit.*, p. 147; Junod, *op. cit.*, Vol. I, p. 193; also Smith and Dale, *op. cit.*, Vol. I, p. 374; G. Dale, " An Account of the Principal Customs and Habits of the Natives Inhabiting the Bondei Country ", *J.R.A.I.*, 1896, Vol. XXV, p. 183.

by the tribe was one of the most important elements, and it was impossible to decide how far this ceremony was designed to make fertile the marriage of the girl herself, or of the fields she would have to sow.[1]

The function of motherhood is also expressed symbolically in nutritional terms. To begin with, as we have already noted, the act of suckling may have its place in ritual as well as physiological life. It definitely implies the social kinship between the mother and child, and a woman is not allowed to suckle an infant which is not her own offspring or that of a clan member. In receiving his mother's milk the baby becomes united to his mother's family, and, according to some observers, the *lobola* paid at marriage is a compensation to the wife's family for just this very reason. The mother has provided the nourishment for the child, and therefore the father's family stands in her debt.

In some communities of the Eastern group of Bantu, we find an interesting expression of the sentiments associated with suckling in the so-called rites of milk brotherhood found among these people. Among the Akamba, brotherhood may be forced on a person by suckling his wife's or his daughter's breasts.[2] Among the Wachagga a milk covenant may be made by members of one clan by drinking the milk of a clan sister in the inside of the hut, the rite being followed by the blood covenant carried out in the open air afterwards. A clanswoman who is suckling a child, squeezes her milk into a bowl of curded cow's milk and this is shared with goat's flesh and blood. " The bond of milk pledges you to stand by your brother." [3] It was also the custom to domesticate children captured in war by making them drink from the breast of a captor's wife.[4]

---

[1] The same is true of the initiation ceremonies of the Valenge tribe of Portuguese East Africa. Cf. E. Dora Earthy, *Proc. Transvaal Museum*, XI.

[2] G. Lindblom, *The Akamba*, 1920, p. 141.

[3] Gutmann, *op. cit*, pp. 254–7.

[4] Gutmann, *op. cit.*, p. 288. Professor Seligman points out to me that in such cultures milk is equated with blood in native belief.

The mother's function of providing cooked food for her children is also expressed during the ritual of initiation among many clans.   Initiation marks the last step in the severance of the boy from his mother's care, and he is sometimes forbidden from eating food cooked by her at this time.   The death of a boy at the initiation camp is broken to the Thonga mother by handing her a broken food bowl when the procession returns from the camp. A similar custom is recorded among the Bamangwato and the Basuto, where the signal of a man's death is always the throwing of a food bowl on the doorstep of the wife or mother.[1]

8.   FOOD AND FILIAL DEPENDENCE

The social functions of maternity in the nutritive scheme lead us on directly to consider the part of the father in the family as a food-consuming unit.   Paternity is conceived in most of the societies we have been describing in terms of the possession and provision of food.   The dependence of the child and the adolescent on the adult head of the group is a directly and overtly nutritive one. This child-to-father relationship is reflected in primitive metaphor and ceremonial usage in the same manner as the social attributes of maternity that we have just described.

The filial sentiment is extended to all those relationships in tribal life in which one individual is directly dependent on another for food.   This phenomenon is particularly marked in most Bantu societies, since the whole structure of government is built on a definitely paternal pattern, and the terms of family usage are constantly applied to those in authority.   The Thonga headman is described as " the father of his people "[2] when he distributes the carcass of an animal in the centre of a kraal.   A Zulu says

[1] J. Chapman, *Travels in the Interior of South Africa*, 1888, Vol. I, p. 43 ; E. Casalis, *op. cit.*, p. 264.
[2] Junod, *op. cit.*, Vol. I, p. 330.

of his chief as " He is their father, they his children ".[1]
The subjects of a Mwila chief are called his *Bana*—or
children—and he is described as " ruling them *kulela* in
food and other things ", *kulela* being the word used to
describe the nursing of a child.[2]   It is also usual that a
poor man attaching himself to the kraal of a rich headman
should address him as " father ".   To the chief and to the
father both hands must be extended, according to Zulu
usage, when receiving food, if a proper appreciation of
the superior's liberality is to be shown, while in a Baganda
State the proper reply to the call of a chief was " Wampa ",
" You have given to me ", meaning, " It is you who have
given me all I have, my wife, food, and clothing ".[3]   In
other words, there is in Bantu society a symbolic use of
the kinship term of " father " to those from whom the
individual expect to receive food.   Conversely the acceptance of food implies a filial attitude on the part of the
recipient, whether he be subject, slave, or stranger.   By
taking the food the man becomes a son in the legal sense.

This fact is just a special case of the general phenomenon
that kinship obligations in a primitive tribe tend to be
expressed by the giving and exchange of food.   Melanesian
material perhaps illustrates this situation more dramatically than that from South Africa.   Malinowski has shown
that no public transaction takes place in Trobriand
society, whether marriage, death, homage to a chief, or
the circulation of the sacred objects in the Kula ring,
without the exchange of large and sometimes equal
quantities of food.   Such acts form a public acceptance
of some legal obligation, and also bind the contracting
parties in a complex relationship.   One gives and the other
outdoes his generosity in exchange, but always with the
expectation of a similar return later.   Thus the parties
are permanently linked by a system of food exchange.
In marriage, this relationship lasts throughout the life of

---

[1] T. B. Jenkinson, *op. cit.*, p. 25.
[2] Smith and Dale, *op. cit.*, Vol. I, pp. 302, 307.
[3] T. Roscoe, *The Baganda*, p. 44.

the wedded pair.   Our own consideration of the sociology of the *lobola* in South Africa led us to describe a similar situation between the two sets of relations-in-law who have received cattle from each other, or hold them in pledge.

Thus on the one hand numbers of the kinship group are actually bound to contribute towards each other's maintenance.   There are certain relatives whom a man must provide with food—his wife and children in nearly all societies, and a wider series of kinsmen among primitive tribes.[1]   On the other hand, these very ties of nutritive dependence make for the symbolization of food itself. The act of giving or receiving food becomes a legal act, representing the formation, or affirmation, of ties between different members of the society—ties which are analogous to those within the family itself.   Among these are reckoned usually the relationships between subject and chief, chief and chief, the families united by marriage, blood brothers, or sometimes members of age groups.   In these different relationships it is food *par excellence* which is exchanged, even in societies which have been for a long time in contact with the money circulation of white peoples.   From its early significance as the object of family obligations, food acquired a secondary value as an article of gift and exchange, which other valuables have not.   For this reason I have included the whole phenomenon of exchange of eatables under the heading of the symbolization of food.

9.   Conclusion

These words bring us, in fact, to the point where we started out on the analysis of the sociological significance of food.   It was my thesis that nutrition in human society cannot be considered as a biological instinct alone, of the

---

[1] I was interested to note that among the Babemba a child is never taught to thank its relatives for food, nor does an adult express any thanks.   "Why," they say, "he is their child.   They are not giving to him from pity.   Why should he salute them ? "   He should salute a stranger if the latter gives him food, but not one of his own clan.

type that actuates the behaviour of the lower animals. Nor, on the contrary, can man's nutritive needs and food-getting activities be divided from the physiological basis on which they rest, as has too often happened in the history of sociological theory.

Nutrition is a biological process in that the constant drive of hunger gives to food-getting an interest and a value quite different from that of any other activity on which man is engaged. Moreover, the earliest tie of child-hood—that of the infant to its mother—is almost entirely a physiological relationship. The structure and bonds of the family in a primitive society are determined to a very large extent by the fundamental biological need of food : since it is within these groups that the child learns from whom he may expect his sustenance, and with whom it must be shared.

But nutrition must also be considered from the socio-logical point of view. From the day of birth, tradition regulates the way in which the child is fed, and this pro-cess continues till adult life, the individual's choice of diet and manner of eating depending on the social customs and values of his tribe.

Further, the nutritive ties of each individual are fixed according to legal rule. Society determines on whom the child shall be dependent for its food, who shall prepare it, and how the whole supply shall be distributed, such bonds of interdependence being one of the strongest cohesive forces in a primitive society. Later, these same family units become the basis of the food-producing system of the tribe. Family is linked to family by marriage, or other ties, in order to facilitate the nutritive quest, or to regulate the ownership and inheritance of food resources, such as land, water, or stock. In further economic activities we find the larger group of the clan co-operating, or at the ultimate limit of expansion, the tribe itself, so that the essential bonds uniting the members of these bigger units must be described as nutritive in the widest sense.

I spoke therefore of the *primary extension* of nutritive ties from the household to the kinship group, as the latter comes to participate in the family function of sharing and distributing supplies. Next I used the term *secondary extension* to describe the formation of yet further nutritive relationships as each adolescent boy or girl becomes a member of the wider food-producing system of clan or tribe, shares in the common ownership of food resources, or accepts the leadership of a single chief in economic activities.

This whole series of institutions and relationships I have spoken of throughout as the *nutritional system* of the tribe. I have tried to show that just as the fundamental drive of sex is shaped by human codes and customs, which regulate the whole relation of man to woman, the legal status and functions of parenthood, the laws of exogamy, and the subsequent education and upbringing of the child ; so also this *reproductive system* is paralleled in the nutritional sphere, the two great physiological needs often being fulfilled by the same institution in a human society, since the family is the starting-point for the formation of all subsequent ties. The analysis of social institutions on the basis of such fundamental biological needs is therefore the end to which the Functional method of anthropological study leads.

I chose a primitive society on which to make this study, but I believe the method so indicated could be applied to a more civilized group. The greater insecurity of the savage man's food supply throws into relief his nutritional institutions, and his whole scale of hopes, fears, and beliefs, as to his daily bread. Further, the simplicity of his system of groupings enables us to see the situation more clearly. I was able to show, for instance, that, in primitive conditions, food itself becomes symbolic of the human relationships which it brings into being. Food is sacred because it is the summit of the primitive man's ambitions and well-being, but also because it represents the ties of kinship by which he is bound. Thus, while I believe a nutritive analysis of modern society would be valuable, especially in elucidating the psychology of the intimate family group, the study of eating customs seems to me an absolute essential if we are to understand the structure and cohesion of a savage tribe. A functional examination of any primitive community is meaningless unless we start from the sociological significance of food in that particular group.

BIBLIOGRAPHY

ABBREVIATIONS

B.S. : *Bantu Studies*, Johannesburg.
E.J. : *Economic Journal*, London.
S.A.J.S. : *South African Journal of Science*, Johannesburg.
T.R.S.S.A. : *Transactions of the Royal Society of South Australia*, Adelaide.
J.R.A.I. : *Journal of the Royal Anthropological Institute of Great Britain and Ireland*, London.
P.R.S.A. : *Proceedings of the Rhodesian Scientific Association.*
J.P.S. : *Journal of the Polynesian Society*, New Plymouth, N.Z.
T.N.Z.I. : *Transactions and Proceedings of the New Zealand Institute*, Wellington, N.Z.
C.N.L.C. : *Report of the Government Commission on Native Laws and Customs*, 1883. Cape Town Parliamentary Papers.

GENERAL LITERATURE

ABRAHAM, K. *Selected Papers of.* (Tr. 1927.) International Psycho-Analytical Library, No. 13. London.
ALVERDES, F. *Social Life in the Animal World.* (Tr. 1927.) London.
ARMITAGE, F. P. 1922. *Diet and Race.* London.

BALDWIN, J. M. 1895. *Mental Development in the Child and in the Race.* New York.
——— 1906. *Thought and Things . . . or Genetic Logic.* 3 Vols. London and New York.
BERNARD, L. L. 1925. *Instinct.* London.
BÜCHER, C. 1924. *Arbeit und Rhythmus* (6te Aufl., Leipzig).
——— 1893. *Die Entstehung der Volkswirtschaft* (IIIte Aufl., Tübingen, 1920). (Eng. Trans. : *Industrial Evolution*, 1901.)

CANNON, W. B. 1920. *Bodily Changes in Pain, Hunger, Fear, etc.*
CRAWLEY, A. E. 1902. *The Mystic Rose* (2 vols., new edition by Th. Bestermann, 1926). London.
——— 1925. *The Tree of Life.* London.

CUNOW, H. 1898. *Die ökonomischen Grundlagen der Mutter-schaft*, Die Neue Zeit XVI.

DEWEY, J. 1922. *Human Nature and Conduct*. London.
DICKINSON, Z. C. 1922. *Economic Motives*, Harvard Economic Studies, Vol. XXIV.
DREVER, J. 1921. *Instincts in Man*. Cambridge.
DURKHEIM, E. 1912. *Les Formes Elémentaires de la Vie Religieuse*. Paris.
———— 1902. *De la division du travail social*. Paris.

ESPINAS, A. 1877. *Des Sociétés Animales*. Paris and Dijon.

FLÜGEL, J. C. 1921. *The Psycho-analytic Study of the Family*. International Psycho-analytical Library, No. 3. London. Vienna.
FRAZER, J. *The Golden Bough* (abridged ed., 1925). London.
FREUD, S. 1918. *Three Contributions to the Theory of Sex*. 3rd Edition. (Eng. trans. by A. A. Brill.) New York and Washington.
———— 1919. *Totem and Taboo* (Eng. trans. by A. A. Brill.) New York and Washington.
———— 1927. *The Ego and the Id*. (Eng. trans. by Joan Riviere.) International Psycho-analytical Library, No. 12. London.

GENNEP, A. van. 1904. *Tabou et Totémisme à Madagascar*. Paris. Bibliothèque . . . Sciences Religieuses.
———— 1909. *Les Rites de Passage*. Paris.
GINSBERG, M. 1921. *The Psychology of Society*. London.
GOLDENWIESER, A. A. 1923. *Early Civilization,—An Intro-duction to Anthropology*. London.
GROSSE, E. 1896. *Die Formen der Familie und die Formen der Wirtschaft*. Freiburg u. Leipzig.

HACHET-SOUPLET P. 1900. *Examen Psychologique des Animaux*. Paris.
———— 1912. *La Genése des Instincts*.
Handbook of Child Psychology, ed. Carl Murchison. Worcester, Mass.
HOWARD, H. E. 1920. *Territory in Bird Life*. London.
HOYT, E. E. 1926. *Primitive Trade : its Psychology and Economics*. London.
HUNTINGDON, ELLSWORTH. 1925. *The Character of Races*. New York and London.

KING, I. 1906. *The Psychology of Child Development.* Chicago.
KOHLER, W. 1927. *The Mentality of Apes.* London.
KOLNAI, A. 1921. *Psycho-analysis and Sociology.* (Eng. trans. by E. and C. Paul.) London.
KOPPERS, P. W. 1921. *Die Anfänge des Menschlichen Gemeinschaftsleben.* München-Gladbach.
KROPOTKIN, P. A. 1902. *Mutual Aid.* London.
KYRLE, R. MONEY. 1930. *The Meaning of Sacrifice.* London.

LOWIE, R. H. 1921. *Primitive Society.* London.

McDOUGALL, W. *An Introduction to Social Psychology.* 21st Edition (first published 1908). London.
MARETT, R. R. 1914. *The Threshold of Religion.* 2nd Edition. London.
MARSTON, W. M. 1931. *Integrative Psychology.* London.
MAUSS, MARCEL. 1923–24. Essai sur le Don. *L'Année Sociologique.* N.S. Tom. I. Fasc. I. Paris.

PAVLOV, I. 1927. *Conditioned Reflexes.* (Trans. G. V. Annep.) London.
PIAGET, J. 1929. *The Child's Conception of the World.* (Eng. trans. by J. and A. Tomlinson.) London.
PILLSBURY, W. B. 1923. *The Fundamentals of Psychology.* Revised Edition. New York.
PREYER, W. T. L. 1893. *The Mind of the Child.* 2 Vols. New York.

READ, CARVETH. 1925. *The Origin of Man.* 2nd Edition. Cambridge.
REINHEIMER, H. 1909. *Nutrition and Evolution.* London.
ROMANES, G. J. 1883. *Mental Evolution in Animals.* London.
ROUSSEAU, J. J. 1922. *Discours sur l'origine et les fondements de l'inégalité parmi les hommes.* Edited by H. F. Muller and R. E. G. Vaillant. New York.

SELIGMAN, E. R. A. 1929. *Principles of Economics.* 12th Edition. London and New York.
SHAND, A. F. S. 1920. *The Foundations of Character.* 2nd Edition, 1920. London.
———— 1921 and 1922. Articles in the *Journal of Psychology.*
SMITH, W. ROBERTSON. 1894. *Lectures on the Religion of the Semites.* 2nd Edition. London.
———— 1903. *Kinship and Marriage in Early Arabia.* 2nd Edition. London.

SOROKIN, P. A. 1928. *Contemporary Sociological Theories.* New York and London.

SUMNER, W. G., and KELLER, A. G. 1927. *The Science of Society.* Yale University Press.

SUTTON, J. BLAND. 1890. *Evolution and Disease.* London.

STERN, W. 1924. *The Psychology of Early Childhood.* (Tr. from 3rd Edition.) London.

TEAD, ORDWAY. 1919. *Instincts in Industry.* London.

THORNDIKE, E. L. 1911. *Animal Intelligence.* The Animal Behaviour Series.

——— 1913. *Educational Psychology.* 3 Vols. New York.

TROTTER, W. 1919. *Instincts of the Herd in Peace and War.* 2nd Edition. London.

VARENDONCK, J. 1923. *The Evolution of the Conscious Faculties.* London.

VIERKANDT, A. 1927. Nahrung und Wirtschaft in *Festscrift Eduard Hahn zum LX Geburtstag III.* Stuttgart.

WALLAS, GRAHAM. 1908. *Human Nature in Politics.* London.

——— 1921. *Our Social Heritage.* London.

WATSON, J. B. 1924. *Psychology from the Standpoint of a Behaviourist.* 2nd Edition. Philadelphia and London.

WESTERMARCK, E. A. 1921. *The History of Human Marriage.* 5th Edition. 3 Vols. London.

——— 1912. *The Origin and Development of Moral Ideas.* 2nd Edition. 2 Vols. London.

WISSLER, CLARK. 1923. *Man and Culture.* London.

AFRICAN LITERATURE

AYLIFF, J., and WHITESIDE, J. 1912. *History of the Abambo, generally known as the Fingos.* Transkei.

BARROW, J. 1806. *Travels into the Interior of Southern Africa.* 2 Vols. London.

BARTER, C. 1879. *Alone among the Zulus.* London.

BARTON, J. 1921. Notes on the Suk Tribe of Kenia Colony. *J.R.A.I.,* Vol. LI.

BAUMANN, H. 1928. The Division of Work according to Sex in African Hoe Culture. *Africa,* Vol. I, No. 3. London.

BRAUER, E. 1925. *Züge aus der Religion der Herero.* Leipzig.

BROWN, A. R. RADCLIFFE-. 1924. The Mother's Brother in South Africa. *S.A.J.S.,* Vol. XXI.

——— 1929. Articles in *Man,* Vol. XXIX.

BROWN, J. T. 1926. *Among the Bantu Nomads.* London.

BROWN, G. ST. J. ORDE. 1925. *The Vanishing Tribes of Kenya.* London.

BROWNLEE, F. 1925. Circumcision Ceremony in Fingo-Land. *B.S.,* Vol. III, No. 2.

BRYANT, A. T. 1905. *A Zulu-English Dictionary.*

———— 1923. The Zulu Family and State Organization. *B.S.,* Vol. II, No. 1.

———— 1929. *Olden Times in Zululand and Natal.* London.

BURCHELL, W. J. 1822–24. *Travels in the Interior of Southern Africa.* 2 Vols. London.

CALLAWAY, The Rev. H. 1870. *The Religious System of the Amazulu.* Natal, Cape Town and London.

CAMPBELL, D. 1922. *In the Heart of Bantuland.* London.

CASALIS, The Rev. E. 1861. *The Basutos.* (Eng. trans.) London.

CHAPMAN, J. 1888. *Travels in the Interior of South Africa.* 2 Vols. London.

COLE, A. W. 1852. *The Cape and the Kafirs.* London.

COLENSO, J. W. 1855. *Ten Weeks in Natal.* Cambridge.

DALE, G. 1896. The Customs and Habits of the Natives inhabiting the Bondei Country. *J.R.A.I.,* Vol. XXV.

DECLE, L. 1898. *Three Years in Savage Africa.* London.

DORNAN, S. S. 1908. The Bechuana. *P.R.S.A.,* Vol. VIII, No. 1.

———— 1925. *Pygmies and Bushmen of the Kalahari.* London.

———— 1928. Rain-making in South Africa. *B.S.,* Vol. III, No. 2.

DRAYSON, A. W. 1891. *Among the Zulus.* 3rd Edition. London.

DUNDAS, C. 1921. Native Laws of some Bantu Tribes of East Africa. *J.R.A.I.,* Vol. LI.

———— 1924. *Kilimanjaro and its People.*

EARTHY, E. DORA. 1925–26. Some Agricultural Rites of Valenge and Vachopi. *B.S.,* Vol. II, Nos. 3 and 4.

ELLENBERGER, D. F., and MACGREGOR, J. C. 1912. *History of the Basuto.* London.

ELMSLIE, W. A. 1899. *Among the Wild Ngoni.* Edinburgh and London.

FAYE, C. 1923. *Zulu References for Interpreters and Students.* Pietermaritzburg.

FLEMING, F. 1853. *Kaffraria, and its Inhabitants.* London.

———— 1856. *Southern Africa.* London.

FRANKLIN, H. 1927. Selection from Notes on Manyika Customs. *Nada*, Vol. V. Salisbury, Rhodesia.
FRITSCH, G. 1872. *Die Eingeborenen Süd-Afrikas.* Breslau.

GALTON, F. 1889. *Narrative of an Explorer in Tropical South Africa.* London.
GARDINER, A. 1836. *Narrative of a Journey to the Zoolu Country.* London.
GIBSON, J. Y. 1911. *The Story of the Zulus.* 2nd Edition. London.
GOULDSBURY, C., and SHEANE, J. H. W. 1911. *The Great Plateau of North Rhodesia.* London.
GROUT, L. 1864. *Zulu-Land.* Philadelphia.
GUTMANN, B. 1926. *Das Recht der Dschagga.* Munich.

HERSKOVITS, M. J. 1926. The Cattle Complex in East Africa. *American Anthropologist*, Vol. XXVIII.
HOBLEY, C. W. 1910. *The Ethnology of the Akamba and other East-African Tribes.* Cambridge.
——— 1922. *Bantu Beliefs and Magic.* London.
HOERNLE, A. W. 1923. The Social Value of Water among the Naman of S. W. Africa. *S.A.J.S.*, Vol. XX.
——— 1925. The Importance of the Sib in the Marriage Ceremonies of the South-Eastern Bantu. *S.A.J.S.*, Vol. XXII.
HOLDEN, W. C. 1866. *The Past and Future of the Kafir-Races.* London.
HOLLIS, A. C. 1905. *The Masai.* Oxford.
——— 1909. *The Nandi.* Oxford.
HOLUB, E. 1881. *Seven Years in South Africa.* Tr. 2 Vols. London.

ISAACS, N. 1836. *Travels and Adventures in Eastern Africa, descriptive of the Zoolus.* 2 Vols. London.
IRLE, J. 1906. *Die Herero.* Gütersloh.

JACKSON, H. M. G. 1926 and 1927. Notes on Matabele Customary Law. *Nada*, Vols. IV and V. Salisbury, Rhodesia.
JENKINSON, T. B. 1882. *Amazulu.—The Zulus, their past history, manners, customs and language.* London.
JUNOD, H. 1927. *The Life of a South African Tribe.* 2nd Edition. Neuchâtel.
——— 1924. Le Totémism chez les Thongas, les Pédis, et les Vendas, *Le Globe* (Geneva).

KIDD, D. 1906. *Savage Childhood.* London.
———— 1908. *Kafir Socialism.* London.
———— 1925. *The Essential Kafir.* 2nd Edition. London.
KROPF, A. 1889. *Das Volk der Xosa-Kaffern.* Berlin.

LAGDEN, G. Y. 1909. *The Basutos.* 2 Vols. London.
LESLIE, D. 1875. *Among the Zulus and Amatongas.* 2nd Edition. Edinburgh.
LICHTENSTEIN, M. H. C. 1812–15. *Travels in Southern Africa in the Years* 1803, 1804, 1805 *and* 1806. Tr. A. Plumptre. 2 Vols. London.
LINDBLOM, G. 1920. *The Akamba.* 2nd Edition. Uppsala.
LIVINGSTONE, D. 1857. *Missionary Travels and Researches in South Africa.* London.

MACKENZIE, C. 1925. *The Spirit-Ridden Konde.* London.
MACLEAN, J. 1858. *A Compendium of Kafir Laws and Customs.* Reprinted 1906. Grahamstown.
MAYR, F. Fr. 1906. The Zulu Kafirs of Natal. *Anthropos,* Vol. I.
MELLAND, F. H. 1923. *In Witch-bound Africa.* London.
MERKER, M. 1904. *Die Masai.* Berlin.
MEYER, HANS. 1909. *Das Deutsche Kolonial-Reich.* Leipzig and Wien.
MOFFAT, R. 1842. *Missionary Labours.* London.
MOLEMA, S. M. 1920. *The Bantu Past and Present.* Edinburgh.

PASSAGE, S. 1907. *Die Buschmänner der Kalahari.* Berlin.
POSSELT, F. W. T. 1926. Native Marriage. *Nada,* Vol. IV. Salisbury, Rhodesia.

RATTRAY, R. S. 1923. *Ashanti.* Oxford.
———— 1927. *Religion and Art in Ashanti.* Oxford.
ROSCOE, J. 1911. *The Baganda.* London.
———— 1915. *The Northern Bantu.* The Cambridge Archæological and Ethnological Series.
———— 1923. *The Bakitara.* Cambridge.
ROUTLEDGE, W. S. and K. 1910. *With a Pre-Historic People : the Akikuyu of British East Africa.* London.

SCHAPERA, I. 1928. Economic Changes in South African Native Life. *Africa,* Vol. I, No. 2. London.
———— 1930. *The Khoisan Peoples of South Africa.* London.
SCHINZ, H. 1891. *Deutsch Südwest Afrika.* Oldenburg and Leipzig.

SCHULZE, L. S. 1907. *Aus Namaland im Kalahari.* Jena.

SHAW, W. 1860. *The Story of my Mission in South-Eastern Africa.* London.

SHOOTER, J. 1857. *The Kafirs of Natal and the Zulu Country.* London.

SHROPSHIRE, DENYS. 1927. Marriage Rites and their Meaning. *Nada,* Vol. V. Salisbury, Rhodesia.

SMITH, E. W., and DALE, A. M. 1920. *The Ila-Speaking Peoples of Northern Rhodesia.* 2 Vols. London.

STANNUS, H. S. 1910. Notes on some Tribes of British Central Africa. *J.R.A.I.,* Vol. XL.

STOWE, G. 1905. *The Native Races of South Africa.* London.

TAYLOR, H. J. 1906. The Amandabele. *P.R.S.A.,* Vol. VI, No. 1.

THEALE, G. M. 1910. *The Yellow and Dark-skinned Peoples of South Africa.* London.

———— 1919. *Ethnography and Conditions of South Africans before 1510.*

THOMAS, N. W. 1917. Some Ibo Burial Customs. *J.R.A.I.,* Vol. XLVII.

TORDAY, E. 1929. Principles of Bantu Marriage. *Africa,* Vol. II, No. 3. London.

TYLER, J. 1891. *Forty Years among the Zulus.* Boston and Chicago.

VEDDER, H. 1923. *Die Bergdama.* 2 Parts. Hamburg.

WERNER, A. 1906. *The Natives of British Central Africa.* London.

WILLOUGHBY, W. L. 1928. *The Soul of the Bantu.* New York.

REPORTS

1883. *Report and Proceedings, with Appendices, of the Government Commission on Native Laws and Customs.*

LITERATURE FROM OTHER AREAS, TO WHICH REFERENCE IS MADE IN THE TEXT

ARMSTRONG, W. E. *Papuan Government's Reports* 1917–1922.

BEST, ELSDON. 1900–01. Spiritual Concepts of the Maori. *J.P.S.,* Vols. IX and X.

———— 1907–09. Maori Forest Lore. *T.N.Z.I.,* Vols. XL, XLI, and XLII.

BOAS, F. *Ethnology of the Kwakiutl.* Bureau of American Ethnology. Annual Report 35, Part I.

BROWN, G. 1910. *Melanesians and Polynesians ; their Life-Histories described and compared.* London.

BROWN, A. R. 1922. *The Andaman Islanders.* Cambridge.

———— 1912. Belief concerning Childbirth in some Australian Tribes. *Man*, No. 96.

CHALMERS, J. 1902. *Work and Adventure in New Guinea.* London.

CODRINGTON, R. H. 1891. *The Melanesians.* Oxford.

FIRTH, R. 1929. *Primitive Economics of the New Zealand Maori.* London.

FOX, C. E. 1924. *The Threshold of the Pacific.* London.

FURNESS, W. H. 1920. *The Island of Stone Money—Uap of the Carolines.* Philadelphia and London.

GRIMBLE, A. 1921. From Birth to Death in the Gilbert Islands. *J.R.A.I.*, Vol. LI.

HOLMES, J. H. 1924. *In Primitive New Guinea.* London.

IVENS, W. C. 1927. *Melanesians of the South-East Solomon Islands.* London.

LANDTMANN, GUNNAR. 1927. *The Kiwai Papuans of British New Guinea.* London.

MALINOWSKI, B. 1912. The Economic Aspects of the Intichiuma Ceremonies. *Festkrift Tillägnad Edward Westermarck.* Helsingfors.

———— 1915. The Natives of Mailu. *T.R.S.S.A.*, Vol. XXXIV.

———— 1921. Primitive Economics of the Trobriand Islanders. *E.J.*, Vol. XXXI.

———— 1922. *Argonauts of the Western Pacific.* London.

———— 1926. *Crime and Custom in Savage Society.* London.

———— 1926. Magic, Science and Religion, in *Science, Religion and Reality*, ed. by Joseph Needham. London. Referred to as " Magic, Science and Religion " in the text.

———— 1926. *Myth in Primitive Psychology.* London.

———— 1927. *Sex and Repression in Savage Society.* London.

———— 1927. *The Father in Primitive Psychology.* London.

———— 1929. *The Sexual Life of Savages.* London.

MARINER, W. 1818. *An Account of the Natives of the Tonga Islands in the South Pacific Ocean.* 2 Vols. London.

———— 1906. *The Todas.* London.

MEAD, MARGARET. 1929. *Coming of Age in Samoa.* London.

PARKINSON, R. 1907. *Dreissig Jahre in du Südsee.* Stuttgart.

RIVERS, W. H. R. 1914. *The History of Melanesian Society.* 2 Vols. Cambridge.

SELIGMAN, C. G. 1910. *The Melanesians of British New Guinea.* Cambridge.

SELIGMAN, C. G. and B. Z. 1911. *The Veddas.* Cambridge.

SPENCER, B., and GILLEN, F. J. 1927. *The Arunta.* 2 Vols. London.

TURNER, G. 1884. *Samoa a Hundred Years ago and long before.* London.

WILLIAMSON, R. W. 1914. *The Way of the South Sea Savage.* London.

INDEX

In spelling the tribal names in this index, I have followed no consistent scheme, but have used that adopted by the different authors quoted in the text.